The Greatest Escape

The Greatest Escape

A Bomber Command Navigator's Story of Survival in Nazi Germany

Martin Barratt

First published in Great Britain in 2023 by
Pen & Sword Military
An imprint of
Pen & Sword Books Ltd
Yorkshire - Philadelphia

ISBN 978 1 39907 527 5

A CIP catalogue record for this book is available from the British Library.

Typeset in INDIA by IMPEC eSolutions
Printed and bound in England by CPI UK Ltd.

Pen & Sword Books Ltd. incorporates the Imprints of Pen & Sword Archaeology,
Atlas, Aviation, Battleground, Discovery, Family History, History, Maritime,
Military, Naval, Politics, Railways, Select, Transport, True Crime, Fiction,
Frontline Books, Leo Cooper, Praetorian Press, Seaforth Publishing,
Wharncliffe and White Owl.

For a complete list of Pen & Sword titles please contact

PEN & SWORD BOOKS LIMITED
47 Church Street, Barnsley, South Yorkshire, S70 2AS, England
E-mail: enquiries@pen-and-sword.co.uk
Website: www.pen-and-sword.co.uk

or

PEN AND SWORD BOOKS
1950 Lawrence Rd, Havertown, PA 19083, USA
E-mail: uspen-and-sword@casematepublishers.com
Website: www.penandswordbooks.com

Dedication

This book is dedicated to the crew of Handley Page Halifax
JB869 DY-H

Sergeant William Bernard Johnson Happold – Pilot
Sergeant Gordon Stanley Bowles – Flight Engineer
Sergeant Joseph Harold Barratt - Navigator
Sergeant John Brownlie – Wireless Operator
Flying Officer John Baxter – Bomb Aimer
Sergeant Duncan Roy McGregor – Air Gunner (mid upper)
Sergeant Thomas Henry Jones – Air Gunner (tail)

And to all the aircrew of Bomber Command 1939-1945

Humility beyond measure
Courage beyond comprehension

Contents

Acknowledgements

In the twenty-four years it has taken me to research for this book I have been fortunate enough to meet a wealth of people whose assistance, support and help have been invaluable to me. It would not be possible to thank everyone I have met along the way, but I would like to give special mention to the following groups of people who have helped me over the years:

The amazing staff at the Public Records Office in Kew for helping me locate and extract information relating to raid reports and operations from the extensive AIR archive of papers that they hold pertaining to RAF Operations across the war years; the RAF Museum at Hendon for their gracious time during various visits to the Bomber Command Hall; The Wolds Gliding club at Pocklington Airfield in Yorkshire; The Commonwealth War Graves Commission; the RAF Personnel Management Centre at Innsworth; Herr Horkens at the Stadt Offices in Monchengladbach.

Steve Heppenstall who helped locate the crash site of my father's Halifax and who kindly provided photographs and details of the location, including translations of contemporary German records detailing the crash and its aftermath; John Griffin who helped with navigational course plotting and interpreting seventy-nine-year-old handwritten navigation notes; Judy Adams at the Irvin Aerospace Company; Ian Foster and Gillian Ashmore at Halifax 57 Rescue; the late Simon Kularatne (102 Squadron researcher); Greg Harrison at The Bomber Command Historical Society; Chris Goss; John Nichol; Oliver Clutton-Brock; Dennis Hoppe; Doug Radcliffe (Bomber Command Association); Mike Wood at the Yorkshire Air Museum; David Brocklehurst at the Battle of Britain Museum, Hawkinge; Barry 'Buzz' Hope author of the '....*And in the morning*' series of Squadron histories and books; Laura Caplan for permission to refer to her father's map of the route of the Death March from Stalag Luft IV in the winter of 1945 and Greg Hatton of the 392nd BG Memorial Association. I would also like to thank Des Philippet for allowing me to reproduce the photos of the graves of members of my father's crew who lie in Rheinberg War Cemetery, Germany.

My wife Janine; ex-wife Sarah; my late mother Marjorie and my daughters Zoe and Sophie; to Dan and Ben and my stepsons Charlie and Oliver who all encouraged and supported me and, when necessary, pushed and prodded me, and also listened to endless anecdotes and stories, books and films on Bomber Command over the years and put up with endless rewrites, edits and changes and my obsessive interest in the various stories. To Janine who became used to her husband's increasingly hermit-like existence spending hours locked in his study reading, researching and drafting only to emerge for food, tea, wine and essentials and then disappearing again; my cousin Adrian Locke who provided extensive details about my father's childhood home in Hednesford; Gordon Walther who provided rare family photos of my father, his siblings and my grandparents.

Heartfelt thanks, and fond remembrance to my grandmother, Elizabeth Barratt. A truly remarkable lady whose devotion to her only son meant that she kept every single letter he wrote from the various camps in Germany where he was incarcerated, every communication from the Air Ministry (including the telegrams advising my father was missing and then a PoW), every reply from the Red Cross asking after news of her son, the letters to my father from Leslie Irving at the Irving Parachute Company, his flying logbooks and other miscellaneous material. It is down to her that such a remarkable and precious archive has survived and as its current custodian it has given me unprecedented insight into not only my father's thoughts and state of mind in those days, but also provided a crucial evidence trail of where he was at key points in the narrative during his time in Germany as a prisoner.

To my friends Michael Leuty, John Riley, Diarmuid Connolly, Simon Robinson, Nick Hahn, Margaret and John Frith (whose father was also a Bomber Command veteran), Paul and Julia Flowers, Richard Cotton and all others who provided encouragement and enthusiasm from the very early days of the project (and at all times thereafter). I would also like to thank my friend and colleague Will Simpson for the initial book cover concept with Jon Wilkinson.

To the relatives of the crew of JB869 – Bill Brownie (Sergeant John Brownlie), Ken Jones (Sergeant Tommy Jones), John Andrews (Sergeant Bernard Happold), Helen McGregor (Sergeant Duncan McGregor), David Youdle (Sergeant Gordon Bowles) and to Alastair Hunter (F/O John Baxter) who provided photographs and, in some cases, original copies of wartime correspondence and PoW letters from their relatives. Thanks to the late Tom Wingham, ex-secretary of the 102 Squadron Association, who was of immeasurable assistance in the early years of my research and put a great deal of time into helping me. I would also like to thank the many former aircrew who knew my father, many now sadly gone, who gave so freely of their time and hospitality, in particular Calton Younger, Bill Pattison, Percy Carruthers, Harry Hughes, Batch Batchelder, Bill Younger, Dennis Emes, Leonard Rose (Stalag Luft IV Ex PoW Association), George Guderley, and also Brian Joseph (son of David Joseph whom my father was in the camps and on the march with).

Heartfelt thanks must go to John Grehan and all the team at Pen & Sword Books for their invaluable guidance and support and for their clear enthusiasm for the project right from the start and for enabling me to tell this story to the widest possible audience.

Finally, to my new grandson Zach – the next generation. For the hope that in future there must be a better way for men to reconcile their differences, that peace and friendship can instead fill the void left by the misery and wasted human potential that conflict brings.

Learn the past, watch the present, create the future.

Introduction

To the living we owe respect,
but to the dead we owe only the truth.

Voltaire

The early hours of Wednesday, 5 May 1943.

I have often wondered what my father's thoughts were, a young man of twenty-six, crouched in the darkness of the nose of his stricken Halifax. Bloodied, far from home and engaged in a desperate struggle for life as the stricken bomber began its fiery plummet to earth. Amid the noise, the flames and the fear I have tried many times to put myself in his shoes in the moments before he finally managed to tear open the escape hatch under him and tumble out into the cold night sky.

For four of the seven-man crew of Handley Page Halifax JB869 DY-H it would mean the end of their story and the end of their short lives, as the aircraft tore itself apart and the blazing fragments fell to earth. For the three fliers who did get out it would mean, quite literally, a leap into the unknown, their initial relief at exiting the aircraft and seeing a deployed parachute canopy above them quickly replaced by a fear of what kind of landing, not to mention reception, awaited them on the ground. It was 1943 and the height of the air war over Europe, the Americans bombing by day and the British by night and as a result allied airmen bailing out over enemy territory were just as likely to meet their deaths at the hands of vengeful civilians on the ground, as they were at the hands of flak batteries and night fighters whilst in the air. Lynchings were increasingly commonplace, as nearly happened to my father as you will read in this book. So were stories of captured airmen, or *Terrorflieger* (Terror-fliers) as the German propaganda machine christened them, being summarily executed within minutes of coming down and either shot, beaten to death or, in some cases strung up from trees and wooden posts.

For my father and his two crewmates at least, they were amongst the 'lucky' ones – the brutal shock of being shot up and their aircraft set alight, of bailing out and wondering what had happened to their friends, quickly replaced by the pain of a heavy landing, the humiliation of capture and the start of their long two years in captivity. One can forgive them for perhaps having thought that the greatest danger was over; little did they know what lay ahead of them.

I am told that my father rarely spoke to others of his wartime experiences, either as a navigator in Bomber Command or as a prisoner of war and preferred (like so many) to try and put what had happened behind him. Few who survived felt that they were able to share those defining experiences with anyone who had not seen what they had seen or had not endured what they had endured. The thrill and the terror of aerial warfare and then the boredom and grind of prison camp life – a life punctuated by episodes of fear, prolonged hunger, unimaginable hardship and physical cruelty. Many ex-PoWs chose only to discuss their experiences with other ex-PoWs, for how could those who had not lived through those times possibly relate to some events so shocking they almost beggar belief?

As a small boy I was only aware that my father had been in the RAF after my mother, clearing out the loft with him in the late '60s in our house in Tettenhall Wood, Wolverhampton, brought down an old, battered suitcase. When she opened it, I remember the flash of blue serge: his RAF uniform complete with Navigator brevet and gold buttons. I remember him trying it on (it still fitted him some twenty-six years after he had last worn it) and then he mentioned that he 'had flown in a Halifax bomber in the war' and that was all he said about it. I had no idea what a Halifax was or looked like and I seem to recall that I was vaguely disappointed that he wasn't a Spitfire pilot like my Uncle David and that he hadn't produced a pair of 'Biggles' type goggles or, even better, the much-prized sheepskin flying jacket, and the subject wasn't mentioned again until I was older.

Around 1976 when I was twelve or so we watched 'The Great Escape', during the days when it was a regular screening on TV, and my mother mentioned that my father had also been a prisoner. Like most boys I was curious and I began to press him for details. Some came willingly enough, that he was a navigator in 102 Squadron and that originally he had been in the Royal Artillery before volunteering for Bomber Command. Eventually he would start to open up about his time in the air, usually the lighter more humorous episodes like getting lost as a rookie navigator while on training flights, or helping to carry a fellow airman out on to the parade ground so he wouldn't crease his tunic or scuff his boots as the 'best turned out' accolade would mean extra leave passes.

Sometimes he would mention prison camp life where he told me stories of the ingenious things men built with whatever they could scrounge or bribe the guards with, and then coyly telling me about one of his several escape attempts and subsequent recaptures. If my questions unwittingly strayed too near the darker episodes that they clearly brought to his mind however, he would abruptly clam up and it was made clear the discussion was over. Similarly, any discussion about the numerous faint scars on his back and legs was utterly taboo and it was some years before I found out that they were a combination of injuries he received when bailing out and ill-treatment when he was a prisoner. He wasn't a member of any veterans associations, eschewed any pomp and ceremony, although he would always sit down quietly and watch the Remembrance Day service from the Cenotaph on TV but was always introspective – almost withdrawn and now I know why.

Many years later I watched a television programme about Air Chief Marshal Sir Arthur 'Bomber' Harris and the Allied Strategic Bombing Offensive. As I watched the programme it dawned on me that this is what my father had been involved in. What struck me most was the realisation that the true, awful reality of the campaign was so different to the images which had formed in a young boy's mind all those years before. This was no picnic, no easy option and no 'great adventure'. It told of an uncertain future haunted almost daily by the prospect of violent and impending death. In 1943 an airman of Bomber Command actively engaged on operational flying could expect a lifespan estimated in weeks (comparable to that of a soldier in the trenches in the Great War). An operational aircrew's existence at that time consisted largely of long flights in the dark and cold in cramped conditions, being deafened by the unrelenting roar of the engines and punctuated by moments of abject terror on the way to, over, and back from the target. Seemingly only a fiery death in an exploding aircraft or captivity as a prisoner of war awaited. Less a case of 'if' more a case of 'when'. I wanted to find out more about this secret battle that my father had taken part in and had (against overwhelming odds) survived where so many thousands of his compatriots and crewmates had met their deaths, and I began to press him for more details.

To my eternal regret I wish I had spoken with him more in the years shortly before his death from cancer in 1988. Writing this book almost thirty-five years later and knowing what I know now of that part of his life, I often reflect on the opportunity I missed. What I wouldn't give to have just one evening with him now, over a glass of his favourite whisky and ask him the endless stream of questions in my fifties that it never occurred to me to ask in my teens and early twenties. I can still remember a holiday to Yugoslavia with my parents in 1978 when I was 14, we were caught in an electrical storm and the worst turbulence I have ever encountered in my life (even now). The Lockheed Tristar bucked and dipped, dropping for what seemed like hundreds of feet (but probably only a few tens) and levelled out with a noisy thud before rising only to drop again. Passengers screamed, even the cabin staff looked green and my mum, bless her, gripped my hand tightly and uttered the rather bizarrely fatalistic 'Well if we all go, we all go together Martin'! I remember thinking 'Hang on…go where??… I haven't lived yet'! But then I glanced at my father, sitting in his seat, calm as you like with not a hair out of place, reading his *Telegraph* and sipping his whisky, moving his right arm – glass in hand – in tandem with the bucking of the aircraft in a vain attempt to avoid spillage. He looked at my mum with a smile then looked at me, chuckled and said: 'We'll be fine boy, don't worry.' He winked at me, carried on with his paper and all was well with the world.

In many ways this has been a difficult book to write, and I have found whilst writing it that it has forced me to confront things about him that I have never properly reconciled. Fundamentally honest (and good) my father was, nevertheless, a complex and often difficult man. A mass of contradictions; at times achingly funny, dry-witted, sharp-minded, informed, insightful and cultured. At other times he could be harsh, cold, distant and often seemingly troubled. The fact that he endured the depravations and unspeakable treatment that I now know he went through, as will be revealed in this book, is further testament to the remarkable reserves of courage and fortitude that he possessed as a man, as did so many others like him. The chapters that deal with his time as a PoW have been the most difficult to write and the sections describing what he and other men went through at times do not make for comfortable reading.

Many Bomber Command veterans returning from war, particularly those who had been through a rough time, seemed for the most part to have buried what had happened to them, re-joining civilian life as best they could and building careers, getting married, starting families and living their lives. What became obvious through my own research however is that many had never fully come to terms with their experiences and in later life those unresolved conflicts inevitably resurfaced. Looking back now I am certain that this was true of my father and, sadly, support for veterans particularly in terms of mental health was fundamentally lacking and many men were left to suffer in silence.

One of my father's closest friends from Stalag Luft VI, Heydekrug suffered terribly in later life. Fred Tees was the rear gunner of Lancaster AJ-C, Pilot Officer Ottley's Lancaster, from 617 Squadron on the famous Dams raid in May 1943. The aircraft was shot down on the way to the target and Sergeant Tees was one of only three survivors from the fifty-six men lost on the Dams raid, himself suffering serious burns. Fred became a barber in Letchworth after the war and is featured in a Pathé Newsreel at a Dambusters twenty-four-year reunion held at Scampton in 1967. Sadly, Fred Tees took his own life on 15 March 1982. He never married and in accordance with his final wishes his ashes were scattered over the graves of his crew who lie together in Rheinberg Forest War Cemetery, Germany.

Primarily this book is the story of my father and his survival in Nazi Germany after bailing out, but it is also the story of the crew of Halifax Bomber JB869 DY 'H-Harry'. It is a story of seven young men in their late teens and twenties, from different lives and backgrounds who were thrown together by chance and who as young aircrew, trained together, lived together, flew together and fought together until fate shattered that brotherhood. It has been said many times before, but men who have experienced combat for any length of time, either in a unit or as a crew, are unusually closely bonded together as evidenced by the story of Fred Tees. Undoubtedly, it's to do with the experiences that they have collectively been through but also, I believe, it must surely be to do with the fact that all placed their life into other men's hands, whether in training or it combat. They relied on the skill of the pilot and flight engineer to get them in the air, to keep them up there, and get them safely down again; the navigator and wireless operator to get them to the target, the bomb aimer to drop the payload accurately, the air gunners to protect the aircraft from enemy night fighters. A failure by any one of them could have devastating consequences for the whole crew.

The sheer scale of the losses suffered by Bomber Command is staggering. Only German U-boat crews suffered higher proportionate losses in the Second World War. Of the 125,000 men who took part, 55,000 were lost.

As to my father's crew specifically, researching this book over a twenty-four year period has allowed me to build a picture of them as men. To speak to the people who knew them, to put faces to simply name, rank and serial number, to put flesh on the bones and to see them as more than simply stark, mute names on a village or church memorial or etched onto a neat, white headstone in Rheinberg Commonwealth Cemetery in northern Germany. I have managed to build a pen-portrait of each of his crewmates. Invariably some are more detailed than others as they rely solely on being able to trace relatives who knew them and could provide key insights into their lives. What emerges however is the picture of a group of young men with an array of talents and abilities (academic, sporting and musical) cruelly wasted. One wonders what they would have gone on to achieve in life had they lived – how many great doctors, scientists, sportsmen, writers, statesmen, inventors, industrialists were lost to the world in the millions of dead that resulted from the last world war. The rows of neat, white headstones are as much individual monuments to profligacy with human life and the waste of potential, as they are to the brave souls who lie beneath.

Finally, it must be remembered that the airmen of Bomber Command were volunteers to a man. I venture that the arrogance of youth has made us all feel at some point in our lives that we were invincible, that we could master and conquer everything that the fates throw down before us and that nothing and no-one would stand in our way. I'm sure that's what my father and his crew believed as they boarded the waiting trucks to be driven out to their aircraft for their nightly ops, even when the reality of operational flying with Bomber Command in 1943 was beginning to hit home and the empty tables in the mess halls across the shires the morning after a raid bore witness to the fact that the reality, for most, was that they would not be coming home.

For Harry Barratt, Bernard Happold, Tommy Jones, Duncan McGregor, Gordon Bowles, John Baxter and John Brownlie – the crew of JB869 DY 'H-Harry' I am happy that I can finally give them a collective voice.

This then, for the first time, is their story.

Martin Barratt
Hydestile Farmhouse,
Hydestile, Surrey
May 2022

Chapter 1

The Barratts of Anglesey Street

T he little terraced house with the grey pebble render is long gone now, demolished sometime in the 1970s, its foundations lie somewhere under an anonymous patch of grass and tarmac which is part of the town's rail station car park. Yet in the early years of the last century No.8 Anglesey Street, Hednesford, Staffordshire was alive with the sounds of family life. Typical of the thousands of properties in mining communities across the length and breadth of the Black Country, the house was home to my grandparents Joseph and Elizabeth Barratt, and their eight children.

No.8 was barely a stone's throw from the ornate and imposing Technical and Mining College, an extension of Cannock Chase Mining College, and a building that would play such a pivotal part in my father's early life. It still stands, largely untouched but now converted to luxury apartments, a far cry from its humble beginnings training miners as part of their initial familiarisation course for life down at the coal seam. A Black Country building in a Black Country landscape.

The Black Country – the name seems to have first come into use in the 1840s and it is believed to have been inspired by the black soot from heavy industry that covered much of the area in a fine powder, but its heavy mining of black coal is just as likely a candidate. There is some debate by traditionalists as to which towns and cities make up the Black Country but today it is generally accepted that most areas of the four Metropolitan District council areas of Dudley, Sandwell, Walsall and Wolverhampton fall within its curtilage.[1]

At the turn of the last century Hednesford (pronounced 'hens-fudd') was in many ways a typical mining town within the burgeoning industrial heartland of the country. The town has its roots in the twelfth century and the reign of King Stephen II. Local legend has it that in Saxon times a man called 'Heddin' (or 'Hedda') constructed, by hand, a ford over a small stream in the area and it became known to travellers as 'Heddin's Ford' which was corrupted over the centuries to the name the town has today. What is certain is that William, the first Lord Paget, a catholic industrialist, built the first blast furnace in the Midlands in Cannock Chase woods near Hednesford in 1561 but it remained only a small village and even by the end of the century its population is estimated to have been no more than fifty.[2] It wasn't until the late 1850s and the expansion of the operations of the Hednesford Colliery Company and the wider Industrial Revolution that the population of the town started to increase significantly. By 1881 the population had swelled to 7,000 people and it is estimated than over 50 per cent of the men in the town were employed in coal mining. Hednesford, like many towns in the Black Country, further expanded as the demand for coal intensified and by the turn of the century the Midlands was one of the most heavily industrialised parts of Britain, served by a network of fast-spreading rail and canal connections.

By contrast the surname Barratt first originated in Lincolnshire in about 1150 after settlement by Norman invaders following the conquest, and the Norman knight John Baret, who is listed in the Battle Abbey Roll, is reputedly a direct ancestor. The name Baret was in turn derived from the Old French for Baraud meaning 'bear hard or strong' and it is believed a large contingent of the Lincolnshire strain joined the Earl of Pembroke Richard 'Strongbow' de Clare's invasion of Ireland in 1172. As a result of that endeavour land was granted to the family in County Mayo and eventually became the Barretts (or Bairéad in Gaelic). To this day it remains one of the more common names in that part of Ireland (along with County Cork). The Barrett family crest *frangas non flectes: virtus probitas* translates from the Latin as 'unbowed, unbroken honour and courage'.

At some point in the 1850s to 1860s it is believed, though conjectural, that my great-grandfather came over from Ireland and settled in the Midlands and in turn my grandparents settled in Hednesford in the house that would become home to my father Joseph and his siblings: Amy, Doris, May, Rose, Sheila, Elizabeth and Gladys. The house in Anglesey Street was, as previously stated, typical of the type and the time and butted up against a detached house which still stands. The front door of No.8 opened straight into the front room and then a door to the right led up the narrow stairs. Through the front room was a living room with a black-leaded grate in the corner, a table and chairs and then doors to the pantry and steps down to the cellar. Another door at the back of the room led down to a small kitchen with a stove and a red stone, rectangular sink housing a single cold-water tap.

The back door faced their neighbour's back door – Mr and Mrs Pritchard – and then the backyard, extending some six or seven metres housed the outside privy and the coal house. Beyond that was a long, thin strip of garden, enclosed at the end by a fence and the railway line at the bottom with Hednesford station some 100m or so further up the tracks. Eventually my grandfather added a gate in the fence, which is there to this day, so that he could access the Ex-Servicemen's club – apparently, he had his own glass behind the bar for his favourite tipple, a pint of mild. He was fond of his Crown Green bowling and used to tend to (and mow) the lawn. A working man in every respect of the word.

Upstairs at No.8 there was a landing and two good sized bedrooms on the left-hand side, at the end of the landing was a step down into another bedroom, likened by members of the family to a ship's cabin. As he grew up this was to be my father's room due to his being the only male child in what was otherwise a house full of sibling sisters and it was here that he did most of his studying. My grandfather died when I was quite young but one of my memories of him, apart from the smell of Players Whiskey Ready Rubbed pipe tobacco, was sitting on his lap watching Westerns with him on a black and white TV (a liking for the genre that he seems to have passed on to my father and he in turn to me) and the fifty pence piece he used to press into my hand when I saw him with the cheery refrain 'All right my pigeon?' In photographs taken of him around the time is the half-hunter fob watch he used to wear with a heavy silver-chain and bowling medal attached. The watch used to sit mounted on a mahogany watch stand, inlaid with yew that my father made in woodwork class at school.[3]

My father, Joseph Harold Barratt (aka Joseph Junior) came into the world sometime in the early morning of Thursday, 22 February 1917. By all accounts he didn't have the easiest start to life and my grandmother told my mother that he had contracted pneumonia as a new-born and was not initially expected to live, spending his first few weeks of life swaddled in a dressing table drawer. It should be remembered that my father was born some three decades before the introduction of the NHS and the welfare state and that at the time of his birth infant mortality was in the region of 90 deaths per 1,000 births[4] compared to just over 3 deaths per 1000 live births in 2020.

His survival at that young age was far from assured but he eventually recovered from this early trauma with little discernible ill effects, although in later life he suffered considerably from bronchial complaints. Arguably it was to be the first of many triumphs through adversity that he encountered during his lifetime.

Life for the Barratt family was tough, as it was for so many families at the time, money was always very tight and feeding a family of ten is undoubtedly a challenge in any day and age whatever the family circumstances, but my grandmother did a superb job with the resources she had available to her. Hunger, however, was ever-present and growing up my father would tell me that he woke up feeling hungry and went to bed the same – a doorstop wedge of bread and jam was the stalwart for warding off hunger pangs but it left its mark on his taste buds and after that and the PoW camps he never touched jam again, proclaiming that he had had 'enough of jam to last me a bloody lifetime'.

Nevertheless, my grandmother always made sure there was food on the table for her husband and growing family and did an astonishing job with very modest resources at her disposal – something my mother, who had nothing but affection and admiration for my grandmother, frequently relayed to me while I was growing up. A kindly, wise and astute lady, my grandmother also had the unenviable job of refereeing the inevitable squabbles between seven daughters (and a son) and did so, according to my mother, by always listening sympathetically to each complainant but never taking sides, which certainly seems to be the most pragmatic solution.

As I am an only child it's hard to imagine what it must have been like growing up with seven siblings, never mind seven sisters, but although he could sometimes be abrupt and stern (as I was to discover as his son) my father was never cruel or vindictive and his sisters were fond of him, and he them, especially the younger ones who looked up to their big brother. As big a family as they were they were also big personalities and my Aunts Doris and May were never too much in awe of him not to put him in his place if he got a little too big for his boots. When I was growing up, Christmases as a kid were truly magical and we would travel back up to the Midlands from our house in Hampshire and stay with the family for the festive period – my aunts' houses all bursting with music, laughter, food, drink and merriment and cousins a-plenty. I vividly recall one Christmas party in the mid 1970s – I'd be about ten – when my father was telling me off for something or other while talking to my Uncle Les. He muttered something to Les about 'bloody kids' just before taking a bite from a vol-au-vent and as he bit into it my Aunt Doris cuffed him one from behind as she was walking past. 'Hey you, watch that language in front of the boy,' she said, at the same time flashing me a smile and a wink as she glided past. My father almost choked on the mouthful of puff pastry, and I can still see the mix of shock and outrage on his face nearly fifty years later! Aunt Doris became my personal heroine at that point and even now when I think of it, I still chuckle at the memory.

For a family that had experienced growing up in the tough times that followed the aftermath of the Great War they certainly knew how to enjoy themselves and celebrate all that life had to offer. Perhaps it was the very fact that they had experienced such austerity and hardship that they made sure they lived life to the full and made the most of the good times as well as stoicism through the bad – something that my father would come to rely on more than once during his time in the air and on the ground at key points in his life.

Life for the Barratts also had the uncertainties that came with coal mining at that time. It has always been a dangerous occupation, accidents were commonplace and my father's birth came less than a year before the Minnie Pit Disaster[5] in the village of Halmer End, near Newcastle-under-Lyme in North Staffordshire. An underground explosion claimed the lives of 155 men and boys and was attributed to the ignition of 'firedamp', the collective name for a number of flammable gases that accumulate in pockets in coal mines and can explode with devastating consequences, burying men alive to slowly asphyxiate or die of terrible burns.

In December 1911 an accident occurred at No.9 Pit, Hednesford mine[6] which at the time belonged to the Cannock Chase Colliery Company Limited. The cause of the fire in which five men lost their lives was never conclusively identified, but it is thought to have been caused by a smouldering lamp wick from a miner's lamp igniting spilt lamp oil on the floor. One of the men who died, Thomas Stokes,[7] was awarded the Edward Medal – a forerunner of the George Medal. Stokes, born in Burntwood in 1870, worked as a stallman at the pit and after the fire broke out and upon hearing five men were trapped he went back to the pithead to help them but was overcome by the smoke and unfortunately was one of those who lost his life.

As a coal miner working at the coal face in Hednesford my grandfather would have been acutely aware of the risks every time he ventured out the front door of No.8 Anglesey Street to go to work. By the start of the 1930s one in every twenty workers in Britain was a coal miner, yet 25 per cent of all workplace injuries happened in mining.[8] At one time the Cannock Chase coalfields were populated by some forty-eight different coal mines. The last of these, Littleton Colliery, closed on 3 December 1993 bringing to an end over 700 years of coal production in the area.

Walking to the pithead every day with his 'snap' at his side[9] and climbing into the meshed cage that would take him and his fellow miners down into the grimy, claustrophobic bowels of the earth, my grandfather would spend hours underground at the pithead clawing at the coal with rudimentary tools before emerging at the end of his shift, black with coal dust, dripping with sweat and eager to get above ground and to let the cool fresh air fill his lungs. The dangers for coal miners were not only confined to fire and explosion underground but also the array of respiratory complaints and disorders they faced from years of exposure to coal dust underground including pleural diseases, emphysema, bronchitis, increased risk of cancer of the trachea, bronchus, lung, stomach and liver and the pernicious CWP (Coal Workers Pneumoconiosis), also known as 'Black Lung' or 'Miners Lung'. All would have a debilitating effect on miners as they reached later life long, long after they had worked their last shift at the seam.

I think that there is, perhaps in some quarters, a certain romanticising of the coal-mining industry in this country and, while the bravery and dedication of the men who went underground is absolutely beyond question, the realities are that it was a bleak, dangerous, dirty and ruinous life for which many men paid with their lives (and many more with their health) in order to provide the fuel for the home fires and the fires of heavy industry.

It was a life that my grandmother was absolutely determined her only son would not follow.

Chapter 2

A Black Country Boy

Against the backdrop of life in 1920s Britain my father had what can only be imagined as being a fairly typical upbringing for a boy of that time growing up in the West Midlands. He spent lots of time playing in the street outside his house, kicking a can around with his mates or fashioning anything they could find into something closely approximating a football and playing for hours until it was time to be called back into the house. When I was growing up he never could understand why my friends and I would prefer to sit in our rooms and listen to records or play with a Scalextric racing set, when we could be out exploring and he would always be doing his best to push me out the door.

Much of his time as a young boy was spent in the fields and surrounding areas around Hednesford Hills, catching tadpoles in jars or building dens and climbing trees around Cannock Chase, disappearing for hours and only returning when it was dark. Often he would sit on the hillsides high above Hednesford and gaze down on the town, watching the comings and goings at the colliery, the slow turning of the giant headstocks and the shunting of the engines taking away the coal. The noise of heavy industry was never far away and the thick black smoke belching from chimneys was a constant reminder of the region's heavy industry – and perhaps also of the life that awaited him as the son of a miner expected to follow in his father's footsteps down to the rich seams underground. On the occasions when he told me about his boyhood he would speak of the times he spent high up on those hills, wistfully musing on what was beyond the horizons of his native Staffordshire.

Covering some 17,000 acres, Cannock Chase, or simply 'the chase' as it is known locally, is the mainland's smallest Area of Outstanding Natural Beauty (AONB). Human activity at the Chase dates back to the Mesolithic Period with the discovery of flint knapping tools and there are remnants of Bronze Age settlements and an Iron Age hillfort occupied between 500BC – 100AD. William the Conqueror designated Cannock forest a royal hunting forest in 1066 and it remained so until 1087[1] and the deer that are present today are only a fraction of the extensive herd present during those times – it's amusing to ponder whether my father's great ancestor (and mine) the Norman knight John Baret ever visited the area that was so beloved of my father, his sisters and countless generations before and since.

By 1546 Cannock Chase had passed into the hands of Sir William Paget (the Catholic industrialist mentioned briefly in the first chapter) who introduced the first blast furnace to the Midlands in the 1560s. The start of the Great War in 1914 saw the establishment of two large military camps, each housing up to 20,000 troops and containing its own transport and services infrastructure. In 1958 Cannock Chase was designated as an Area of Outstanding Natural Beauty and remains a stunning and restful place with sweeping hills and views containing an abundance of wildlife, flora and fauna.[2]

More pertinently Cannock Chase is also home to the German Military Cemetery in the village of Brocton and contains the graves of over 5,000 German, Austrian and Ukrainian nationals who lost their lives in the two world wars. By a strange quirk of fate the cemetery also contains the graves of the three German airman who died when their Heinkel He-III was shot down on 19 April 1941 and crashed only about a mile from the author's current house in Hydestile, Surrey.[3]

When he wasn't out exploring the Chase, fishing with his pals or swimming in the local lakes and ponds that dotted the local area my father was doing what most youngsters did at that time – waiting for the weekend. Saturday mornings were spent at the local cinema, either the Electric Picture Palace a few hundred yards down Anglesey Street, or the Picture House (later the Empire) in Rugeley Rd. The Electric Picture Palace was preferred due to its proximity – a scruffy and rather austere wooden building, it had started life as a skating rink in 1910 before incorporating a cinema two years later. Eventually it was completely rebuilt in the Art Deco style in the 1930s and renamed 'Tivoli', becoming something of a landmark in the area. The building survived until 1963 before its eventual demolition in favour of some or other anonymous supermarket, also now long gone.[4]

Back in its heyday in the 1920s however Saturday morning at 'The Palace' was kids' matinee time and, as was the case up and down the breadth of the county for many decades, a rowdy assortment of local kids would cram into the cinema for a couple of hours to give their parents a break. Staple diet for the young matinee audience at that time were the Hal Roach produced comedy shorts 'Our Gang' about the adventures of a ragbag group of poor kids growing up in an American neighbourhood. The shorts were interspersed with snippets of the great silent movie stars of the day, Charlie Chaplin, Harold Lloyd, the Keystone Cops and my father's favourite, Buster Keaton. How much watching they actually did though is open to conjecture as my father once described, in between raucous laughter, what tended to happen:

We'd be crammed in like sardines, dozens and dozens of grubby little kids all jostling each other waiting for the first picture to come on. As soon as the lights went down the screaming from all these kids would be absolutely deafening and then you'd get down on your hands and knees and scrabble about under the seats to see how far you could get to the rows behind. The idea was to try and tie some kids' shoelaces together and then get back to your seat before the lights went up and the usher told you off.[5]

Life wasn't all football, tree-climbing and movies though and like practically all boys at that time my father had a number of chores that he was responsible for, from bringing in coal from the coal house, generally cleaning and fetching and carrying, to outside chores in the garden. Like most working men at the time my grandfather kept a few chickens (bantams) for eggs and occasionally for the table and my father's designated job was to feed them. Anyone who has kept chickens, as I have, knows that, while rewarding, they also take a reasonable amount of looking after and that bantams – especially the cocks – can be demanding and sometimes vicious birds, especially if they feel their territory is being encroached upon.

I remember my father telling me about the trials and tribulations of feeding time.

> *Bantams are feisty little things – the old man had this one*
> *particular bird who would gather all the hens up behind*
> *him and then puff himself up ready – he would fly at your*
> *face with his spurs so you had to hold a metal bin lid up*
> *like a shield while taking the corn and grain in and you*
> *could hear him rat-tat-tatting on the lid trying to peck*
> *you, so you had to be a bit quick.*

In the hardships that followed the end of the First World War working conditions and wages for miners had fallen year on year in real terms and so every bit of extra food and money coming into the house was invaluable. It's helpful to understand some of the historical backdrop that caused so much disillusion and resentment by the mineworkers and much of the accompanying hardship for so many families, including my father's.

At the outbreak of the Great War former mineworkers' leader and trade unionist Keir Hardie had opposed Britain's participation, viewing it as a capitalist enterprise of which the average working man was merely an unwilling pawn, and he tried unsuccessfully to organise a national strike, appealing specifically to the mine workers (at the time the largest single group of workers in the UK and with a tendency to be more militant in their outlook).

Coalmining, along with other key work areas, was considered a reserved occupation in the Great War, as it was to be in the Second World War, as Britain's mineworkers were vital to keep the fires of industry burning (literally). Joining up to fight was not compulsory; however in the early years of the conflict an increasing number of mineworkers left to enlist and swap their pickaxe for a rifle. By March 1915 some 191,710 mineworkers had answered General Kitchener's poster-boy call to take up arms and join up and coal production had fallen accordingly.[6] To protect output the national coal industry had been privatised by the government of Lloyd George which, to a large extent, protected miners' pay, safety and working conditions and helped ensure a stable and steady supply of coal to power the country's needs including the production of munitions and heavy industry.

Understandably after the end of the war miners and the trade unions were keen for this situation to continue, however Lloyd George bowed to pressure from the mine owners and the mines were subsequently denationalised and returned to private hands on 31 March 1921.

Almost immediately the mine owners began demanding pay cuts and increases in working hours to mitigate the impact of foreign competition in the rebuilding period that followed the Great War and tensions began to mount. The miners, backed by their trade union, appealed to the railwaymen and transport workers to join a strike planned for 15 April 1921. The strike never materialised due to wavering by the other two unions and the miners were eventually forced back to work having had to accept a cut in pay. Resentment increased and at the end of June 1925 the situation was further inflamed by mine owners announcing the unilateral imposition of new working conditions, including a cut in wages and an increase of an extra hour on the working day. In the face of this the miners and their fellow workers in transport and on the railways held firm and Stanley Baldwin, then Prime Minister, headed off industrial action by agreeing to subsidise mine owners to ensure that miner's wages were protected.

The return to the Gold Standard in 1925, introduced by then Chancellor Winston Churchill, and the worsening relations between the miners, the unions and the government accelerated the problems of a depressed economy and with ever increasing cost-saving measures the conditions for a national strike were set. On 4 May 1926 this became a reality and what was destined to become the largest industrial dispute in British history – the General Strike – began, after strike action was called by the Trades Union Congress. Striking miners were locked out of their coal mines by the owners and summarily dismissed from their jobs. Some estimates place the number of strikers anywhere between one-and-a-half and one-and-three-quarter million men.

For the miners of the Cannock Chase Mining Company, my grandfather among them, it meant an uncertain and worrying time. The General Strike itself was called off after only nine days but the stoppage in the Midlands is said to have lasted some twenty-six weeks until miners gradually trickled back to work, having no other choice, only to face longer hours and lower wages. Many miners had large families to feed and clothe and, in those times they were often the only breadwinner which put a considerable strain on the family budget. For the ten-strong household at No.8 Anglesey Street it must have been a particularly difficult time and not for the last time in his life my father, then aged nine, experienced with his siblings the familiar pangs of hunger that saw him off to bed at night and were waiting to greet him when he awoke in the morning.

School provided a welcome distraction and my father showed real ability and aptitude for his subjects and had a natural inquisitiveness married to a determination to do well that stayed with him throughout his life. Remembering him now I recall that he had a very broad spread of life skills and could turn his hand to pretty much anything from drawing and painting to sports, woodwork and carpentry. When he turned 12 he enrolled in the 1st Hednesford Scout Troop, formed in 1908 by local man Tom Patchett and still going strong today.[7] Scouting proved to be an ideal outlet for an outdoor boy like my father who, when he wasn't studying, spent most of his time around the chase and surrounding areas. By all accounts he enjoyed his time and contributed actively to the various activities and events that Scouting had to offer.

Academically he was a gifted mathematician and excelled also in Physics and English. He was well-read given the means at his disposal and was astute, interesting and possessed a broad general knowledge, having the ability to contribute to pretty much any conversation, however obscure the subject matter. Over the years I heard from my aunts just how dedicated he had become in his studies the older he became, spending hours poring over books at the local library, keen to expand his knowledge and try new things. Money in the house was always tight and didn't stretch far enough for books, but my grandmother started doing part-time jobs here and there to earn some money and some of that was used to help pay for his books – his small and select personal library was further expanded by the addition of books that he was awarded as prizes in school competitions and examinations, ranging from Shakespeare to Byron, Kipling to Shaw and various mathematics and science texts. These volumes now sit in my own library in my study at home.

Towards the end of his schooling his thoughts no doubt began to focus on future employment. I have the original of his final school report from West Hill Boys School in Hednesford, dated 31 March 1931 when he had just turned 14, and it is suitably glowing and would set him up well for his first foray into work.

To whom it may concern,

Harold Barratt has just completed his final term at the above school. He has reached the highest standard, and for the last three months has been engaged chiefly upon special individual work. The subjects in which he excelled are mathematics and science, while at such practical subjects as gardening and woodwork, he has shown great interest and enthusiasm. He has entered into the social life of the school wholeheartedly and for the past season has been Captain of the school football team. He is a lad I can thoroughly recommend as being honest, trustworthy, and considerably above the average in all round ability.

I am,
Yours faithfully S. Edwards (Class Teacher)
West Hill Boys School, Hednesford

I recall growing up as a boy when this revered document would be produced by him as an example of application around the time that my own end of year school report was due – school report day for me largely consisted of thrusting the envelope under his copy of *The Telegraph* at the breakfast table and making myself scarce as quickly as possible. My father's academic bent towards mathematics and science were, it must be said, in very stark contrast to my own as a literature and arts graduate. However, it's easy to see why he would later excel as an Air Navigator. All I can usefully add on the matter is that it is fortunate that he, and not I, was called upon to guide his crew across the night skies of Europe – were it left to the author then in truth I doubt very much whether we would have ventured far from the end of the runaway before becoming lost, such is my terrible sense of direction.

As much as the report from his teacher outlines his academic prowess it also gives an insight into his inherent ability in (and love for) 'the beautiful game', football. Like most kids he played from an early age and graduated from kicking cans and rags about in the street to playing for his school team. At that time local professional teams often provided kit (shorts/shirts) for local schools, as many do today, and West Hill Boys School was no exception. They were supplied by founder members of the football league and seven times FA Cup Winners Aston Villa FC and my father proudly wore the claret, white and blue as a schoolboy. Football not only gave my father a respite from his studies but also an important introduction to working as a team, winning together and losing together, each doing his job and relying on those around him – neither getting carried away when things were going too well nor becoming despondent when they went awry 'meeting with triumph and disaster and treating those two imposters just the same' as Kipling would put it in 'If'. ('If', a much-referenced poem in the slim hardbound volume 'The Kipling Reader', a book prize that my father won at school and later gave to me as a boy of twelve).

Later in life I'm glad to say that my father's allegiance transitioned to the oldest, greatest and most famous of the Midlands teams, Wolverhampton Wanderers. One of his friends from an early age was Hednesford-born Tommy Galley, an England international who signed for Wolves in 1933 and went on to make 183 appearances in the famous old gold and black, scoring 41 goals. My father was a season ticket holder at Molineux stadium for many years and witnessed the great Championship winning sides of the 1950s and those stirring victories under the floodlights on a chill, foggy night where the likes of Puskas's Honved were put to the sword by the likes of Billy Wright, Ron Flowers, Peter Broadbent, Bill Slater and little Johnny Hancocks and his ferocious right foot. My father introduced me to Tommy Galley at a family party in 1987 shortly before he passed away, his love of football and his beloved Wolves undimmed.

Later, as a prisoner of war in the camps, he would once again spend many hours of his life kicking a football about. Percy Carruthers DFM, MiD, author of *Of Ploughs, Planes and Palliasses* was with him in various camps and remembered him very well when I wrote to him in 1996. We shared a great correspondence and, like all of the veterans I spoke to or wrote to, he was incredibly generous with his time. He described my father to a tee in one of his letters:

> *I knew him quite well. He was one of the most popular and well-liked members of any camp in which he was incarcerated. He was an excellent exponent at football and a most humorous storyteller you can imagine.*[8]

Dennis Emes, shot down on 13 May 1943 in a Halifax from 51 Squadron raiding Bochum, also recalled my father in the letters we swapped and shared details in his correspondence with me that he was instrumental in helping to organise football in the camps and other sports activities.[9]

In the early 1930s in England school leaving age was set at 14 and once he left school my father was expected to secure employment quickly so that, like some of his siblings, he could contribute financially to the household. My grandfather was keen for his son to follow his own path and earn his living as a miner. My grandmother was, I gather, determined that her son should not follow his father down the mines and she actively encouraged him to continue his studies and reach out for new experiences and opportunities. At various times this apparently caused some degree of friction between father and son but the die had already been cast and the more knowledge he acquired the keener my father's appetite became for more.

In 1931 after leaving school he enrolled on an engineering course at Cannock Mining College and at some point shortly afterwards he began work as a Wages Clerk at the Hednesford Mining Company. As ever he took his studies very seriously and split his time between applying himself to his job and locking himself away in his room with his studies. Speaking with a few of my aunts over the years they recalled how everyone in the house had to be quiet at certain points when he was studying for fear of inviting a stern look or a cross word from him when he was trying to concentrate (something I remember only too well from my time growing up on the occasions I interrupted him whenever he was working on his quarterly VAT return).

By 1933 he was no doubt enjoying his work as a clerk in the wages office and as a young man of sixteen was starting to think about what he wanted to do with his life and how he would make his way in the world. All this, against the backdrop of a global economic depression and a Britain that was still largely recovering from the effects of the Great War, the loss of almost a million men killed in combat, and countless others who came home but would never be quite the same again.

Meanwhile, on 30 January 1933, some 800 miles across the Channel in Germany, a 44-year-old Austrian-born German politician and First World War veteran by the name of Adolf Hitler was being installed as Chancellor of Germany.

After his war service Hitler had entered politics, joining the German Workers Party in 1919[10] before becoming head of the

National Socialist German Worker's Nazi party in 1921. His part in an attempted coup in Munich in 1923 led to five years imprisonment during which he was to write what effectively became his blueprint for the Reich, the toxic, rambling and anti-Semitic *Mein Kampf.* After his release he began to rebuild the Nazi party and by 1932 they were in the ascendancy. His appointment as Chancellor in 1933, albeit reluctantly, by President Von Hindenburg set in motion a train of events that would alter the course not only of my father's life but also millions of people around the world.

Ever the political opportunist, Hitler took advantage of the fire that gutted the Reichstag building on 27 February 1933[11] to convince Hindenburg that the nation was threatened by a communist inspired insurgency and that draconian powers were needed to extinguish the threat. The elderly Hindenburg loathed Hitler but felt compelled to act and consented to one of the most punitive and restrictive pieces of legislation ever passed in Germany. The resultant Reichstag Fire Decree[12] effectively extinguished civil liberty in Germany and cleared the way for dictatorship. The decree saw the suspension of freedom of speech and of a free press, the end of the right to assembly, incarceration of dissidents without charge, the abolition of political parties and complete autocracy over state local government institutions. The newly opened Dachau concentration camp, the first to be built, housed political prisoners and 'undesirables'. The first insidious steps against the Jewish Community were manifested in the ban on Jews in the civil service but, as history shows, worse was yet to come, much worse.

Books were revered by my father as rare possessions to be valued and looked after, they represented not only a gateway to knowledge but also an investment of hard-earned money. The organised burning of books by the Nazis in the Opernplatz in Berlin 1933, as shown in the newsreels of the time, would have been anathema to him. One of the authors burnt was Heinrich Heine, a German essayist of Jewish descent whose words in 1821 were to prove grimly prophetic:

> *Dort, wo man bucher verbrennt, verbrennt man am Ende auch Menschen* (Where they burn books, they will, in the end, burn human beings too).[13]

In August 1934, with Hindenburg now dead, Hitler proclaimed himself Führer of Germany and in another five short years Britain would again find itself embroiled with Germany in a devasting global conflict that would cost millions of lives. In the intervening years, Hitler embarked on an aggressive programme of rearmament and rebuilding, reducing unemployment rates in Germany, strengthening the German economy (in the early years at least) and galvanising the nation behind National Socialism by tapping into the heart of the Volkish ideology and using the humiliation of the Treaty of Versailles to further stoke the fires of national pride.[14]

Hitler now fixed his focus firmly on expansionism and on reclaiming the territories that had been taken from Germany as a result of the treaty. Talk of a coming war in Europe was an unpalatable thought for British families who were still dealing with the economic consequences of the previous conflict and the decimation of a generation of young men in the mud of Ypres, Flanders Passchendaele and Verdun. For British politicians appeasement became the order of the day and they clung forlornly to the hope that Herr Hitler's aggressive posturing regarding expansion and reunification were nothing more than exhibitionist sabre-rattling for domestic consumption only. With the *Anschluss Österreichs* on 12 March 1938 and the military occupation of Czechoslovakia in March 1939 (following the annexation of the Sudetenland in 1938), there can have been little doubt remaining for even the most optimistic of people that war in Europe was coming and that it was only a matter of time.

In Anglesey Street, Hednesford, as in so many other homes the length and breadth of the nation, young men and women regarded the growing tensions with Germany with a sense of foreboding and unease. Gone was the cheery, patriotic ardour of men clamouring to enlist to go and fight over twenty years before. The joyous mass enlistments of the 'Pals' Battalions – legions of men who enlisted with their friends as part of the great adventure to 'give the Hun a bloody nose' on the Western Front – were replaced by a numbed sense of shock as most left their broken and bloodied bodies in the mud of France, some with no known grave. The story of the Accrington Pals is a grim reminder of the realities of warfare at that time. In 1916 on the opening day of the Battle of the Somme 700 Accrington Pals took part in the attack. In just twenty short minutes, 580 of the Pals lay either dead or wounded.

At home Prime Minister Neville Chamberlain made a statement in the House of Commons on 31 March 1939 which amounted to a guarantee to Poland that if the country were to be attacked by Germany, Britain and France would step in and take direct military action to help protect that country:

> *... in the event of any action which clearly threatened Polish independence, and which the Polish Government accordingly considered it vital to resist with their national forces, His Majesty's Government would feel themselves bound at once to lend the Polish Government all support in their power. They have given the Polish Government an assurance to this effect. I may add that the French Government have authorised me to make it plain that they stand in the same position in this matter as do His Majesty's Government.*[15]

Prime Minister Neville Chamberlain, March 1939.

As an uneasy stand-off between the countries of Europe, the British Government introduced conscription on 27 April 1939 and the later introduction of The Military Training Act meant that men like my father were required to take six months military training as preparation for the expected conflict. My father duly enlisted in the Territorial Army and was no doubt manifestly shocked at just how poorly equipped they were and ill-prepared for any forthcoming occasion when it may be called upon to provide support to the regulars.

In the early hours of Friday, 1 September 1939, after several false flag incidents, German troops crossed the border into Poland supported by Stuka dive bombers and heavy armour and the invasion of Poland began in earnest. At 9pm Prime Minister Neville Chamberlain directed Sir Nevile Henderson, the British Ambassador in Berlin, to serve Von Ribbentrop with an ultimatum to withdraw troops from Poland. The next morning millions of people woke up in the towns and villages across the length and breadth of the UK to begin what my mother called 'one of the strangest weekends I can remember'. At the end of a working week life went on much as it always had done with people going about their daily business but there was a quiet and sombre mood. My mother Marjorie Corson, then a girl of 14, lived with her parents above their newsagents and tobacconist shop 'Corsons' on the Dudley Road in Wolverhampton.

During one of my discussions with her she remembered that apart from cigarettes and pipe tobacco people were most keen to buy papers and to read of the latest developments concerning the situation playing out in Poland. In nearby Hednesford my father spent Saturday in the saloon bar of his favourite haunt, the Anglesey Hotel, with his best friend and neighbour Bob Pritchard. The two men smoked cigarettes, supped beer and mulled over the probability of armed conflict with Germany and what that could mean for them both and many of their mates.

In Poland, President Moscicki upgraded the previous day's state of emergency to a state of war and as the Germans continued their Blitzkrieg campaign, Britons monitored the grim reports coming through on the radio regarding the deteriorating situation in Poland. At 9am on Sunday morning, with no response from Germany to the British Ambassador's ultimatum issued the preceding Friday, Chamberlain appealed one final time to Herr Hitler to announce by 11am that he would withdraw his troops and avert what now seemed to all other people in Britain to be inevitable. War.

Chapter 3

Standing Alone

We and France are today, in fulfilment of our obligations,
going to the aid of Poland, who is so bravely resisting this wicked and
unprovoked attack upon her people. We have a clear conscience...
.....And now that we have resolved to finish it,
I know that you will all play your part with calmness and courage.

Neville Chamberlain, 3 September 1939

At 11.15am on a bright, sunny, Sunday morning in late summer of 1939, millions huddled around their wireless sets the length and breadth of Britain to hear their Prime Minister Neville Chamberlain, in a voice sounding thin and strained, confirm what many had already suspected:

I am speaking to you from the Cabinet Room at 10
Downing Street. This morning the British ambassador
in Berlin handed the German government a final note
stating that unless we heard from them by 11 o'clock that
they were prepared, at once, to withdraw their troops from
Poland, a state of war would exist between us. I have to tell
you now that no such undertaking has been received, and
that consequently this country is at war with Germany.

Prime Minister Neville Chamberlain 3 September 1939

In fact, no response of any kind was ever received from Germany to Chamberlain's ultimatum. Hitler simply ignored it as he was convinced that Britain would not carry out its threat of a declaration of war. Hitler had always viewed the little island across the Channel as having very similar values, character traits and cultural heritage to the German Volk. He admired the British for their colonial and empiric past and believed that this was primarily due to their shared Anglo-Saxon bloodlines. Also, throughout the 1930s relations between the two countries had been relatively cordial and Edward VIII was well-known for his pro-Nazi sympathies. Even after his abdication in 1936 the following year the (now) Duke and Duchess of Windsor began their infamous and ill-fated tour of Germany, being feted by the Nazi leadership and pictured at various staged events and walkabouts throughout the nation. The propaganda benefits of the tour would have been obvious to Hitler, and especially to Joseph Goebbels, whereas for the Windsors it was no doubt a welcome positive reception and salve to the ego having been given the cold-shoulder by the British aristocracy and the public's unwillingness to accept the American divorcee Wallis Simpson.

There is, perhaps, another reason for Hitler's initial unwillingness to pursue a war against Britain and in it lies the rather curious story suggesting that Herr Hitler allegedly owed his life to a British 'Tommy' who spared him in the trenches during the First World War. Private Henry Tanday VC DCM MM, 5th Battalion, Duke of Wellington's Regiment, had fought from the early days of the Great War and served with great distinction at Ypres, The Somme and Passchendaele. During the latter months of 1918 he took part in the capture of Marcoing, where he earned his Victoria Cross, and on 28 September the story goes that he happened across a wounded, retreating German soldier and took aim but decided not to fire.[1] The fortunate soldier is said by Tanday to have nodded his thanks and moved on.

Years later a painting of a British soldier (Private Tanday) carrying a fellow wounded British officer on his shoulders at the Battle of Ypres was painted by the Italian artist Fortunino Matania. It is reported that Hitler had a copy of this painting and indeed showed it to Neville Chamberlain upon his visit to the Berchtesgaden in Bavaria in 1938, exclaiming that Tanday was the man who had saved his life. For some the story remains apocryphal, but others believe that there is evidence that it happened and that Tanday carried with him regret for his actions for the rest of his life. After witnessing first-hand the destruction of Coventry and London during the Blitz in 1940 he was reported as forever regretting his decision all those years earlier.[2]

As the nation's wireless sets crackled following Chamberlain's broadcast on that Sunday afternoon 3 September 1939, Tanday's story, if true, is indeed darkly ironic. In Dudley Road, Wolverhampton my mother Marjorie Corson ran to my grandfather William 'Billy' Corson, a veteran of the Great War, flung her arms around him and sobbed, 'You're not going Dad, they're not taking you!'[3] He smiled and reassured her that he was 'too old to fight this time around', but over the next seven years my mother was to lose many family friends, and latterly some school classmates who were old enough to fight but who, sadly, did not return home. Like many young girls of that time she confided that, in her late teens, although she would happily dance with 'service boys' as she called them, she would not allow herself to get involved in case they were lost.

> When I was at school in Wolverhampton I used to sit next to this boy who used to push me off the bench onto the floor and get me into trouble with the teacher. He was a grubby little devil and used to really get on my nerves and pull at the bows in my hair. Years later I was at a tea dance with Audrey and this very attractive RAF boy came up to me and asked for a dance – very handsome he was and he smiled and said 'You don't recognise me, do you Marjorie'? It was him!!! We danced and agreed to meet the following week but he never showed up, shortly afterwards I heard from a friend that he had been posted as missing, after that I never allowed myself to get too close, it happened to so many of those poor young boys.[4]

The sense of surrealism on that September day in 1939 when war was declared was further compounded by a test air raid warning in London at 11.27am that saw people scrambling for the newly-constructed air raid shelters. As the country began its life on a war-footing and mobilisation for the impending conflict ahead, young men and women across Britain began to think about what effect the war would have on them and how, and where, they could assist as part of the war effort. Despite Britain and France's assertion that they would go to the aid of

Poland, in reality very little practical assistance was provided and on 29 September, twenty-eight days after the invasion began, the Polish capital Warsaw finally fell into German hands.

By 6 October the German Army, assisted by Russian units, seized control of the entire country. Britain, meanwhile, was amassing its expeditionary force (the BEF) ready to go to France to help protect and assist France in the likely expectation of a German attack. By 27 September 152,000 men, 21,242 vehicles and 36,000 tons of ammunition had landed in France and further reinforcements added over the following months would swell that number considerably.[5] Despite fears of air raids and an assault on Britain, in the first eight months following the declaration of war very little fighting happened other than a few isolated engagements. What followed was essentially a prolonged stalemate, 'The Phoney War' as it became known, and was characterised by a period of frustration for those at home as they were forced to live under a raft of government restrictions, including the introduction of food coupons/rationing and constraints on movements, while life otherwise continued largely as normal.

For those who lived through it, it must have seemed the strangest of times with war raging only a short distance across the Channel and the devastation being wreaked throughout Europe, yet an eerie sense of normality continued in Britain while people prepared, filling sandbags, taping windows, making blackout curtains and waiting to see what would happen.

The declaration of war also saw the introduction of the National Service (Armed Forces) Act, requiring all medically fit males between 18 and 41 to register for service and wait for their papers. Joseph Harold Barratt, then 23, enlisted into the British Army on 15 March 1940, transferring from the Territorial Army, and after his initial training was complete he was posted to Shorncliffe in Kent, home of 22nd Field Regiment, Royal Artillery.

Part of the British 4th Infantry Division, 22 Field Regiment was one of the units sent to France as part of the British Expeditionary Force, under the overall command of General John Vereker, 6th Viscount Gort. Perhaps fortuitously my father joined too late to be sent over to France and was instead stationed on the outskirts of Dover, where his time was largely spent practising drills with his gun crew in case they should be redeployed across the Channel or required for home defence, as seemed increasingly likely. Like many he was watching with a keen eye the developments in France and the Low Countries as the German army continued its seemingly unstoppable march through neighbouring countries, pushing aside all in its path.

On 10 May German forces swept virtually unopposed into Luxembourg and then pushed out into Holland and Belgium. The Dutch army surrendered on 14 May prompted by the heavy aerial bombing of Rotterdam by the Heinkels of Kampfgeschwader 54, which completely destroyed the centre of the old city, killing 900 civilians and leaving over 85,000 people homeless. The Dutch had seen what had happened to Warsaw and feared what may become of other Dutch cities – Reichmarshal Göering lost no time in capitalising on these fears and had threatened that Utrecht would be the next city to be obliterated if the Dutch did not immediately lay down their weapons. Few doubted that he would do precisely that unless the aggressor's terms were met.

With the surrender of Holland, the German advance then swept aside Belgian resistance and pushed further into France. The speed of the Blitzkrieg stupefied the French and the combination of fast-moving mechanised infantry supported by German armour and effective air power made for an unstoppable force that made gains at an astonishing rate.[6]

Such was the speed of the German advance, especially the divisions led by Generals Heinz Guderian and Erwin Rommel, exceeding even the most optimistic projections from the high command, that at one stage Hitler himself tried to halt the advance, fearful that they may be over-reaching themselves. Nevertheless, Guderian pressed on and his determination to drive his armoured corps as far as supply lines allowed, the so called 'race for the sea', is largely credited with ensuring that that the remaining elements of the British Expeditionary Force and French ended up being trapped on the beaches at Dunkirk. It is estimated that at one point over 500,000 men were camped on the beaches, doing their best to survive the constant attack from German dive bombers and hoping against hope that they would somehow be rescued.

Operation Dynamo, the evacuation of troops from the beaches of Dunkirk, has been written about extensively in other books but the accomplishments of that day, including the mobilisation of the armada of naval vessels and small ships that crossed the Channel to help take men home, was certainly miraculous. Between 26 May and 4 June over 338,000 troops had been successfully rescued from the beaches in France. So many things aligned over those days to ensure success where seemingly disaster was the more likely scenario facing the nation – a calm sea, a period of good weather, a determined rear-guard action from British and French troops that frustrated the German advance. But also an order from Hitler (due to astrological prompts according to some) that the Armoured Corps should halt on 24 May.

While the saving of so many lives and the ability to recover such a large portion of the British Army intact was, effectively, priceless, the financial cost in lost equipment was to prove colossal as men were forced to abandon whatever they had in France; many only returned to England with their rifles and left everything else behind. It is estimated that 64,000 vehicles, 20,000 motorcycles, 76,000 tonnes of ammunition, 400,000 tonnes of supplies and 2,500 artillery pieces were left in France,[7] and although much of the equipment was disabled or spiked by retreating troops the Germans were able to recycle and re-use much of it.[8]

On 4 June, to a subdued House of Commons still reeling from the losses in France, Prime Minister Churchill delivered the second of the three key speeches that he made during the Battle of France. It is famous for the stirring oration at the end and defiant pledge to 'Fight on the beaches, (we shall) fight on the landing grounds', but earlier in the speech he also referenced the events of Dunkirk and the importance of air supremacy, which was to be so roundly tested in the weeks and months ahead during the Battle of Britain. The events of Dunkirk have often been portrayed in the time-honoured fashion of turning a crushing defeat into a victory of sorts and to Churchill's credit he resisted the temptation to do so in his speech:

We must be careful not to assign to this deliverance the attributes of a victory. Wars are not won by evacuation. But there was a victory inside this deliverance, which should be noted. It was gained by the air force. Many of our soldiers have not seen the air force at work...they underate its achievements. I have heard much talk of this; that is why I go out of my way to say this.

Winston Churchill, 4 June 1940

The beleaguered and battered remnants of the BEF stuck on the beaches had been embittered that there appeared to be no sign of the men of Fighter Command at Dunkirk, leaving them to be pounded incessantly by dive bombers on the beaches. The popular myth of the 'absent flyboys' persisted for many years, but the RAF was indeed there flying over 2,700 fighter sorties, losing 87 airmen and 100 aircraft during the course of the evacuation. The men of Fighter Command made a significant contribution to Operation Dynamo and suffered heavy losses as a result.

The sentiment in Churchill's speech cannot have been lost on those returning home from France or those men waiting for what now seemed the certainty of invasion, my father among them. He was stationed near Dover during the evacuation and watched as tens of thousands of bedraggled troops disembarked after being snatched from the beaches of Dunkirk. They had their rifles but very little else and he eyed them intently as they filed forlornly past, faces etched with grime – many streaked with blood – each face a stark testament to the horrors they had witnessed as an army in full retreat.

Of the 338,000 men lifted off the beaches in Operation Dynamo over 200,000 passed through Dover alone. I recall asking him about his army service prior to joining the Royal Air Force and he recounted in some detail his experience of watching the seemingly never-ending columns of men filing past. A ravaged army in retreat is never a pretty sight but having already seen what the Wehrmacht were capable of while smashing through the Sudetenland, Czechoslovakia, Poland and now France it must have been a particularly sobering experience. My father recalls the general sense of unease:

> *I felt sorry for them, we all did, seeing them filing past gave you the jitters as you could see that they had clearly all had a pretty rough time of it. We gave them our cigarettes, chocolate, whatever we had. It was a worrying time, you had a sense then of what was coming and just how stupidly ill-prepared we were. As I watched them filing past us and the scale of it all became clear I remember thinking – Christ, if they could do that to the main bulk of the army, what would they do to the rest of us?[9]*

On 18 June, Waterloo Day, Churchill had again addressed the nation in the House of Commons with what was to become known as his 'Finest Hour' speech and in it he pulled no punches, few doubted not only the steely resolve but also the stark threat in his words:

What General Weygand called the Battle of France is over: I expect that the Battle of Britain is about to begin. Upon this battle depends the survival of Christian Civilisation. Upon it depends our own British life, and the long continuity of our institutions and our Empire. The whole fury and might of the enemy must very soon be turned on us.

Following Dunkirk, talk of impending invasion was on everyone's lips as the nation waited for the anticipated onslaught that would surely precipitate an invasion of Britain. With Poland, Denmark, Norway, Belgium, Holland and now France all occupied, and the core of the British Army ragged and mauled, few believed that the country would be capable of mustering any form of sustained defence. At 5.20am on 6 July Dover was bombed and the town eventually became known as 'Hellfire Corner', suffering terribly from enemy bombing raids and dive-bombers attacking merchant ships in the Channel. For my father routine drills with his gun crew were now replaced with orders to form a defensive line with other units and be prepared to repel whatever came across the Channel. Armed with their Lee Enfield .303 rifles the remnants of his unit were one of many ordered to defend Dover alongside a makeshift force of new recruits, regulars and men of the LDV (Local Defence Volunteers) and recently formed Home Guard.

The events of these few months were to prove formulative in his eventual decision to leave the army and volunteer for aircrew as he told me one day while we were watching a programme about the circumstances leading up to the Battle of Britain. I vividly recall his derision when talking about the state of readiness of the country to repel the expected assault from the Germans by land, sea and air:

> *It was idiotic really; we were told that we were the front line and had to defend against the invasion and that we were 'not to retreat but to fight where we stood'. Half of the blokes with us weren't even regulars and didn't even have a rifle as there weren't enough to go around. So you had a ragbag of old men and boys with pitchforks and staves mixed in with a load of green recruits like us and we were supposed to fight off well trained and well-armed German parachutists! It really was laughable when you think about it, what on earth did they expect us to do? If they had have invaded us it would have been all over very quickly I'm pretty sure of that.*

As time passed and Hitler delayed his plans for invasion the British Army was given much-needed breathing space to re-equip. Reasons for Hitler's dalliance are debated even to this day. Some claim that he was nervous about launching an invasion without first securing air supremacy over the skies of England, others that he was fearful of having overreached himself and his astrological advisors had insisted that invasion was not prudent. Yet another strain of thought contends that

Hitler still held out hope that Britain would eventually agree to some kind of neutrality in return for allowing Hitler to operate unopposed in Europe (if true the events of Dunkirk would no doubt have bolstered his expectations). Other historians have claimed that Hitler had simply overstretched his supply lines and, with Britain no longer seen as an immediate threat, it was felt that a decision could be left until such time as the men in the field were rested and re-supplied.

Whatever the real explanation either one, or most likely a combination of all the above to some degree, the delay gave Britain vital breathing space and by the time the eventual invasion plan of Britain, *Unternehmen Seelowe* (Operation Sealion), was put into effect in July 1940 the country had had precious time to recover and to re-equip. As a prerequisite for invasion Hitler had insisted on air superiority and Göering had rashly promised to deliver it. The dogged resistance of Fighter Command and the heavy attrition rates suffered by the Luftwaffe allowed further scope for recovery and by the height of the Battle of Britain in September the army could muster a full sixteen divisions spread across the South East of England to defend against invasion from sea or airborne assault.

Fighter Command's frontline squadrons themselves grew stronger towards the end of the battle and with mounting losses inflicted on his aircrews and air supremacy an ever-distant hope, Hitler postponed Sealion 'until 1941', eventually abandoning the idea altogether and casting his eyes towards the east with *führerdirektiv 21* – Operation Barbarossa, the planned invasion of Mother Russia.

Nevertheless, despite the staving off of invasion, there was among many a wider sense of impotence and never more so than in the case of my father. With the threat of invasion receding, he told me that he and his gun crew were mostly deployed filling in bomb craters around Dover and clearing rubble from the sporadic bombing. Journeying back to the Midlands on leave in the autumn of 1940 he witnessed first-hand the devastation wrought on the city of Coventry, only 35 miles or so from Hednesford, that saw almost two-thirds of the city's buildings destroyed and hundreds killed and wounded. Seeing the devastation of Coventry seemed to have had, my aunts later told me, a profound effect on my father and he became impatient to do something that would allow him to strike back – to do something tangible that would see the death and destruction around him avenged with attacks on Germany itself.

In the early years of the war at least, the only force deemed capable of doing precisely that was the RAF and, more specifically, Bomber Command. At some point my father's mind was made up and he made the decision that he wanted to transfer from the army and volunteer for the RAF. The wheels were duly set in motion and he put in for a transfer from the army to volunteer for RAF aircrew. On 17 April 1941, while still in the South East, he was given a special leave pass, signed by Captain E.T.P. Ford and told to make his way to the Aviation Candidates Selection Board in Oxford.[10]

Packing up his kit he was to report to Sergeant Jarrett at Portsmouth Station at 19:45 hrs and he joined other candidates on parade before boarding the 20:30hrs train from Portsmouth to Oxford. At Oxford he spent the night at Cowley Barracks, home of the Oxford & Buckinghamshire Light Infantry, with orders to report to the Aircrew Selection Board at the Old Clarendon Laboratories Building, Oxford at 08:30hrs on the morning of Friday, 18 April 1941, to be assessed for suitability as aircrew. The selection process itself took two days during which my father went through an RAF medical examination to check his overall fitness and from there sat the General Intelligence Test (G.I.T) and thence the Elementary Maths Test (E.M.T). He passed all three with ease and after a final interview with the Aircrew Selection panel he was accepted and recommended for training as a pilot.

On Saturday, 7 June 1941 former Artilleryman Joseph Harold Barratt now became AC2 (Aircraftsman 2nd Class) Joseph Harold Barratt, Service Number 657168 RAFVR (Royal Air Force Volunteer Reserve). On the following Saturday he arrived at the newly formed 9 ITW (Initial Training Wing) at Stratford-upon-Avon for basic training, which included the usual drill instruction as his introduction into the Royal Air Force, but also basic instruction on a range of subjects including flight theory, mathematics, navigation and basic meteorology plus he took his initial flights in a de Havilland Tiger Moth.

After his initial period of instruction was over he was, like so many young men, destined to pass through the British Commonwealth Air Training Plan that would see him leave England for Canada to be put through his paces and learn his craft away from the risks of enemy attack in the air. The British Commonwealth Air Training Plan (BCATP), otherwise known as 'the Plan', remains to this day one of the most ambitious and large-scale aviation training programmes in history. Between

1940 and 1945 almost half of the aircrews who served in the RAF, RCAF, RAAF, RNZAF and Fleet Air Arm (whether as pilots, navigators, gunners, bomb aimers, wireless operators or flight engineers) had been trained under the programme.

Host countries included Australia and New Zealand, Canada, and the United States, South Africa, Rhodesia and Bermuda. Unlike the UK, which was considered not suitable for aircrew training due to the risk of attack from the air, poor weather and ongoing air operations by the RAF, these far-flung locations allowed crews to be trained in relative safety, in good weather and in geographical locations that offered vast amounts of space for both flight, gunnery and navigation training. They were immensely popular with the crews.

On 2 August 1941 my father was promoted to LAC (Leading Aircraftsman) and after a short period of leave would board one of the large cruise liners that had been hastily pressed into service as troop ships (an array of luxury liners that included the Titanic's sister ship the *Britannic*, the *Queen Mary* and the *Queen Elizabeth*) to take thousands of young Air Cadets to Canada to train as aircrew.

The start of the long and arduous process of training for his part in Bomber Command had now begun in earnest.

Chapter 4

Owls and Bloody Fools

Only Owls and Bloody Fools Fly at Night

Group Captain Tom Sawyer DFC

As my father embarked on one of the many cruise ships from Portsmouth bound for Canada it must have been a strange time for him. It was the first time in his life that he had left his native shores, in any capacity, but he was finally doing something that he wanted to do, to fly and to contribute to the war effort. His apprehension at undertaking such a long sea voyage (another first) during wartime was no doubt tempered by his natural inquisitiveness and excitement at visiting a country on the other side of the world that he had studied and read about at school and seen some of the culture on the newsreels and features. He would also have been looking forward to life in the RAF, learning to fly and being afforded opportunities that he almost certainly would not have experienced had his life followed its former peacetime course and the natural progression of an Estimating Clerk at the local colliery. By all accounts he relished the task ahead and was determined to apply himself to whatever lay before him.

On Monday, 25 August 1941, he arrived at No.1 Manning Depot, Royal Canadian Air Force (RCAF) in Toronto, Canada and the following day he reported to the American Consulate in Toronto as an Official Student (Aircrew Under training) where under application 2156 he made his application for a non-immigration visa to P.W. Clough, Vice Consul, for a six month visa. My father was based at the Naval Air Station at Pensacola for the start of his Pilot training.[1] Built in 1913 the NAS is known as 'The Cradle of Naval Aviation' and over the years countless US Navy, Marine and Coast Guard Pilots have passed through this esteemed facility.

Boarding a Canadian Pacific Railway train from Toronto for Pensacola on 27 August, his papers checked by US Immigrant Inspector Arthur P. Hodson, my father settled down for the 1,200 mile 19 hour journey from the edge of Lake Ontario to the Florida coast. On Thursday, 28 August The Louisville & Nashville Railroad Dining Car Service offered a special meal for the RAF pilots en route to Florida including Fresh Vegetable Soup to start and the choice of Ocean Snapper with a Creole sauce or Sirloin of Beef followed by Ice Cream and Coffee.[2] My father enjoyed his food and in later life always had the best (as a young boy I recall the local 'high quality' butcher delivering to the house, always finest steak and the best cuts of lamb and pork – I put this down to the regular hunger he felt as a boy, and then the deprivations he suffered as a PoW, but I also smile at the thought of his undoubted delight at the meals served up in Canada and the US compared to what he was used to being served in wartime England). Upon reaching Pensacola he would begin an intensive period of training where he was assessed for suitability as a pilot or other aircrew. During this time he became fully acquainted with two aircraft that left a lasting impression on him – the North American Harvard and, his personal favourite, the Boeing Stearman.

The Harvard was a stalwart of the aircrew training programme and over 17,000 of these versatile, robust airframes were built – 5,000 alone were supplied to the British and Commonwealth Air Forces. Powered by a single Pratt & Whitney R-1340 Wasp radial engine delivering 600hp the Harvard had a top speed of 208mph with a service ceiling of over 24,000ft. It was popular with cadets and instructors as the cockpit felt and looked like a combat aircraft. North American designed the aircraft to be exactly that, but also to make it more forgiving for those just learning to fly and who were 'learning the ropes' before graduating to the real deal.

The Boeing Stearman biplane was produced in much smaller numbers (approximately 10,600 were built) than the Harvard but it was to become the go-to pilot trainer during the Second World War. Rugged, hard-working and dependable, many Stearmans were retained as crop-dusters after the war, and many are still in use today in flying schools, in private ownership and as stunt aircraft. Compared to the Harvard the Stearman was infinitely more sedate, powered by a Continental R-670 radial engine delivering 220hp. It had a modest ceiling of just over 11,000 feet, but pilots loved them for their accessibility, strength of design and ability to soak up anything that rookie pilots could throw at them.

It is said that they were deliberately hard to control to ensure they were given a healthy respect by their pilots and an 'aversion to complacency'. Certainly, my father always spoke very highly of the aircraft and enjoyed his time flying in it. In the 1970s he spoke several times about wanting to take refresher flying lessons, obtain his pilot's licence and buy an aircraft (and nearly did so as a sharer with a former Spitfire pilot at Blackbushe Aerodrome) and the Stearman was high on their list of potential acquisitions, such was his regard for the old aircraft. Despite opting for training as pilot at the end of his training my father was marked out as more suitable as an Air Observer (Navigator) and so was recommended in his final assessment for training as an Air Navigator – a common occurrence it would seem – and so he began to prepare for the next phase of his training.

It is worth remembering that at this stage of the war the United States was still neutral and celebrated aviator Charles Lindbergh (he of 'Spirit of St Louis' fame) was particularly outspoken in his belief that the USA should stay out of the war. Lindbergh was a leading figure in the 'America First' committee and believed that Britain, despite its rhetoric and propaganda, was now losing the war.[3]

For some time it looked like Lindbergh and the AFC were indeed winning this particular argument, but all this was to change at 7:48hrs (Hawaiian Time) on 7 December when a mix of fighters, bombers and torpedo bombers of the Imperial Japanese Navy, 353 aircraft in all, attacked the naval base at Pearl Harbor. By the time the attack ended they had sunk four American battleships, three cruisers, three destroyers, two other ships and destroyed over 175 aircraft. In total 2,403 US navy personnel were killed and 1,178 wounded – 1,177 men were lost on the USS *Arizona* alone, the majority still lie within its sunken hull today. For Lindbergh the shock waves of the Pearl Harbor attack ran deep and although the stain of anti-Semitism and association as a Nazi sympathiser often come to the fore whenever his name is mentioned, what is clearly evidenced in the historical record is that, though refused recommissioning into the services (reputedly on the instruction of The White House) he is believed to have participated in fifty combat missions as a civilian and is credited with shooting down a Mitsubishi Ki-51 observation aircraft in July 1944.[4]

On Friday, 16 January 1942 my father was confirmed as being recommended for instruction as an Air Navigator and he was posted to 31 ANS (Air Navigation School) based at Port Albert Ontario and so embarked on the return journey to Canada to complete his training. On Monday, 26 January 1942 he finally arrived at 31 Air Navigation School Port Albert, Ontario where he began the intensive training that would eventually see him become a qualified navigator in a frontline squadron in Bomber Command. Originally based in Wales at St Athan, No.31 Air Navigation School suffered heavily from attention by Göering's Luftwaffe during the Battle of Britain and as a result it was relocated to Port Albert, Ontario Canada. Opened in October 1940 and becoming operational in November, No.31 Air Navigation School was located on the east coast of Lake Huron and went on to produce 1,964 student navigators and observers, the vast majority of whom went on to form part of the backbone of Bomber Command's frontline crews.

Students were instructed in the use of the Astral compass as well as the basics of course plotting and target location. His new 'office' for the next few weeks would be that other stalwart of the training schools, the Avro Anson. The twin-engine monoplane, originally conceived in the mid-thirties as a maritime reconnaissance aircraft, was deemed obsolete for front line duties and so was relegated to training, but the young aircrew loved it. Powered by two Armstrong Siddeley Cheetah radial engines the Anson was capable of a pedestrian cruising speed of 158mph with an operational ceiling of 19,000 feet.

In the 'Annie' they had an aircraft that was durable and dependable, spacious, adaptable and relatively easy to fly with superb visibility. I recall my father often spoke of the Anson with great fondness and enjoyed his flight time in the aircraft while he was putting into practice in the air what he had been learning in the classroom.

My father's journey to the stars as a navigator started in earnest on Tuesday, 10 February 1942 at 9:20hrs when he walked out with Pilot Officer Simpson for the first of his 'Air Experience' flights. As they walked towards the row of bright yellow Avro Anson trainers neatly parked up outside the vast hangers, the sheer scale of the facilities must have had an impact on him. Anson R9714 was destined to be the first of many examples of the marque that he flew in. Between 10 February and 8 May his logbook shows that he amassed a total of seventy-five hours flying time in the sturdy little aircraft (fifty-four in daytime flying) in thirty-seven separate flights and, bar a few exceptions, taking to the air in a different Anson for each flight which highlights how just sizeable the roster of aircraft possessed by the training school must have been.[5]

The early flights in February and March saw him primarily focused on basic map reading, association of time and distance, drift taking and air plots and then on 19 March, as 2nd

Navigator in Anson N9592 piloted by Sergeant Staton, he had his first experience of taking plots, fixes and winds by use of Astro Compass fixes. Monday, 25 May saw him take his first night flight, this time in Anson R9650 piloted by Flying Officer Cast. Leaving the ground at 20:07hrs they took a short two-hour flight and this was followed the following day with another two flights, one during the day and one at night to practise night map reading.

As March rolled into April the flights became more frequent and detailed with a focus on DR navigation techniques. DR, or 'Dead Reckoning' navigation to give it its full name, is the process of calculating the current position of a moving object (an aircraft in this case) by using a previously known position ('fix') and then using estimated values of airspeed, heading direction and course over an elapsed time taking into account 'drift' (the effect of wind on an aircraft). The ability of a navigator to be able to fix the position of his aircraft accurately in the air and to keep his pilot constantly informed with course changes or corrections was naturally key and my father seems to have been particularly capable in this regard. As he neared the end of his initial training at 31 ANS his final few flights were a mix of daytime and night navigation exercises, finding a pre-ordained 'target', checking positions by use of Astro compass and then recce and photography to prove that the correct target had been found and marked.

On 8 May aboard Anson N5008 with Flight Leader Appleton at the controls, my father made his final short night flight of the course. In his assessment he obtained 1221 out of a possible 1600 marks (75.7%) and passed the Air Observers Navigation Course, described by Chief Instructor Squadron Leader W.J.V. Branch as 'an above average navigator'. After successfully completing the basic training course my father then began the Advanced Navigation Course, still at 31 Air Navigation School, and from 18 May to 5 June 1942 he completed a further 33 hours flying time making 14 separate flights in the trusty Anson, this time focusing on navigation by the stars, sight taking and plotting Astrograph fixes.

On the final day of his training in Canada on 5 June 1942, under clear blue skies, my father climbed out of Anson K8774 pulled off his helmet, swept his fingers through his hair and realised, with a smile, that he had finished that leg of his journey – he passed his Advanced Navigation Course and his logbook was signed off once more by Squadron Leader Branch with the added note 'Recommended for night bombers'.

LAC (Leading Aircraftman) 657168 Joseph Harold Barratt was now qualified as both an Air Navigator and an Astro Navigator and two days later on 8 June 1942 he received his promotion from leading aircraftsman to sergeant. Glancing down at the newly sewn stripes on his uniform he was now ready to return to the United Kingdom to begin the next phase of his training. However before he returned to home shores, like many airmen who perhaps had never been abroad before, he wanted to see the States and he took a short period of leave where he visited New York and took in the sights and sounds of a bustling city. On the way through he took a trip, first to the top of the Empire State Building – built only twelve or so years before and the world's tallest building, and then to Macy's the famous department store where he picked up some gifts for his seven sisters. Finally on Tuesday, 30 June 1942 he boarded one of the many troop ships in Brooklyn for the two-week voyage across the Atlantic back to England.

Arriving in wartime Portsmouth on 14 July, a warm and sunny summer day, as he walked down the gangplank, he must have wondered what had changed in the time he had been away. Heaving his kit bag over his shoulder he caught a train to Bournemouth and headed for 3 PRC (Personnel Reception Centre) which was a central mustering point for literally thousands of aircrew returning to the UK after their training in Canada was concluded. Men were housed in requisitioned hotels and buildings. Unfortunately, this did not go unnoticed by the Luftwaffe who often targeted the town for special attention accordingly.[6]

Following a wait of three or so weeks he was then ordered to report to No.1 (0) AFU (Advanced Flying Unit) based at RAF Wigtown in Dumfries and Galloway. The airfield cuts a somewhat desolate if peaceful picture today, most of the site itself has returned to agricultural use, but the ghostly and derelict control tower and a few buildings can be seen dotted across the landscape. In 1942 it was a very different picture that greeted my father and the many other airmen who found themselves posted to the station. Constructed on the Machars Peninsula just east of Stranraer, RAF Wigtown would eventually find itself home to several operational squadrons including 174, 175 and 182 Squadrons, equipped with rocket-firing Hawker Typhoons in 1943. However, in this period of its life it was a training station preparing trainee airmen fresh home from Canada for the next phase of their progression through RAF training.

On 7 August 1942 my father presented himself at RAF Wigtown and one week later at 12:15hrs strode out with pilot Sergeant Minchin to continue the next phase of his training, once again on the trusty old Avro Anson that equipped the base. Over the next three weeks his logbook records thirteen flights taken while at 1 AFU notching up an additional twenty-eight hours on Ansons, fourteen of those flying at night and with exercises concentrated primarily on DR navigation, map reading, drifts and plots. His last flight was at 14:22hrs with Warrant Officer Steele piloting and a few days later he was marked as having passed the course, and noted as a 'consistent marker'.

Having completed his allotted training time on the archaic Ansons he was now to enter into the final phase of his training, in preparation for joining a frontline squadron of Bomber Command and on 8 September he was posted to 20 OTU (Operational Training Unit) based on the coast at Lossiemouth, North East Scotland. As well as a new set of faces and landscapes, this posting would also mean the introduction of a new aircraft type for my father to get used to – the Wellington Bomber, in which he would spend the next twenty-five training flights.

This superb two engine long-range medium bomber was designed at Brooklands near Weybridge in Surrey in the thirties by a team that included Barnes Wallis, designer of the famous bouncing bomb used in the Dams raid by 617 Squadron. Wallis was principally responsible for the development of the intricate geodetic airframe, something that is widely regarded as chiefly accountable for the Wellington's reputation for robustness and its ability to soak up a good deal of punishment, but still bring its crew safely home. The aircraft was well liked by aircrews and became known affectionately as the 'Wimpy' after the portly character of hamburger-eating sidekick 'J. Wellington Wimpy' in the Popeye cartoons of the day. Hardly any examples survive today – the RAF Museum at Hendon has a superb example (used in the 1955 film 'The Dambusters') but she saw no operational action. However back in 1985 Wellington N2980 'R-Robert' was successfully recovered from the bottom of Loch Ness having ditched there in 1940 following engine failure while on a night flying training exercise.[7]

Compared to the relatively open and airy interior of the Anson, the Wellington – a considerably larger airframe – must have come as somewhat of a shock to my father. Cramped and cluttered, many crews found it to be a claustrophobic 'office' in which to work but, as with the Anson, my father always spoke of the Wimpey with a smile and was enthusiastic about its performance in the air.

As well as new aircraft it would also mean the instigation of the 'crewing up process' where men would finally begin the process of forming themselves into crews. By 1943 the nucleus of would-be Halifax crews would form at this point – pilot, navigator, bomb aimer, wireless operator and a gunner. Flight Engineers had already been sent on to the Heavy Conversion Units to learn the specifics of the four engine Halifax and with the addition of the mid-upper gunner the five men would become seven. Operational Training Units were just that, each man had already proven their individual aptitude within the initial training postings – now they were being melded into coherent crews, with a rigorous training programme designed to prepare men for operational night flying in a frontline squadron of Bomber Command.

On arrival they were billeted in the various Nissen huts that scattered the camp – cold, damp and furnished with iron bunks, a few sticks of furniture and a stove, they were nevertheless 'home' for next few weeks. In the briefing room the following day the new intake of 20 OTU was assembled, my father amongst them, and the excited chatter was quickly hushed as the instructors outlined the content of the next few weeks – initially it would be classroom instruction and intensive sessions on all aspects of navigation, followed by all the other skills essential to operate a heavy bomber: aircraft layout, controls, parachute training, dinghy drills, low-level flying, bombing, navigation and flight training.

However, the initial session the following morning would be devoted to 'crewing up'. One would perhaps have expected the RAF to divide the men into crews automatically, but it was generally felt more advisable that they should mingle and find their own way. Either way the trainees were instructed to report to one of the large aircraft hangers the following morning and ordered to peel off and get themselves into crews. With a bemused air the young airmen duly filed in to No.2 hanger at Lossiemouth and slowly the process began until eventually my father saw a young, dark-haired airman walk smartly up to him and, with a broad smile, thrust out his hand and confidently announced himself:

'Morning. Bernard Happold – I'm a pilot.'[8]

My father smiled back and returned the customary firm handshake. 'Harry Barratt, I'm a Navigator.'

'So then Harry,' continued my father's new-found friend 'Don't suppose you know any of the Bomb Aimers or Wireless Op's yet do you?'

My father laughed. 'Not had much chance yet, what about that bloke over there?'

The two men sauntered over to introduce themselves: 'Hello – we're looking for a Bomb Aimer and a Wireless Op for our crew, how are you fixed?'

The young Scot shook hands with the two men and instantly the duo had become a trio: 'I'm John Brownlie, I'm a Wireless Op, I'd be happy to pitch in with you if you'll have me.' At that point he immediately beckoned over another airman who had been watching them intently.

'I met this fellow this morning – he's another John, and another Scot, John Baxter, he's a Bomb Aimer. Pleased to meet you lads.'

And so the laughter, the banter and the introductions continued. After a while the four aircrew realised that they still needed to complete their crew and at some point they bumped into the plucky little Welshman Thomas Jones, a rear gunner, who had the stature and athleticism needed to get in (and out) of the tail turret and he was duly welcomed into the fold. In a scene that was to be repeated countless times in mess halls across the country, men came to know each other and cement themselves as a crew – chatting, laughing, swapping stories and jokes and starting to forge the bonds that, they hoped, would galvanise them in the air as well as on the ground.

The crew of five, as they now were, began to get to know each other, they would pick up their Flight Engineer and mid-upper gunner at the Heavy conversion Unit (as neither position was required for Wellingtons) but for now, they nevertheless represented five-sevenths of a complete Halifax crew. With the classroom sessions complete the partial crews moved into the second part of their final training.

At 9:45hrs on Sunday, 1 November 1942, as 2nd Navigator, my father took his first flight in a Wellington under the stewardship of Sergeant Burroughs. The aircraft for that trip was R1060, one of the training unit's oldest aircraft, but one that would go on to provide faithful service for a good many aircrews during its lengthy career.[9] Focusing primarily on night flying cross country, exercises and local bombing practice, he would spend almost the next two months in the air virtually every other day fine-tuning the skills that he had developed since the early training days in Canada. He was also developing the night-flying navigation skills that both he and his crew would eventually need (and rely on) for the arduous five and six hour flights to targets across the length and breadth of Germany.

As they walked out to the aircraft the Wellington's heavily weathered and oiled appearance, its engine nacelles shining silver where the dark paint had been worn away over many years, was evidence of its extensive operational service before being transferred to instructional duties. In many ways this would see the start of one of the most dangerous periods of flying for the newly formed crews as the combination of elderly and essentially clapped-out aircraft and rookie crews accounted for the disproportionately high number of Bomber Command airmen killed before they had even taken part in a single operation over enemy territory. Over 10 per cent of Bomber Command's losses happened in training and as one crew member recalls, often finding a serviceable aircraft to fly on a night-time training op was 'sometimes a matter of going from airframe to airframe' to find one that was deemed serviceable enough to take into the air. Sadly, for many crews luck did not hold out and over 5,000 trainee aircrew died as a result of flying accidents while on training flights, mostly a mix of pilot error and mechanical failure.

His initial flight on R1060 as a 2nd Navigator was to acclimatise him to the Wellington and for the next month or so he would fly as 2nd and 1st Navigator on a variety of exercises, all of them cross country and the majority would be on night flying. Looking up at the noticeboard for the day's training and crew pairings on Monday 16 November my father was with Sergeant Happold. Take off time was 09:50hrs.

The fledging crew of Bernard Happold, my father, John Brownlie, John Baxter and Tommy Jones climbed into Wellington HD945 and headed out from Lossiemouth on a five-hour flight, the usual cross country and marking exercise which would become standard for all crew over the next few weeks. The following day my father was again in the air, this time with Pilot Officer Burroughs as pilot (his third outing with him) to ensure that he was making good progress and in the same vein subsequent flights with different pilots followed including, on 25 November, a trip aboard another of the units' old warhorses with Flight Lieutenant Lodge. Wellington W5690,[10] now an elderly aircraft, was a veteran of many bombing raids across Germany in 1941 and had several esteemed Bomber Command pilots at her controls before eventually being transferred to training duties with 20 and then 15 OTUs.

On 2 December Sergeant Happold was once more the pilot as my father and the crew took part in a night cross country exercise on Wellington 1089. From this point forward he made a further twelve flights to complete his training at Lossiemouth. The pilot for eight of these flights was Sergeant Happold as the crew finally melded into shape.

On 15 and 18 December my father completed his final flights with 20 OTU, both with Bernard Happold as the pilot, in Wellington R1707[11] and N2758[12] respectively. His logbook summary, signed off by Wing Commander Martin, Training Wing OC (Officer Commanding), shows that he had completed twenty-nine and a half hours day flying on Wellingtons and forty hours forty-five minutes of night flying.

With his training now complete my father and the rest of his crew packed their kit ready to report to 1652 HCU (Heavy Conversion Unit) in Yorkshire, for their final period of training on the four engine Halifax prior to beginning operational flying.

Chapter 5

Band of Brothers

We few, we happy few, we band of brothers;
For he today that sheds his blood with me
Shall be my brother; be he ne'er so vile,
This day shall gentle his condition:

Henry V, Act IV, Scene III

Wednesday, 30 December 1942 was a cold and frosty day, with the daytime temperature just a degree or so over freezing, when my father and his fledgling crew mates arrived from Lossiemouth to report to 1652 HCU (Heavy Conversion Unit) at Marston Moor.

Named after the nearby site of the 1644 Civil War battle that saw Cromwell's Ironsides rout the Royalist cavalry under Prince Rupert of the Rhine, the RAF base was approximately halfway between the towns of Harrogate and York and would become their home for the next couple of months or so, until they were deemed ready to be posted to a frontline squadron. Formed by the RAF in late 1941, Heavy Conversion Units were intended to be the final stepping stone between formal training and operational flying, and they gave crews the chance to get accustomed to the switch between the two-engine medium bombers like the Wellington that they were used to at the

OTUs, to the more powerful four engine 'heavies' that they would soon be flying over the night skies in Germany.

Each Heavy Conversion Course consisted of a period of instruction on the ground supplemented by time in the air where the new crew would be joined by instructors. These instructors were usually experienced flyers who had completed their tour of thirty ops and who were then trained as instructors before returning to ops at a later date to undertake their second 'tour'. When they were satisfied that their new charges under training were sufficiently competent, the crews would be allowed to undertake further flights on their own to complete their training.

Conditions at the base were rudimentary and the crews were assigned one of the many Nissen huts that were dotted around. Sparsely furnished with iron bed frames, basic racks for clothes and a central stove for warmth, they were cold and draughty, but for each of the crews it was home and a place for them to gel and get used to each other. Throughout history and pretty much in any circumstances, men thrown together in combat formed a bond that was also unique. They were fiercely loyal to each other, both within the service and within their unit. In a specialist team like a bomber crew each man was honed in his particular trade, be that as pilot, navigator, gunner, air bomber or whatever and they all knew that their survival depended upon their individual ability to do their own job and to function collectively as a team. As aircrew they would hang out together, drinking, eating, sleeping, socialising, training and flying together and that meant they had to quickly adapt to and absorb their individual, foibles and idiosyncrasies. They had to learn to be around people who ordinarily they would probably never have socialised with – they had to learn tolerance of each other and to accept the small differences that, perhaps, in civilian life would become irritants or cause tension. There could be no room for personality clashes, grudges, grievances or petty disagreements in the air, their lives depended on each other's ability to function and do their job – of not wanting to let the other fellow down and to engender a feeling that, whatever happened, they would be able to count on themselves and on each other when the going got tough.

However, one of the first things that had to happen was that the 'five' men from Lossiemouth rapidly needed to become a full crew of seven to operate the Halifax operationally. For this they needed to find a Flight Engineer and a Mid Upper Gunner.

Unlike at the OTU in Lossiemouth where they had been largely left to their own devices to form would-be crews, once they reached the Heavy Conversion Unit each crew would be assigned a Flight Engineer and an additional gunner. For some this was the preferred option as it removed the need to spend time 'finding' someone suitable, whereas for others there were concerns about having crew members foisted upon them – what if they didn't gel? What if they weren't quite up to scratch and would be a potential weak link in the crew? For Bernard Happold, my father and the rest of the crew they appeared to have struck gold on both occasions. Their Flight Engineer came to them in the form of the tall, fair-haired Gordon Bowles. Handsome, thoughtful, calm and affable, the others took to him straight away and Bernard Happold was particularly pleased to have him on board as his right-hand man in the cockpit. In a Halifax (and also in the Lancaster and Stirling) the Flight

Engineer was capable of flying the aircraft should anything happen to the pilot, as well as tackling any issues in the air and so having someone with the temperament to match his technical skillset was of paramount importance.

Though only twenty years of age he had impressed with his cool-headedness and seemed wise beyond his years. He had married his eighteen-year-old sweetheart just four days before my father and the other crew had arrived at Marston Moor. All the crew needed now was to find another air gunner who would occupy the mid-upper turret.

At just nineteen Air Gunner Duncan Roy McGregor – Roy as he preferred to be called – was destined to become the youngest member of the crew. Originally from Uxbridge in Middlesex, Roy's father, Dr John Roy McGregor, an ex-Scottish Rugby International, was Medical Director at Harefield Hospital (then a sanatorium for Tuberculosis) and the family lived in the large house in the grounds of the hospital. Speaking in 1997 his sister Helen remembered him as a kind, thoughtful, dedicated but quite reserved man who had been very proud to join the RAF and wanted to do his bit for the country. Though young, he was sporty, confident and enthusiastic and keen to demonstrate his capability within the Boulton & Paul powered gun turret and to protect the aircraft and the crew with the snarl of its Browning machine guns. Roy would have been conscious of being the youngest (by some seven years) but he was well-liked by his crewmates and liked those he had fallen in with.

Duly introduced, the full crew no doubt retired to the mess facility or their hut to swap cigarettes, stories and catching up on what each had been up to and what lay ahead for them. Gazing out across the windswept fields in the fading winter light, the dark shapes of the Halifaxes dotted around the base would have been silhouetted against the winter skies, lying in wait for their rookie crews. Wartime bomber crews made for an interesting cross-section of society – men drawn from all walks of life, social strata and parts of Britain (two Scotsmen, a Welshman and four Englishmen in the case of the Happold crew). They were strangers who were thrown together by adversity but who, within a few weeks, would form a bond of brotherhood in the air that is unlike any other.

For many they inhabited different worlds in peacetime and their life experiences and interests would be very different. My father, a miner's son with little access to books but a keen intellect and a desire to progress in life, bunked next to his skipper – Bernard Happold – the son of a banker who had enjoyed the fruits of comfortable living, a public-school education and everything that went with it. From what I gleaned from my father during our infrequent discussions about his war service, and from what his siblings told me, Bernard and my father hit it off almost immediately at Lossiemouth and got along famously – a mutual love of books and sports gave them much to talk about and for two young men with such different backgrounds they just appeared to click.

Bernard Happold, a Sergeant pilot, would have the job of skippering the crew – of getting them into the air, over to the target and back home again safely. At just twenty-two years of age Bernard was typical of that band of young men who had volunteered enthusiastically for a life in the RAF. Originally from Hartley in Westmoreland, he was the only son of William Leonard and Clara Eleanor Happold. As a young boy Bernard was fascinated by aeroplanes and flying and filled his bedroom with models and drawings of various aircraft. He had a natural gift for painting and art – making gifts of his work to friends and family. His father was a bank manager at the Midland Bank in Kirkby Stephen, Cumbria, and so had the means to pay for private education and to send his young son away to public school. Bernard attended Sedbergh School in Cumbria. Founded in 1525 and re-established in 1551 as a grammar school, Sedbergh thrives to this day. The alma mater of such notables as ex-England Rugby Internationals Will Carling and Will Greenwood, the dramatist John Arden and no less than three recipients of the Victoria Cross, it's motto 'Dura Virum Nutrix' (A Stern Nurse of Men) gives a clue, perhaps, to the stoic values instilled in its young men (and, since 2001, into its young women also).

Like many public schools Sedburgh advocated the 'house' system and believed that it creates and sustains a sense of belonging, community, team-work and pride, inspiring confidence, developing social skills and a strong sense of pride in team and community – values that would have been instilled in Bernard Happold from an early age no doubt and which would certainly have helped him in his future role as Skipper of his crew, both in terms of the standards that he would have set for himself and also for the rest of his crew.

A member of Powell House, named after old Sedberghian and school benefactor, Sir Francis Sharp Powell and created in 1916, the young master Happold was a boarder at the school from May 1935 to December 1939 when he left at 18. By all accounts he was a conscientious and diligent student and applied himself well to his studies. During his time there he took an active part in boxing, cricket and rugby and his contemporaries remembered him as easy-going, sociable and kind. After leaving Sedburgh and with the war two months old Bernard appears to have joined the local Home Guard and in 1997 one of his cousins, John Andrews, related to me the details of one of his first duties. It appears that Bernard was asked to stand, rifle slung over one shoulder, in the pouring rain near his home having to guard the wreck of a Westland Lysander that had come to grief. Initially proud to be asked to guard the wreck of an aircraft it quickly became apparent that he had been placed there due to the distinct lack of interest among the more senior members of his platoon because of the appalling weather conditions. Nevertheless, by all accounts Bernard stuck doggedly to the task and guarded the stricken aeroplane for some hours until it was recovered, despite being soaked to the skin and freezing cold.

At some stage, like all of the men who volunteered for aircrew in Bomber Command, he must have decided that he wanted to do more and, in Bernard's case, his love of aircraft would no doubt have driven him to consider exchanging the khaki uniform for air force blue.

Volunteering for the RAF and for aircrew in particular Bernard joined up on 18 February 1941 at Lord's Cricket Ground in London and, like so many, found himself posted to Canada as part of the same Commonwealth Air Training Plan that took my father and countless others along the same path.

On his return to the UK Bernard reported to 12 PATU (Pilot Advanced Training Unit) and from there on to Lossiemouth to join 20 OTU to fly Wellingtons where his and my father's paths would cross.

Joining Bernard and my father in the 14-foot-long nose section of the Halifax would be the two Scots in the crew. The first, John Baxter the Bomb Aimer, was the oldest and most senior member of the crew, a Flying Officer at 27 and the only officer amongst an NCO crew. Born in Glasgow on 15 April 1916, John Baxter was the only son of David and Jessie Baxter and he had two older sisters. Like my father, John was a bright boy and a keen student and seems to have taken very well to his studies, attending the prestigious Albert Road Academy in Pollockshields. Popular, kind and well-liked as a boy he joined the Boys Brigade and according to his family was continually bringing home prize books for being the 'best boy'. An accomplished pianist, family members have told me that he could play 'by ear' without reading music.

Outside the classroom John was a good athlete and gifted footballer, playing for Queens Park reserves, no doubt he and my father would have enjoyed the discussions about football. Sometime after leaving school John appears to have favoured a career in journalism and he joined the *Scottish Daily Express* as a trainee. As war clouds approached, he married Dora McLeod, a nurse, on 17 November 1939 and enlisted in the British Army. John's father David Baxter had served in the King's Own Scottish Borderers regiment in the First World War. Unfortunately, his time in the Army seemed to have been frustrating for him and, according to his family, he spent much of his time on a variety of mundane pursuits including looking for deserters (apparently chasing one through the streets of Glasgow) and like so many young men he quickly became bored and decided that he wanted to transfer to the RAF and to join Bomber Command as a pilot. Like most others he was sent to Canada for his pilot training, but he was not selected as a pilot and returned as a Flying Officer and retrained as an Air Bomber (Bomb Aimer).

The second Scot in the crew was another John. Hailing from Aberdeen, John Brownlie was the Wireless Operator for the crew and would eventually follow the same path as my father from Luft VI to Luft IV and the final march across a freezing Germany to liberation.

The final position in the aircraft was that of the rear gunner, occupied by the diminutive Welshman Tommy Jones from Rhymney in Gwent. It was arguably one of the most demanding roles in any wartime bomber crew and certainly the most uncomfortable. Tail gunners had to sit for hours on end, isolated from the rest of their crew, unable to move, in cold, cramped turrets all the time scanning the skies for the tell-tale signs of German night fighter activity. A moment's inattentiveness over enemy territory could spell disaster for a crew and keeping focused for such extended periods of time was a challenge in itself.

By this point the fledgling crews assembled at Marston Moor had already been through around two years of intensive training to get them this far. They had travelled first to Canada and then to Scotland, each receiving comprehensive training for their chosen 'trade'. As a crew they could have been forgiven for thinking that the hard training was over, and in some ways this was true as they were now competent in their individual disciplines – but they were all still to experience flying in what would become their work 'office': the four engine, Merlin 20 powered, Handley Page Halifax.

As with the ageing Wellingtons that they had flown at Lossiemouth, the Halifaxes that lay in wait for them at Marston Moor were for the most part old, battle-worn aircraft that had seen heavy service in frontline squadrons and were now deemed too elderly, had too many flying hours (or too many faults) to be held any longer on full operational roster. Accident rates for crews in training at OTUs and HCUs were notoriously high due to a culmination of inexperienced crews and various mechanical failures. Taking these tired aircraft into the air was a risky endeavour in its own right and almost all had some form of issue, although the maintenance crews did their best to keep them in the air. Oil and glycol coolant leaks were commonplace and in general problems ranged in severity from minor electrical glitches through mechanical and engine problems and, in the worst cases, major structural failure down to stresses put onto the airframe from hard landings.

That aside poor weather often accounted for many crews, three such causalities, all from 1658 HCU at Riccall, happened on the night of 23 November 1943[1] during a night navigation exercise. Severe weather and storm force winds caused icing on the control surfaces of Halifax JB926 and the aircraft broke apart in mid-air with the loss of all crew. Investigations at the crash site later established that the port outer wing had broken away entirely, tearing off both engines and elevators in the process, leaving the crew no chance of escape. Halifax DT578 came down in similar circumstances, killing all on board and a third 1658 aircraft, Halifax DT541, managed to make it back to the airfield before crashing and catching fire. Fortunately the crew managed to extract themselves from the aircraft before it caught fire and was destroyed. The cause in all three cases was severe icing.

Such incidents were a sobering reminder for all, if it were ever needed, that training flights often carried comparable risks to operational flying. For my father he would no doubt have reflected on his time since that first flight in Canada back in February 1942, gaining his first air experience aboard Avro Anson R9714 under Pilot Officer Simpson. My father had since amassed almost 198 hours flying time (88 of those hours on night flying). After first taking to the air as a trainee navigator in the trusty Avro Anson came the many hours aboard the Vickers Wellington at Lossiemouth and now he was about to experience flying in the Handley Page Halifax – which, along with the Lancaster and the Stirling, was destined to be a workhorse of Bomber Command.

At 10:52hrs on Monday, 2 February 1942, under Warrant Officer Lee, my father took the first of his two flights as 2nd Navigator on the Halifax. His Observer's logbook from the time notes that they were in the air for three hours fifty minutes on a Cross Country (G manipulation) exercise. Three days later at 10:45hrs he was again in the air, this time aboard Halifax 'U Unicorn' piloted by Sergeant Griffiths[2] for another G manipulation exercise, lasting four hours and forty-five minutes.

During the course of their HCU training, it was usual for the pilots of the rookie crews to accompany a frontline crew on an operational mission to get a feel for what it was like to fly in combat. On the night of 28 February pilot Bernard Happold was detailed to fly as second pilot on HR663 DY-T Tommy which was one of ten 102 Squadron Halifaxes detailed to attack St Nazaire. T-Tommy's pilot that night was Warrant Officer Towse who guided the Halifax successfully there and back, bombing at 12,500 feet and reporting large fires with accurate TI marking.[3]

All of 102's aircraft returned safely that night, with each claiming to have successfully hit the target. Looking at the declassified raid reports for the month it shows that several of the Halifaxes carried second pilots that night. One of the other ten aircraft flying on that raid was destined to become Bernard Happold and his crew's first aircraft, Halifax W7912 DY – G-George. Warrant Officer Younger was the pilot on the night and reported in their debriefing that the target was attacked at 14,200 feet and 'a good deal of the attack had fallen West of the town'. However, at some point over the target the aircraft was struck by falling bombs from another aircraft causing damage to the fuselage. The damage was described by the crew as minor but it's interesting to note that they didn't fly again operationally for a month or so, so it is possible that the damage was more serious than first reported.

For the rest of Bernard's crew it must have been a nerve-jangling time watching the horizon for T - Tommy to return after the raid and to ensure that their skipper was safe and sound. My father in particular must have been anxious as the two men had flown together since the early days of training at Lossiemouth on Wellingtons and both liked and trusted the other's abilities in the air. It would have been a bitter blow indeed to have seen that partnership dissolved before they had even had chance to fly together in anger as part of a full crew.

On Tuesday 2 March, on a sunny and windy morning in Yorkshire they were again in the air, this time in 'W-William' for the first of three Cross Country exercises in as many days. Finally, on 5 March at 11:25, on yet another windy day they climbed aboard Halifax 'X-Xray' and completed the last of their Conversion Unit Flights.

In total my father completed nineteen hours flying time at Marston Moor and with his final flight his training had officially come to an end. As an interesting footnote his logbook was signed off by the CO at the time who was none other than Squadron Leader Wally Lashbook. Squadron Leader Lashbrook was already something of a cause celèbre for 102 Squadron having joined them in December 1941 helping the pilots to convert from the outgoing Armstrong Whitley bomber to the new Halifax. He further cemented his status after his successful evasion from the Germans after being shot down on the Pilsen raid on 17 April. Making his way through Belgium and into France he was able to make contact with members of the French Resistance, finally arriving at the British Embassy in Spain in June who arranged for his return to England. An exceptional story and an exceptional man, the author was lucky enough to correspond with Wally Lashbrook in the late 1990s while researching for this book.[4]

With their time at Marston Moor complete Bernard Happold, my father and the rest of the crew were officially posted to 102

Squadron, based at Pocklington on 8 March 1943. The long days and nights of training were finally over and what lay ahead of them were the uncertainties of combat flying. Everything that they had spent the last two years training for was now about to come to fruition. For the first time they would be an operational crew, on their own and flying over enemy territory. Each man would be forced to confront the possibility of being shot down, of becoming a prisoner or, perhaps, a realisation that they faced the very real possibility of death. Of the veterans spoken to by the author – and also discussions with his father – it was a subject that they preferred not to dwell on at that time and many chose to keep their own thoughts to themselves rather than create worry amongst their fellow crewmates. In company they preferred to treat such concerns in a casual, light-hearted way, almost gallows humour, but I have no doubt that on the occasions where they were alone their minds would have turned to the task ahead and also, once they reached their frontline operational squadron, to a gradual realisation of the terrible attrition rates that were being suffered amongst the crews of Bomber Command in 1943 as the bomber war was starting to reach its height.

Although they would not be aware at the time, 102 Squadron would go on to suffer the second highest loss rate amongst all the 128 squadrons on roster with Bomber Command.

Chapter 6

Of Bombing Offensives and RAF Heavies

From Hell, Hull and Halifax
May the Good Lord Deliver Us

– Yorkshire Proverb

The Allied Strategic Bombing Offensive is worthy of several volumes in its own right and there exist a number of excellent books covering the subject in forensic detail that can be found in the bibliography. It is beyond the remit of this book to try and cover the campaign in the same level of detail, however it is nevertheless important to cover something of the chronology and main details of the campaign as it sets my father and his crew's story in context and also goes some way to explaining the increasingly harsh treatment meted out to those Bomber Command aircrew who were unlucky enough to fall into German hands (particularly civilians) as the bombing campaign intensified in 1943. What follows therefore is an overall summary highlighted by some individual raids that show the developments in central bombing policy that led to the adoption of the area bombing policy.

By 1943, Bomber Command had changed markedly from the force of only three years before. Air bombing in the early years of the war had been a largely haphazard and ineffective affair and, despite the extraordinary courage of the crews, it soon became clear that the combination of rudimentary navigational aids, naive strategy and ageing, below standard aircraft was yielding increasingly disappointing and ineffective results – not to mention the heavy and unsustainable losses suffered across the participating squadrons.

Bomber Command's fleet of aircraft at that time (1939-1940) was split into its two-engine light bombers (the Bristol Blenheim and Fairey Battle) and its force of medium bombers the Handley Page Hampden, Armstrong Whitworth Whitley and the Vickers Wellington. All proved to be woefully inadequate for the task of daylight ops and fell easy prey for the faster and more manoeuvrable single-seat fighters, the Messerschmitt 109 and the Focke Wulf 190, and also the larger, twin-engine Messerschmitt 110, not to mention German flak batteries.

Although the trusty Wellington would continue as part of the later night offensive throughout the war (and would remain as the mainstay of the Operational Training Units) the rest were quickly withdrawn from daylight sorties. Two infamous and costly raids during December 1939 virtually ensured the abandonment of daytime bombing by the full bomber force, although the light bombers continued to venture over enemy territory for some considerable time. On 14 December 1939 a force of twelve Wellingtons set out to attack the German cruisers *Nürnberg* and *Leipzig*. Of those aircraft that set out for the target around half of them failed to return.

On 18 December a force of twenty-four Wellingtons led by Wing Commander Kellett set out for Heligoland, north of the Friesian Islands, to look for suitable shipping targets. Once again, a little over half of the attacking Wellingtons were lost[1] either over the target itself or falling prey to German fighters on their way home. The vulnerability of the aircraft to fighter attack in daylight raids was becoming increasingly apparent, but change was slow to come into effect.

Worse was to come. In France the ten Fairey Battle squadrons that comprised the Advanced Air Striking Force (AASF), later supplemented by six Bristol Blenheim squadrons, were given the task of protecting the British Expeditionary Force (BEF) as they waited for the invading German troops to sweep through France and the Low Countries. What followed over the coming weeks was little short of disastrous for Bomber Command as the deficiencies of both aircraft when used in daylight raids were laid bare and they proved easy pickings for the faster and more manoeuvrable German fighters and anti-aircraft fire from flak batteries on the ground. Losses were appalling, in one raid against pontoon bridge works at Sedan, forty of the seventy aircraft detailed to attack were lost (thirty-five of them Fairey Battles) in what was to prove to be the single highest loss rate suffered in any major bombing operation of the Second World War. In total over 137 Battles had been destroyed in daylight operations in France and they were finally withdrawn from the Battle of France on 15 June 1940.

During the Battle of Britain, and with the threat of invasion across the Channel looming, Bomber Command under the leadership of its then Commander-in-Chief Sir Charles Portal oversaw a campaign of attacking various so called 'Panacea' targets in the industrial heartland of Germany, mostly oil refineries, factories and marshalling yards. Looking back, this was the early birth of the strategic bombing offensive that would, by 1945, have reduced an increasing number of German towns and cities to rubble and ashes. The charge at this still early stage in the air war was being led by the twin-engined bomber fleet – the venerable Wellington, Hampden and Whitley and although the crews made valiant and determined efforts, a lack of clear direction in bombing policy meant that they were detailed to attack an ever-increasing manifest of seemingly random targets including storage depots, aircraft production factories, ports and shipping which only served to further dilute an already increasingly disparate campaign.

Through 1940 and early 1941 Bomber Command continued with its policy of precision bombing with aircraft detailed to attack specific targets. Reports from the crews as they sipped hot tea and smoked cigarettes at the crew debriefings on arrival back at their bases suggested a high degree of accuracy, and crews confidently reported that they had bombed the target they had been sent out to destroy. Cameras on aircraft were in their infancy at this time and so the reports from the crews remained the primary source of info for collation by the squadrons, which was then reported back to Group and thence onwards to Bomber Command HQ.

Whilst well-intentioned, all of this contrived to mask the true picture of target accuracy within the context of the wider bombing campaign in 1941. However, there was a sense of growing unease and concern, both within the High Command of the RAF and also within the War Cabinet, that claims made about bombing accuracy did not appear to be be borne out and aerial reconnaissance was starting to undercover a worryingly different picture entirely. Finally, Lord Cherwell, Chief

Scientific Advisor to the Cabinet and a friend of Churchill, commissioned one of his assistants, David Bensusan-Butt, to undertake a study of over 633 photographs taken over various targets by attacking aircraft and then comparing them to the bombing claims made by the crews themselves.

The results were shattering and confirmed what many had privately felt to be the case regarding bombing accuracy – that the notion of precision bombing was a noble but unachievable ambition at that point in time. Butt's report, released on 18 August 1941, exposed the stark reality of the staggeringly poor return for the losses suffered by the bomber force. Analysis revealed that only one in three bombers attacking enemy targets ever got within five miles of the target area – for the Ruhr this figure was nearer to one in ten.[2]

Additional post war studies confirmed Butt's findings and concluded that 49 per cent of bombs dropped by Bomber Command between May 1940 and May 1941 actually fell into open country and caused little to no damage. Only three bombs in every hundred dropped fell within five miles of the aiming point. Though many senior figures in the Command expected a less than glowing report, the sheer scale of the failings shocked many and they braced themselves for the inevitable backlash. The cost in raw materials, aircraft and munitions (and in men) had been colossal and though it had been the only service capable of carrying the attack into Germany itself, it now became clear that the vast majority of its efforts and those of its valiant crews had, for the most part, been entirely ineffective. Questions were even raised at the very highest level about the future of Bomber Command itself as a viable or even a necessary force. Speaking in the House of Commons in early 1942, Lord Privy Seal and Leader of the House Sir Stafford Cripps made it clear that serious questions now existed over the most prudent use of the country's valuable raw materials:

> *Another question which has been raised by a great number of Members is the question of policy as the continued use of heavy bombers and the bombing of Germany (and) whether the continued devotion of a considerable part of our effort to the building up of this bomber force is the best use that we can make of our resources. I can assure the House that the Government are fully aware of the other uses to which our resources can be put, and the moment they arrive at a decision that the circumstances warrant a change, a change in policy will be made.*[3]

For the senior figures of Bomber Command the lessons so clearly laid out in the Butt Report needed to be taken on board quickly and its findings acted upon. Not least this would mean that significant improvements were required in the area of aircraft navigation – crews had been trained to fly, for the most part, in daylight before the switch to night operations (due to the heavy loss rates). With the basic navigational aids available at that stage in the war it was now obvious that navigators were struggling to accurately fix positions in the air and get near to the target so as to make bombing effective.

The first major breakthrough in navigation came with the development and introduction of Gee, a radio-based system that allowed navigators to more accurately calculate the position of their aircraft by noting the time signal delay from three separate ground stations. Though rudimentary in many respects and far from perfect, it did at least mean that a competent navigator could ensure that he could get his aircraft to the approximate area of the target to a level that had not previously been possible.

The other key shift for Bomber Command in early 1942 was the appointment of a new Commander-in-Chief, Air Marshal Arthur Harris or 'Bomber' Harris as he became known. Originally from Gloucestershire, he had emigrated to South Africa as a 17-year-old in 1910 and saw action in the First World War with the 1st Rhodesia Regiment. Returning to England he subsequently joined the Royal Flying Corps, the precursor to the RAF, leading a fighter squadron and then working his way up through the ranks in the post-war years. Gruff, single-minded and largely indifferent to dissenting voices, Harris fully embraced his new role as C-in-C and moved quickly to make his mark and re-assert Bomber Command as a key force. Although open-minded to attacks against specific 'precision' targets (provided that they could be effectively bombed) he felt that the true purpose and calling of the bomber was when marshalled in large numbers against targets that could be relatively easily found from the air and then pulverised accordingly.

Even with the recent introduction of Gee, Harris recognised the ongoing difficulties for his crews of finding obscure targets at night from the air and decided to switch the bomber force to attack coastal cities which he believed would be easier to accurately identify as their coastlines were easier to make-out and hit en masse. Two cities were earmarked for the attack that marked the new approach for Bomber Command. The first was the northern German City of Lübeck, once the cradle of the Hanseatic League, a cultural city with many historic buildings and churches and a high prevalence of half-timbered houses in narrow streets which would combust easily.

On 28 March 1942, Palm Sunday, a force of 234 aircraft from Bomber Command including 146 Wellingtons and 26 of the newer Short Stirling four engine bombers attacked the city in three waves. In total more than 400 tons of bombs (including incendiaries) were dropped on the city and as predicted, the part-wood construction of the houses quickly resulted in a devasting firestorm. Thirty per cent of the built-up area of Lübeck was believed to have been destroyed in the raid and 62 per cent of all buildings received damage ranging from complete destruction to superficial damage. German sources estimated that up to 320 people were killed in the raid and 648 injured.[4]

A few weeks later on 23 April 1942 the second City, Rostock, was bombed over a period of four separate nights by a heavy force from Bomber Command including over 161 aircraft on the first night. In total across the four days of the raids the RAF estimated that 1,765 buildings and 60 per cent of the main town area had been destroyed with 204 people killed and 89 injured. Martin Middlebrook and Chris Everitt note in their excellent book charting the RAF campaign in its entirety that, for the first time, German press used the term *Terrorangriff* (Terror Raid) to describe the attack and that even master propagandist Joseph Goebbels wrote in his diary that 'Community life in Rostock is practically at an end'.[5]

Having demonstrated what a combined bomber force could do Harris now set his sights on a third, much bigger raid that would not only send out a devasting signal to the enemy but would also send out a clear notice of intent to any who still doubted Bomber Command's renewed sense of purpose and direction. Operation Millennium was duly conceived as a major show of strength and an ominous portent of what could be delivered by the men of Bomber Command. Harris's plan was to mobilise a bomber force of one thousand aircraft over the target. Of course, Bomber Command did not have a front-line strength of anything remotely approaching that number of aircraft (it was actually closer to 400 at that stage) and so virtually anything that could fly and be put into the air was pressed into service, including aircraft from the OTUs with aircrew still under training taking part.

The target Harris selected for the raid was the 2,000-year-old city of Cologne, one of the largest and most populated of Germany's cities. On 30 May 1942 1,047 aircraft of Bomber Command took off from airfields the length and breadth of Britain and made their way to the target. RAF records show that 868 were successful in reaching the target dropping 1,455 tons of bombs of which two-thirds were incendiaries. The attack on Cologne was utterly devastating, resulting in significant damage to buildings and civilian accommodation as well as accounting for 469 deaths with over 5,000 people injured.

For Bomber Command's C-in-C Arthur Harris it also marked the effective abandonment of the previous policy of precision bombing and heralded the adoption of an area bombing strategy (also known as carpet bombing) as the new approach that he believed was needed. Steeped in controversy to this day, it would focus on bringing maximum destruction to

German towns and cities and would eventually culminate in the firestorms in Hamburg later in 1943 and the virtual obliteration of Dresden in 1945.

The subsequent arrival of the US Eighth Air Force 'The Mighty Eighth', across airfields dotted around East Anglia (and other parts) in the middle of 1942 saw the beginning of so-called 'Round The Clock' bombing – the Americans by day in their formations of Boeing B17 'Flying Fortress' bombers, bristling from nose to tail with machine guns and accompanied by P51 Mustang fighters, and the RAF continuing their offensive by night.

During this period Harris continued his push for better navigational aids that would allow his crews to reach further into the heart of Germany and attack, accurately, larger and more heavily defended targets. One of the next key developments was the formation of the famous Pathfinder Force. Initially opposed by Harris due to an unwillingness to consolidate his best navigators into a more elite group, he eventually relented and instructed Group Captain (Later Air Commodore) D.C.T. Bennett to develop the concept into an operational force.

Central to the Pathfinders concept was the ability to correctly identify and mark targets for following 'waves' of bombers to attack and so a system of Target Indicators ('TIs') was developed that saw a range of different coloured flares dropped over the target area which would ignite at a predetermined height, usually a few hundred feet. Colour combinations were frequently changed and only notified to aircrews on the night of a particular raid to frustrate German attempts to use decoy flare patterns and light decoy fires. Like Harris, Bennett was passionate about wanting to harness the ongoing developments in navigational aids that had led on from the earlier Gee system. Also, like Harris, he possessed the force of personality to see that plans were carried through to fruition.

The first of these additional navigational aids, 'Oboe', was to all intents and purposes a ground-controlled blind bombing system. It had been perfected in late 1942 and first used by a force of six Oboe-equipped de Havilland Mosquitos attacking a power station near the German border on 20 December 1942. The first use was in March 1943 and the target was the Krupp works in Essen. Two ground stations sent out radio signals that were picked up by separate transponders fitted to bomber aircraft and, in essence, aircrews were guided along a prescribed 'arc' that went through the middle of the target. They could carry out course corrections based on a series of morse code signals that indicated how far the aircraft was in the air from the correct 'arc' of the path.

The improvements in both navigational and target marketing aids were also matched by the introduction of new aircraft into frontline service. From 1941 onwards the RAF four engine 'Heavies' had started to enter the fray, replacing the retiring Whitley and Hampden. The Short Stirling was the first of these new heavies and although it proved to be a popular aircraft with its crews due to good manoeuvrability in the air, it was nonetheless underpowered, cumbersome, had a relatively poor service ceiling and attrition rates were high.

It was to be some time before the famous Avro Lancaster was to appear in service and in the interim two other bombers had both appeared on the roster. The first of these was the resultant Lancaster's forerunner. The ill-fated twin-engine Avro Manchester. Chronically underpowered, unstable in the air and with a plethora of electrical and hydraulic gremlins, it developed a deserved reputation as being unreliable and was universally hated by its crews. Withdrawn from frontline service as early as 1942 it is indeed testament to the efforts of all at Avro that all these shortcomings were to be addressed in the resultant Avro Lancaster which became the standout airframe of Bomber Command in the Second World War. Powered by four Rolls Royce Merlin engines the 'Lanc' was easier to fly, easier to maintain, had a high operational ceiling and was capable of carrying a much larger bomb load than its contemporaries.

Along with the Stirling, 1941 also saw the introduction of another four-engine 'heavy' and this was the aircraft that would be destined to take my father and his crew into combat over the night skies of Northern and Central Germany, the Handley Page Halifax. From a design originating in the late 1930s the first prototype of the Halifax (L7244) was completed in Autumn 1939 and the aircraft finally came into frontline service in 1941. Victor Bingham, an ex-Flight Engineer, wrote fondly of the aircraft and in his book *Halifax – Second to None* recalls a letter sent to him by Flight Commander P.A. Gilchrist, a pilot with 35 Squadron who took part in the first Halifax raid on 10 March 1941 after attacking Le Havre, praising the aircraft.[6]

Certainly, the Halifax (or Halibag as she was affectionately known) proved popular with her crews and my father always spoke fondly of the aircraft and the time that he flew in the marque. It is also true that statistics have shown that aircrew were more likely to be able to bale out of a stricken Halifax than they were a Lancaster, possibly due to the Lancaster's smaller escape hatches, narrower fuselage and infamous main wing spar that ran through the fuselage and proved a major obstacle to climb over by airmen in cumbersome flying gear. Freeman Dyson, War Office statistician concluded that Halifax crews had a 25 per cent chance of getting out whereas that figure was only 15 per cent for Lancaster crews.

That said the Halifax was not without its detractors – or its problems – and early B.I examples suffered from a range of issues including problems with lift caused by Handley Page seemingly ignoring advice from Rolls-Royce on the most effective place to position the four Merlin 20 engines on the wings (resulting in reduced lift and severe vibration) and also with the tail fin and rudder design causing its own headaches to new crews, especially those at the conversion units who found the aircraft prone to swinging on take-off, coolant leaks and engine vibration problems.[7] Various modifications were carried out to the aircraft in 1941 and 1942 in an attempt to remedy the problems, these were only partially successful and undercarriage collapses continued to dog the Halifax for much of its production life.

The newer B.II Series I (Special) Halifaxes that my father would fly at least made inroads into addressing the issues of drag. The bulky and ugly dorsal turret was replaced (and done away with all together on some aircraft) and the nose turret was dispensed with, opting instead for a smoothed over 'Z' type fairing, also referred to as a Tollerton nose, which gave improvements in performance and top speed.

Halifax fins and rudders continued to give problems and rudder overbalance claimed the lives of training and operational crews alike. Essentially the problem was that the fins were small and easily overpowered by the rudders which would induce a large sideslip effectively 'locking' the latter and stalling the fins with catastrophic consequences. The problem was only finally solved on much later versions of the Halifax where the triangular fins were replaced by the 'D' shaped or lozenge design which gives the fin a much larger surface area.

For the beleaguered engineers and management at Handley Page there was an additional and potentially much larger problem – irritation at the issues encountered with the Halifax and its operational limitations was growing within Bomber Command and Harris was scathing about both the Halifax and the Short Stirling which had fallen short compared to the better-performing Lancaster. In a letter to Sir Archibald Sinclair, Secretary of State for Air, in December 1942 Harris welcomed the news that production of the Stirling was to cease and urged that the Halifax, which he castigated as 'a deplorable product' should go the same way and that resources should switch fully to production of the Lancaster.[8]

Of course, this was never really an option as too much had been poured into production of the Halifax and the various assembly facilities, but it did allow Harris to vent his frustrations and it served as a warning shot to Handley Page that improvements to the Halifax were needed urgently. In fairness they responded to the criticism, explored all avenues and used all endeavours to bring the Halifax up to the mark and later versions of the aircraft were much improved on the initial offering.

Chapter 7

Suicide but Fun – Pocklington 1943

And when you come to 102
And think that you will get right through
There's many a fool who thought like you
It's suicide but it's fun!

102 Squadron Mess Song.

By early 1943 when my father, along with Bernard Happold and the rest of the crew had completed their training, Bomber Command had begun to further refine its ability to strike targets in the heart of Germany with a large, combined force and with increasingly devastating results. Pivotal to this ability was the ongoing development of the aforementioned navigational aids like Gee, Oboe and later on H2S, with bombing spearheaded by the Pathfinder squadrons like the Oboe-equipped de Havilland Mosquitos of 109 Squadron.[1]

Bombing accuracy had now increased exponentially since the haphazard days of the early years of the air war, but for the RAF precision bombing had now well and truly given way to area bombing (carpet bombing as it was to become known) which focused on the large-scale destruction of factories and de-housing of the civilian population. A pivotal part of this

campaign was to become known as the Battle of the Ruhr –
a concentrated attempt by Bomber Command over a period
of four months to wreak havoc in what was easily the most
industrialised area of Germany. The factories of its great
towns – such as Essen, Duisburg, Dusseldorf, Dortmund and
Wuppertal – were to be specifically targeted in an attempt to
disrupt the production of the special steels vital to the Reich.
Almost two thirds of Germany's total supplies came from these
factories.

For Harris and Bomber Command the Krupps Steel works
in Essen became targets of particular interest. Originally
established in 1819, the Krupps works had steadily become one
of the largest producers of armaments and associated works and
were instrumental in supplying the German military machine
during the 1914–1918 war. In 1939, as the war clouds gathered
once more over Europe, Krupps was again gearing up to supply
the new Reich.

Goering's fanciful boast that no enemy aircraft 'would ever
bomb' Reich territory would, of course, come back to haunt
him as German towns and cities felt the full extent of Bomber
Command's onslaught during 1943 and 1944. Ironically a
Lancaster of 467 Squadron (R5868 S–Sugar, currently a static
exhibit in the Bomber Hall at RAF Museum at Hendon)
completed its 100th operational sortie on 12 May 1944 and
bears the taunting nose art 'NO ENEMY PLANE WILL FLY
OVER THE REICH TERRITORY' underneath 100 carefully
painted bombs denoting its operational prowess.

For the crews of Bomber Command the new phase of
the offensive would mean an intensification of night flying

and regular journeys into the very heart of the most heavily defended targets in Germany and the correspondingly heavy concentrations of flak and enemy night fighters. In the period from 5/6 March to 24 July 1943 Bomber Command conducted over 23,401 operational sorties dropping an average bomb tonnage over the period of 57,034 tons. Over a thousand aircraft were lost by Bomber Command during this period, 640 of these directly over Ruhr targets.[2]

Bomber Command's C-in-C Arthur Harris began what became known as the Battle of the Ruhr on 5 March 1943 when a combined force of 442 aircraft attacked the Krupp works at Essen – it was Bomber Command's 100,000th sortie of the war. Although 56 aircraft were destined to turn back due to various issues en route (including three of the Oboe equipped Pathfinder Mosquitos), the remaining Pathfinders got through and marked the target perfectly with Target Indicators. Halifaxes led the first wave of the attack, including twelve aircraft from 102 Squadron. Reconnaissance photographs the morning after the raid revealed around 160 acres had been razed, with German sources claiming 3,018 houses destroyed, a further 2,166 damaged and up to 482 dead. Tellingly the number of dead exceeded the thousand bomber raid total from the watershed raid on Cologne in 1942 and marked the beginning of four months of relentless bombing of the Ruhr that would test both RAF crews, flak batteries, night fighter crews and civilians to the limit.

My father and his new crewmates were about to receive a baptism of fire and, in due course, be thrown headlong into one of the most ferocious battles of the air war. The train journey from Marston Moor to Pocklington was short, only 26 miles or so, and on arrival at Pocklington station, sadly long since closed, the seven airmen climbed from the train and Bernard Happold, carrying the travel warrant, looked around for the LAC sent from the base to collect them. Contact having been made, the crew were loaded into the transport and held on as the RAF truck lurched its way out of the station for the short drive to the airfield. First point of call for all such aircrew reporting was the Guardroom and thence to their accommodation, the ubiquitous Nissen hut, as sparsely furnished and dank as ever, but it was, nonetheless, home. Each crewman grabbed a bed and started to unpack their kit. When all done those that wanted to made their way to the Sergeants' Mess, said their hellos and queued for something to eat.

Rookie crews, 'Sprogs' as they were known, were always curious anomalies in frontline squadrons – anxious to meet other more experienced crews to find out 'the gen' and to get a feel for combat flying, they were often surprised at the reactions of their battle-hardened comrades which ranged from seemingly cold disinterest, even aloofness, to black-humoured attempts to rattle the new postings. In reality both were commonplace amongst all three services – Army, Navy and Air Force – in combat units that had been in action for any length of time. It was perhaps, in their own way, a defence mechanism by members of the surviving crews to distance themselves from the new faces and not to get too close.

In 1943 the life expectancy of an RAF bomber crew operating in a frontline squadron of Bomber Command was between eight and twelve operations and countless new faces would be seen and then abruptly disappear on bomber stations dotted all over the country. Getting too close to people was risky as if they got 'the chop' over the target it could start to affect one's own mental health and the effects could be debilitating, so most, apart from within their own crew, kept themselves to themselves. So began a curious life for the men who had recently completed training and awaited their first operation and, as well as noticing the disappearing faces in the mess hall, sometimes the dangers of flying in general were brought starkly to life.

On the evening of 29 March 1943 Halifax JB848 DY G-George, fully laden with fuel and bombload, crashed shortly after take-off on the outskirts of Pocklington with the loss of all crew. The pilot, Flight Sergeant Comrie and his crew had only been posted to the station from 1652 Heavy Conversion Unit on 8 March along with my father and his crew, and both Comrie and his navigator were regarded at the HCU as exceptionally capable airmen. Weather conditions on the night were recorded as being very poor with driving rain and low temperatures leading to icing problems. It is believed that Comrie had taken evasive measures to avoid hitting another aircraft and, realising he was coming down, had steered the aircraft away from a residential area, coming down in a field just outside of Pocklington. The explosion was heard throughout the surrounding area and it must have been a sobering realisation for the remaining crews of just how dangerous operational flying was – even before they had left the relative safety of their own county.

As March turned into early April the recently arrived crews began to prepare for their first operation on Saturday, 10 April 1943. Their names appeared on the crew list for ops that evening with thirteen Halifaxes from 102 Squadron taking part in operations that night.

As Bernard Happold and my father filed into the briefing room for the navigation briefing, they must have been full of apprehension ahead of their first operational raid as a stand-alone crew and a realisation perhaps that everything they had trained for in the past 18 months, from Pensacola in the United States, Alberta in Canada through to the wilds of Scotland and now North Yorkshire, was culminating in this moment. When the curtains were pulled back revealing the 'Target for Tonight' they would see, for the first time, what part they would have in Bomber Command's War – their first chance to do 'their bit'. For my father, who had eschewed the relative safety of filling in bomb craters in Dover during his Royal Artillery days to volunteer for Bomber Command, this is what he had been waiting for. This was his chance to do, as he had said to his friends and his family, 'something that would make a difference'. For Bernard Happold also, obsessed with aeroplanes since a small boy, this would be his moment to lead his crew into attack.

With a sweep of the arm pulling aside a large black curtain Frankfurt was revealed as the designated target for the evening's operation. Over 500 aircraft from Bomber Command were detailed to take part in the attack – 144 Wellingtons, 136 Lancasters, 124 Halifaxes and 98 Stirlings.

As navigator my father would not have had the distraction of thinking too much about the night ahead, at least not at this point. Navigation briefings on the nights when ops were on were busy periods and would see all navigators flying that night busily drawing in the route on their plotting charts, calculating course times to the target and back again and marking in any reports of flak concentrations or the like. Of keen interest would be the briefing given by the meteorologist who would advise on such things as wind speeds, expectations over cloud cover, all crucial to a navigator's ability to keep his aircraft on track and on time when flying out to the target (and, hopefully) when heading back.

Bernard Happold had already had a taste of operations on the St Nazaire raid at the end of February, flying as a dickie pilot in HR663 and had no doubt briefed his own crew on what to expect, but this was different – this would mean a trip deep into Germany. Looking at the roster noticeboard they had been assigned Halifax W7912 DY G-George – an older aircraft that had already had somewhat of a chequered history, but one that had a reputation for always getting her crews home.

After the initial briefing was concluded Bernard Happold and my father joined the rest of their crew for the main briefing and then began the process of preparing for the night's ops – drawing their flying kit, making sure they emptied their pockets of any personal items or anything that could be of use to the enemy and then preparing themselves mentally for what they were about to undertake. It would be their first time in the air together as a fully operational crew, placing their lives in the hands of each other and trusting that each had learnt the skills of their individual roles thoroughly and would perform to the levels required when the time came. Perhaps for my father there was a realisation that, apart from the pilot, the core responsibility to get them to the target area and safely home again would rest squarely on his shoulders.

Looking at his flying logs, my father was classed as an above average navigator in his training assessments, and this must have given him a degree of reassurance (not to mention his crew also) to settle any initial nerves, but the hours before take-off must have been stressful. At their allotted time the crew of seven climbed into the back of the covered RAF truck that would take them to their aircraft – having completed their air test earlier in the day they were happy that DY G-George was serviceable and as she should be. Nevertheless, with older aircraft there was always the nagging suspicion of some kind of mechanical gremlin that would jangle the nerves and stay in the back of the mind, particularly as they were embarking on their first operation.

Arriving at the hardstanding, G-George sat waiting for them, fuelled up, bombed up and ready for the long hours in the air. The crew prepared to climb aboard the aircraft while Bernard Happold undertook the customary walk round her to check control surfaces and that he was happy with the aircraft. Signing the Form 700 to take control of the airframe he motioned to the crew and one by one the seven men clambered into the dark and cramped interior that would be their home for the next few hours. My father went through his pre-flight ritual of making sure he had everything he needed to hand, pencils, charts and maps. Removing his thick fur-lined gloves he carefully took off the silk under gloves favoured by aircrew and massaged his fingers before slipping his gloves back on followed by the gauntlets and then settling down to prepare for the flight. Many men had their rituals preparing for combat, this was his.

Near their allotted take off time, the engines of W7912 DY G-George slowly coughed and flamed into life and she joined the steady stream of taxi-ing aircraft before turning onto the main runway at Pocklington. Rising into the night skies over Yorkshire one can only guess at how each of the seven men felt – for certain they would have been focused on their own particular job in hand, especially Bernard Happold and Gordon Bowles the Flight Engineer whose eyes would be scanning the dials and flight engineer's instrument panel, alert for any issue the aircraft may encounter while in the air. For my father, bent over his desk studio maps and looking at the tiny oscilloscope Gee display, I'm sure his thoughts would primarily have been focused around ensuring that he was able to keep his pilot informed with timely and accurate course settings and corrections to ensure that G-George was exactly where she needed to be in the bomber stream.

For John Brownlie, the Wireless Operator, he would lean round his station away from his R1155 Radio receiver and give my father a quick nudge to make him look up from his maps, followed by a thumbs up. My father laughed and shook his head before returning to his maps (something that would become a ritual for Sergeant Brownlie, perhaps part of the superstitions that would increase for many airmen as the campaign grew in magnitude). For gunners Duncan McGregor and Tommy Jones there was nothing to do but wait and prepare – once they were over the North Sea and approaching enemy airspace then their task became infinitely more crucial, continually scanning the night skies for the first sign of enemy night fighters and ready to alert their pilot to take evasive measures should something be seen. The standard manoeuvre in such circumstances was the corkscrew and gunners would either yell 'Corkscrew Left – Go'! or 'Corkscrew Right – Go'! depending upon from which direction the fighter was seen to be attacking.

'Corkscrewing' was an effective but also terrifying experience for crews as the pilot would first put the aircraft into an immediate steep dive to port/starboard and then into a climb followed by another dive to either 'lose' a pursuing fighter or cause it to overshoot. It was a violent 'all or nothing' manoeuvre, requiring brute physical strength from the pilot and strong stomachs from the rest of the crew who had to hang on for dear life, the G forces pinning them against the sides of the aircraft in the pitch-black night. Anything that wasn't fixed or tied down flew around the interior. Apart from the stress put on the crew it also put a tremendous strain on the airframe which could cause other issues, particularly if the aircraft had been damaged in the initial attack.

As G-George pressed on into the night the intercom crackled: 'Navigator to skipper – we should be approaching the Dutch Coast in about 12 minutes.' Everyone on board tensed – for all of the crew of G-George apart from Bernard Happold this would have been their first foray over enemy airspace. It would be the furthest they would have flown in an aircraft and they were effectively on their own, charged with delivering a bomb load on target and then finding their way home to

Pocklington, unaware of what they may face on the way. The intercom crackled again and like so many navigators before and after him my father uttered the immortal phrase: 'Navigator to skipper – enemy coast ahead.'

Along with the main force, the Halifaxes of 102 Squadron encountered only very light flak on the way to the target. For some crews in other squadrons problems on the outbound route would prove to be more hazardous than flying over the target. A Wellington from 424 Squadron, HE159 QB P-Popsie developed severe engine trouble, the pilot eventually giving the order to bale out before the aircraft crashed and burst into flames 15 miles SSE of Maidstone. The rear gunner, Sergeant A.G. Lees baled out at 600 feet and landed close to the wreckage, making several attempts to reach crewmembers but was beaten back by the flames.[3]

Meanwhile about 30-40 minutes from the target Flight Engineer Gordon Bowles was becoming increasingly concerned about one of G-George's four Merlin 20 engines:

'Skipper – the starboard inner is losing oil pressure.'

Bernard Happold glanced over his shoulder and responded: 'What do you want to do?'

Gordon Bowles looked at the bank of instruments in front of him and made the call: 'I think we should probably shut it down, skipper.'

His pilot readily confirmed: 'Agreed – standby to feather the prop.'

Debriefing notes report that 25 minutes from the bombing run the decision had been taken to shut the problematic engine down – it would put an increased load on the remaining three

Merlins, but they could not afford the risk of failure of the affected engine or, worse, the chance of failure followed by a potentially catastrophic fire. With the decision made the problematic engine was shut down and the propeller feathered[4] to eliminate drag. Turning for home was not an option as it would mean potentially turning across hundreds of other aircraft in the bomber stream and the ensuing collision risk was high. Also not bombing the target meant the trip would not 'count' as part of their operational tally and so the crew pressed on with their attack.

Slowly G-George approached the target at a height of 18,000 feet and Bernard Happold steadied the aircraft while Bomb Aimer John Baxter prepared for his bombing run. The 'whump' of anti-aircraft fire could be heard around the target area lighting up the night sky and the aircraft jolted and rattled as they prepared to make their bombing run. For John Baxter there was full cloud cover over the target which made it impossible to see anything happening below. Many of the other crews reported seeing the red Target Indicator flares around the area of the target and bombed on sight of those plus ETA (Estimated Time of Arrival) calculations from their navigators.

John Baxter pressed the bomb release and clicked his microphone on. 'Steady, hold her, that's right. Steady, BOMBS GONE!'

The crew felt the aircraft lurch upwards as the heavy bomb load fell away from under them and the photoflash unit in the bomb bay was triggered to take a picture to be studied by the reconnaissance unit (though rendered useless by the 10/10 cloud cover over the target). Once released the aircraft then swung for home and now the gunners were primed to scour the skies looking for fighters. Flak over the target and on the way back was reported as light to moderate, but the primary concern was the increased stress on the remaining engines of their ageing aircraft as a consequence of shutting one down. As they crossed the Dutch coast on the homeward journey Flight Engineer Gordon Bowles was concerned about further issues, as my father told me:

> *On that first raid I wasn't sure what the issue was, after they shut down one of the engines the Flight Engineer and the Pilot said it was something to do with a leak, I can't really remember but I know that they reckoned we wouldn't make it back to Yorkshire and so I was asked to plot a course to the nearest RAF Station where we could get down.*

Flying back on three engines would mean the Halifax would take longer to get home and was a potential target for enemy aircraft so strict radio silence was observed for most of the journey home. The need to find a suitable base in England to land was paramount and morse-code signals were sent and received to a nearby candidate. Fate would decree that the station where they would set down would be the airfield at RAF Hawkinge, the famous Battle of Britain fighter station, located approximately seven miles west of Dover in Kent. In April 1943, Hawkinge was home to 41 Squadron flying the Supermarine Spitfire Mark XII.

After signals were exchanged between Hawkinge and Wireless Operator John Brownlie aboard G-George, Bernard

Happold guided the Halifax down onto the runway at Hawkinge and her wheels hit the tarmac at 6:50hrs. As she turned at the end of the runway the aircraft was met by ground staff and escorted to a hardstanding. Once the three running engines were shut down the crew let out a collective sigh and one by one began to clamber from the aircraft. Once outside they were met by two airmen from the station who raced across the tarmac in an RAF car: 'Bit out of your way here aren't you, who's the skipper?'

Bernard made himself known to the two airmen and the crew stretched tired limbs and lit up cigarettes while waiting to be driven to the mess. A sentry was posted to keep guard on G–George and the crew were collected and taken to one of the main stations at the base. Bernard Happold's first job was to notify the Ops Room at Pocklington that they were safely down but that the aircraft would require repair to one of the engines. A subsequent report was given to be included in the Ops report for the night:

> *Attacked primary target at 18,000 feet. 10/10 cloud tops 6,000 feet. Results unobserved. One engine feathered due to low oil pressure twenty-five minutes before bombing. Landed at Hawkinge.*[5]

Although they were not to know it at the time, and despite optimistic reports in the debriefing sessions from most returning 102 Squadron crews, the Frankfurt raid was ultimately deemed to be unsuccessful. Thick cloud cover over the target meant that none of the photographs showed the target below and Bomber

Command essentially had little idea where the bombloads had fallen. German reports at the time suggested that most of the bombs had fallen well to the south of the city itself with only very light casualties – the lack of photos meant that it was impossible to determine what level of damage had been caused. Of the 500 aircraft that took part twenty-one had been lost including three Halifaxes, but all 102 Squadron aircraft returned safely from the riad.

Filing into the debriefing room at Hawkinge the exhausted crew of 'G-George' were offered somewhere to sleep, but first the customary breakfast of eggs and bacon and mugs of hot tea while the squadron mechanics identified and then started to work out how to repair the problem with the problematic Merlin.

My father remarked that:

> *The fighter boys were all intrigued with the size of the Halifax and wanted to know what it was like to fly and this and that – I don't think they'd seen a bomber close up before to be honest – the place was full of Spitfires.*

With nothing to do my father and his crew were granted a twenty-four-hour leave pass to enable them to go off the base while their aircraft was repaired. Unsurprisingly, the very recently married Gordon Bowles took the opportunity of visiting his new wife and turned up at her doorstep in his flying kit, staying the night before returning to Hawkinge the next morning.

For the rest of the crew, after a sleep, the most appealing option was the pub and, possibly at the suggestion of their fighter command colleagues, they ended up at The Jackdaw, a short drive away. Then known as the Red Lion it was a country pub in nearby Denton (about seven or so miles from Hawkinge) and remains so to this day. Still in their flying kit, the six men trooped into the pub. My father takes up the story:

> When we walked in there were a few locals in there and they just looked at us as we were all still in our flying boots and jackets and what have you – I don't think they knew what to make of us really. Next minute they were smiling and joking, pushing us to tables and shoving pints in our hands and offering food. It was amazing really, we were served with as much food and beer as we wanted by the landlord and by locals, they couldn't do enough for us.[6]

The amount of beer consumed that day is of course unrecorded, but it must have been a welcome relief after their first experience of combat flying and struggling home with an engine down. The next day, re-joined by Gordon Bowles they returned to Hawkinge and awaited the repair of G-George. Once the aircraft had undergone repair at some point to the troublesome Merlin the crew took off and made the short flight back to Pocklington for a full debriefing and to prepare for their next op. True to form G-George had returned home again safely with one of her crews and they had completed their first op as full crew.

G-George continued as an operational Halifax for some time, always bringing her crew home, although Bernard Happold and his crew never flew in her again. Eventually she was officially retired from frontline operational duty and transferred to 1658 HCU as a training aircraft.[7] This became the fate of many elderly airframes that survived in their respective squadrons and, as previously highlighted, the heady cocktail of worn-out aircraft married to inexperienced crews probably accounted for the high number of casualties as a result of training accidents during the war years. Bomber Command lost 3,986 aircraft alone between 1939 and 1945 in non-operational accidents.[8]

An interesting footnote to the Frankfurt raid is that JB869 DY H-Harry, the Halifax that Sergeant Happold and his crew were to make their final flight in, was also in the air that night as one of 102 Squadron's complement of Halifaxes and returned safely from her third operation, her crew successfully bombing the target.

Handley Page Halifax JB869 was built as part of contract ACFT/1808/C4 by the English Electric Company at their assembly plant in Samlesbury near Preston. A BII Series (Special) she was fitted with the famous 'Z' nose fairing (also known as a Tollerton nose after the company that carried out the work).[9] Taken on charge by 102 Squadron on 24 March 1943 and designated H-Harry, JB869 first appeared on the operational roster for the Essen raid on 3 April where her bomb aimer on her first operation was none other than the late Tom Wingham DFC (later to become the Honorary Secretary of 102 Squadron and a friend of the author). H-Harry was again in action over Kiel the following day, and then made two further trips: Stuttgart on 14 April and Pilsen on 16 April. On both occasions she was skippered by Warrant Officer Lee who had been the pilot during two of my father's last training flights with 1652 HCU.

Having blooded themselves successfully on the Frankfurt raid Bernard Happold and his crew were keen to get more ops under their belt. Most crews were, as it meant one more to the magic figure of thirty ops and the end of their 'tour'. Their next opportunity was Tuesday 20 April, a fine day with light cloud and light winds, which boded well for the night's operations. The crews checked the notice board to see who would be on ops that night and sure enough, the names of Happold, Barratt, Baxter, Brownlie, McGregor, Bowles and Jones appeared on the roster sheet. It was fairly usual for crews to be moved around between aircraft so it was perhaps no surprise to them to see that they had been detailed to a new aircraft – JB869 DY H-Harry. By now she was already a veteran of five operations and was well and truly 'flown in'.

At the briefing the target for the night had been revealed as Stettin; 339 aircraft in total would be detailed to attack the target in what turned out to be the most successful attack by aircraft of Bomber Command beyond the range of Oboe during the whole of the Battle of the Ruhr. Bombing was effective due to the lack of cloud cover over the target and the target marking by the Pathfinders had been particularly accurate.

Unfortunately for the crew of H-Harry their second operation never got off the ground (quite literally). As Bernard Happold prepared to sign the Form 700, Flight Engineer Gordon Bowles noticed an ominous stench accompanied by a dripping sound and a tell-tale pool of aviation fuel was seen collecting on the ground below the aircraft. Stettin was a long-distance target, over 600 miles away, and the aircraft had all been fitted with overload tanks which were located in the bomb bay. The only effective remedy was to drain and patch or remove the tank and refit with a new one – impossible in the time available and the only course of action left was to scrub any participation in the raid for H-Harry and her crew.

Cursing their luck, and with no spare aircraft available, all that was left was for the crew to decamp from the aircraft and wait to be picked up and driven back to the crew room to get out of their flying kit, return their maps and equipment and return to their quarters to sit out the evening. 'Scrubbed' raids did not count towards the magical thirty ops total and so, effectively, the day's preparation and trepidation of the night's ops had all counted for nothing. No flight meant no number chalked off the tour.

For the crews that weren't flying on ops the waiting around proved to be interminable and they had to occupy themselves as best they could. For my father things would get worse as he was experiencing debilitating pangs in his stomach from a developing medical problem that would see him taken into hospital for an emergency operation before the crew were to fly together again. Not wanting to worry his crew he attempted to dismiss it as nothing more than indigestion. Hours later returning crews spoke enthusiastically about how they had been able to hit the target and that was borne out by later photo reconnaissance which showed huge fires burning over the target. German reports showed that 13 industrial premises and 380 houses had been destroyed and 586 people had perished in the raid.

With no ops scheduled for a few days the crews of 102 spent their time as best they could, but for my father things were coming to a head and on Sunday 25 April, he was forced to report to the station MO (Medical Officer) and admitted to the sick bay for observation. With no immediate improvement he was transferred to hospital for surgery on Monday 26 April.

For the time being Bernard Happold and his crew faced the prospect of going into combat with a replacement navigator.

The Barratt Family c.1932. L-R: Gladys, Doris, my father, my grandfather, Amy, my grandmother, Rose and in front Betty and May (Sheila had not yet been born).

My father's boyhood home. 8 Anglesey St, Hednesford c.1920. Their house is the end of terrace to the left of the seated neighbour, Mrs Pritchard.

31. 3. 31.

To whom it may concern,

Harold Barratt has just completed his final term at the above school. He has reached the highest standard, and for the last three months has been engaged chiefly upon special individual work.

The subjects in which he has excelled are mathematics and science, while at such practical subjects as gardening and woodwork, he has shown great interest and enthusiasm.

He has entered into the social life of the school whole-heartedly, and for the past season has been captain of the school football team.

He is a lad I can thoroughly recommend as being honest, trustworthy, and considerably above the average in all round ability.

I am,

yours faithfully,

S. Edwards

(Class teacher)

School Report from Mr Edwards, West Hill Boys School 1931.

31 ANS (Air Navigation School), Canada, January 1942. My father is seated in the front row, 4th from the left.

My father (on the left) sightseeing atop The Empire State Building, New York, June 1942.

Form No. 257
Established August 1940

Application No. _____ **2156**

AMERICAN FOREIGN SERVICE

At _____ TORONTO CANADA _____ Date __26th August__ 19~~1~~41

APPLICATION FOR NONIMMIGRANT VISA

I declare that the following statements are true and correct:

Name _____ Joseph Harold BARRATT

Place of birth __Hednesford, Staffs. England__ Date of birth __22nd. Feb. 1917__

Nationality _____ British.

Travel document R.AF. Identity Card No. 782727 issued at Startford England

Accompanied by _____ No One

Present legal residence No. 1 Manning Depot. R.C.A.F. Toronto Ontario, Canada
(Street, city, and country)

Address (if any) in the United States _____ Naval Air Station,

Pensacola Florida.

Purpose of entry _____ Air Crew under training

Length of stay _____ Approx SIX (6) Months.

I have not previously been refused a visa, deported, or excluded from admission into the United States.
The statements included in my application for registration under the Alien Registration Act, 1940, are hereby incorporated in and made a part of this application.
I understand that I shall be required to depart from the United States at the end of my temporary sojourn.

Harold Barratt

Harold Barratt
(Signature of applicant)

Subscribed and sworn to before me this 26th

day of _____ August _____ 194~~1~~

R. N. Clough

VICE CONSUL
of the United States of America.

Nonimmigration visa No. _____ issued __26th August 1941__ under Section 3(1) of the
Immigration Act of 1924. Service numbers _____

U. S. GOVERNMENT PR

2150

13526
13527

Canadian Visa issued 26 August 1941 in Toronto.

Date	Hour	Aircraft Type and No.	Pilot	Duty	REMARKS (Including results of bombing, gunnery, exercises, etc.)	Day	Night
					Time carried forward:—		
10/2/42	0920	ANSON K9714.	P/O. SIMPSON	NAVIGATOR	AIR EXPERIENCE	1. - 15.	
14/2/42	10.30	ANSON N.9650.	P/O McCARROLL	NAVIGATOR	MAP READING & AIR EXPERIENCE.	1. -45.	
22/2/42	10.48	ANSON N9597	P/O ACKEROYD	NAVIGATOR	MAP READING & ASSOCIATION OF TIME & DISTANCE. (O.M.2.)	2.25	
4/3/42	14.05	ANSON N5012	S/L. BURBRIDGE	NAVIGATOR	PILOT NAVIGATION. (O.M.3.)	2.05	
5/3/42	13.32	ANSON N.5012	F/O. APPLETON	2ND NAVIGATOR	MAP READING & DRIFT TAKING.	2.00	
7/3/42	10.49	ANSON N9985	W/O. WOOD	1ST NAVIGATOR	NAVIGATION BY TRACK & C/S. W/V (O.D.4.)	2.05	
8/3/42	10.29	ANSON N.9871	F/L WILLIS	1ST NAVIGATOR	MAINTAINING TRACK BY DRIFT. (NOT COMPLETED. EXERCISE WASHED).	1.35.	
10/3/42	0931	ANSON N.9602	P/O. REYNOLDS	1ST NAVIGATOR	MAINTAINING TRACK BY DRIFT (NOT COMPLETED)	1.15	
11/3/42	09.44	ANSON N.9838	P/O. SIMPSON	1ST NAVIGATOR	MAINTAINING TRACK DIRECTION By D.R.	2.00	
12/3/42	14.09	ANSON N.9856	F/O. APPLETON	1ST NAVIGATOR	AIR PLOT AND WINDS BY DOUBLE DRIFT (O.D.6).	2.05	
					TOTAL TIME....	18.20	

The first page of my father's logbook, detailing his first training flights aboard the Avro Anson in February 1942.

Date	Hour	Aircraft Type and No.	Pilot	Duty	REMARKS (Including results of bombing, gunnery, exercises, etc.)	Day	Night
					Time carried forward:—	80.20	47.00
1/11/42	09.45	WELLINGTON R.1060	P/O. BURROGHS	2ND NAV.	L.W. 18. X COUNTRY.		
14.11.42	10.05	WELLINGTON D.V. 711	P/O. BURROUGHES	NAV.	LOCAL BOMBING.	2.50	
16.11.42	10.00	WELLINGTON D.V. 711	P/O. BAKER	1ST. NAV.	L.W. 18. X COUNTRY	4.50	
16.11.42	09.50	WELLINGTON HD.965	SGT. HAPPOLD	1ST. NAV.	L.W. 17. X. COUNTRY	5.00	
17.11.42	19.00	WELLINGTON Z 8802 W5690	P/O. BURROUGHS.	2ND NAV.	L.W. 6. X. COUNTRY.		4.05
25.11.42	08.05	WELLINGTON D.V. 711	F/LT. LODGE	1ST. NAV.	LOCAL BOMBING.		.25
18.11.42	02.00	WELLINGTON W5690	SGT. ASPDEN	2ND NAV.	L.W. 18. X. COUNTRY.		4.40
26.11.42	21.00	WELLINGTON R.2139	SGT. HUNT.	1ST. NAV.	X COUNTRY		3.40
21.11.42	18.45	WELLINGTON W5690	SGT. ESDALE	2ND NAV.			.30
28.11.42	19.30	WELLINGTON	SGT. HUNT.	NAV.	LOCAL BOMBING		.30.
29.11.42	18.55	WELLINGTON R.707	P/O. BERNEY	NAV.	LOCAL.		.50.
2.12.42	20.10	WELLINGTON 1089	P/O. BERNEY	NAV.	LOCAL.		1.35.
2.12.42	21.45	WELLINGTON 1089	SGT. HAPPOLD	1ST. NAV.	X. COUNTRY		5.00
					TOTAL TIME....	93.00	68.40

Training as 1st Nav on Wellingtons at 20 OTU, Lossiemouth, November 1942.

The Crew of Handley Page Halifax JB 869 DY-H 102 Squadron, May 1943.

Above left: 1092623 Sgt William B.J. Happold (Pilot).

Above right: 1070175 Sgt John Brownlie (Wireless Operator).

Left: 657168 Sgt Joseph H. Barratt (Navigator).

Above left: 127296 F/O John Baxter (Bomb Aimer).

Above right: 1219595 Sgt Gordon S. Bowles (Flight Engineer).

Above left: 1602585 Sgt Duncan R. McGregor (Air Gunner).

Above right: 1338943 Sgt Thomas H. Jones (Air Gunner).

My father's nightly 'office' – The navigator's station on board a Halifax.

Handley Page Halifax Mk II TL- P 'Popsie' of 35 Squadron, 1942.

DATE	AIRCRAFT TYPE & NUMBER	CREW	DUTY	TIME Up	TIME Down	DETAILS OF SORTIE OR FLIGHT	REFERENCES.
	W.7934	PILOT F/S. McKINLEY T. NAV. SGT. SUTHERLAND F.A. W/Op. SGT. MILLAR A/G. SGT. O'GRADY M.L. ENG. SGT. SHAW H.F. BOMB. SGT. ALLIBONE F.	DUISBURG	2443	0253	Attacked primary target at 19,000 feet heading 190°M 160 IAS 10/10 cloud tops 21,000 feet. Steady red TI markers and reflection of green seen. Bombed on these and ETA.	
	HR. 668	PILOT NAV. F/O. CRANWELL E.W. P/O. FENTON A.E. W/Op. F/S. MUNRO A.G. A/G. SGT. FAULKES P. ENG. SGT. HOPKINS R.W. BOMB SGT. ASHBROOK J.	As above	2148	0250	Attacked primary target at 18,500 feet heading 195°M 165 IAS 10/10 cloud at 19,000 feet. Bombed on ETA. Thick cloud over whole of route and heavy flak over target area. Unsatisfactory trip.	
0.4.43	.13 aircraft detailed to attack		FRANKFURT.	10/10 cloud vary from 6/10,000 feet.			322
	JB. 835	PILOT P/O. BARKER G.C.E. NAV. F/O. DOTHIE J.R. W/Op. SGT. BROWN R.E. A/G. SGT. LONG R.E. ENG. SGT. HURST J. BOMB. SGT. PERRY J.	As above	2335	0117	Returned early owing to port outer engine developing glycol leak at 0016 hours. Captain proceeded out to sea and jettisoned bombs.	
	JB. 868	PILOT F/L. INGRAM G.F.H. NAV. SGT. RICHARDS S.C. W/Op. SGT. CARNOCK E.A. A/G. SGT. MOULESONG J. ENG. SGT. WHITE K. BOMB. P/O. RUSHBROOK J.	As above	2332	0610	Attacked primary target at 17,000 feet heading 035°M IAS 165 10/10 cloud tops 6/7,000 feet. Landmark and preliminary warning flares seen on approach. Red T.I. at target seen through cloud. Centre of red T.I. in bomb sight. Successful trip if T.I. markers were right.	
	W.7912	PILOT SGT. HAPPOLD W.G.J. NAV. SGT. BARRATT J. W/Op. SGT. BROWNLIE J. A/G. SGT. McGREGOR R.A. ENG. SGT. JONES T.H. BOMB SGT. BOWLES G.S. SGT. BAXTER	As above	2343	0650 HAWKINGE	Attacked primary target at 18,000 feet. 10/10 cloud tops 6000 feet. Results unobserved. One engine feathered due to low oil pressure twenty five minutes before bombing. Landed at HAWKINGE.	
	JB. 894	PILOT SGT. HALE R.R. NAV. SGT. HUTH A.C. W/Op. SGT. HOBBIS W.A. A/G. SGT. LOWINGS J.L.S. ENG. SGT. QUEVILLAR R. BOMB. P/O. WILCOCK. E.D.	As above	2336	0636	Attacked primary target at 18,000 feet heading 038°M IAS 170 10/10 cloud tops 6/8000 feet. Timed run from green markers Bombed on E.T.A. results not seen.	
	HR. 667	PILOT P/O. YOUNGER A.S. 2nd. PILOT L. FOWLE F.R.C. NAV. F/S. PELTIER J. W/Op. F/S. SHARPE A A/G. SGT. BELL W A/G. P/O. McARTHUR T.J.	As above	2347	0617	Attacked primary target at 16,500 feet heading 045°M IAS 180 10/10 cloud tops about 10,000 feet. Preliminary warning steady green seen but difficult to distinguish yellow ground markers. General glow beneath cloud at target. Aimed at centre of glow which contained green and red patches. No results observed.	

Raid report on Frankfurt, 10 April 1943 – forced landing at Hawkinge.

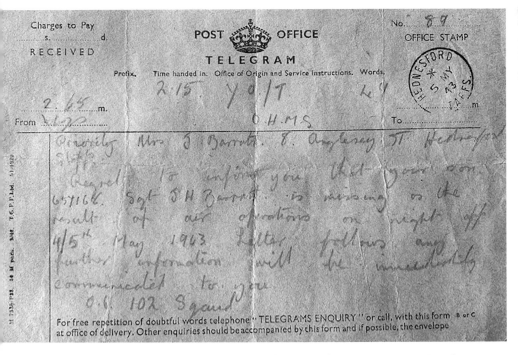

Original pencil written telegram advising that my father was missing after the Dortmund raid 4/5 May 1943.

WAR ORGANISATION
OF THE
BRITISH RED CROSS SOCIETY and ORDER OF ST. JOHN OF JERUSALEM

President:
HER MAJESTY THE QUEEN.

Grand Prior:
H.R.H. The Duke of Gloucester, K.G.

WOUNDED, MISSING AND RELATIVES DEPARTMENT

Chairman:
THE DOWAGER LADY AMPTHILL, C.I., G.B.E.

TELEPHONE NO. :
SLOANE 9696

TELEGRAPHIC ADDRESS :
"WOMIREL, KNIGHTS, LONDON"

S/AEW
RAF C.7098
In replying please quote reference :

7 BELGRAVE SQUARE,
LONDON, S.W.1

15th June 1943.

Dear Mrs. Barratt,

We have not, so far, received any news of your son, Sergeant J.H. Barratt, No.657168, but we feel we should let you know that information has reached us from the Air Ministry that one member of your son's crew, Sergeant T.H.Jones, has been officially reported as a prisoner of war.

We are therefore endeavouring to get into touch with him and should we eventually succeed in obtaining any helpful additional news from this source, we shall of course, communicate with you again.

We are sure you will understand, however, that our enquiries to prisoners of war are now very much delayed and it is possible that the family of this airman may hear news of your son from him before we ourselves receive any reply.

Should you receive news in this way, we should be most grateful if you would be good enough to let us know.

Yours sincerely,

Mrs. E.Barratt,
8, Anglesey Street,
Hednesford,
Staffs.

Margaret Ampthill.

Chairman.

---

8 Anglesey St.
Hednesford
Staffs.
July 6. 1943.

Dear Mrs Brownlie,

I am so very pleased to hear you have had the good news that your son is safe it is grand. I do wish they could all have been saved, it is terrible to hear that four out of seven have lost their lives, it is a very sad loss. I have not heard any news from my son since receiving his card, but a letter from the British Red Cross Society says he is a prisoner of war, wounded, in German hand

Yours Sincerely,
E. Barratt.

Letter from my grandmother to the Wireless Op's mother, 6 July 1943.

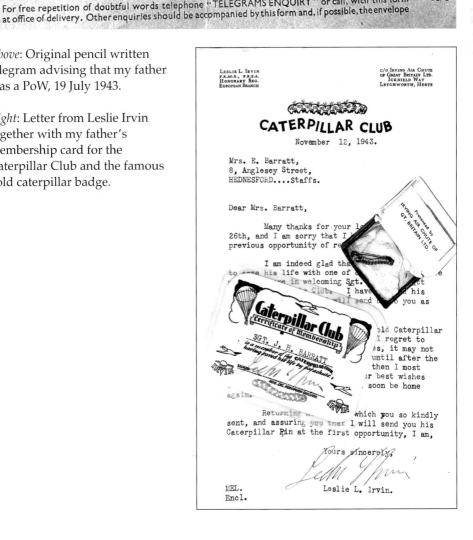

Above: Original pencil written telegram advising that my father was a PoW, 19 July 1943.

Right: Letter from Leslie Irvin together with my father's membership card for the Caterpillar Club and the famous gold caterpillar badge.

Kriegsgefangenenlager   Datum 19.5.43

Dear Mother and Dad   You have probably heard
by now that I am quite safe and in
good health but I thought I'd just drop a
line to tell you not to worry unduly.
I'm being treated fairly well but am
naturally anxious to be home again.
Will write a letter as soon as I'm settled.
                    Love Harold

                    x x x x x x x x

Left: Handwritten letter from my father to my mother advising that he was safe (note date, the letter did not reach her for over 2 months).

Below left: From my father's PoW diary – 'The Baltic Cruise' 1944.

Below right: 'Gefangenenschaft' Life as a PoW, a poem by my father, 1944.

15

IN DAYS TO COME WHEN I AM FREE
ON LOOKING BACK I'LL SOMETIMES SEE.
THE "INSTERBURG" BY MEMEL QUAY.
THAT BORDERS ON THE BALTIC SEA.

I'LL SMELL AGAIN THAT STIFLING HOLD
WHERE NEAR A THOUSAND PRISONERS BOLD
WERE STOWED AS SLAVES IN DAYS OF OLD
IN TRANSPORT TO ANOTHER FOLD.

THREE NIGHTS I SPENT THERE SICK AND SORE
HUDDLING ROUND THE DIRTY FLOOR
WONDERING IF I EVERMORE
WOULD SEE AGAIN OLD ENGLAND'S SHORE.

BUT SUCH IS LIFE IN MANY WAYS.
TEMPT NOT THE FATES IT NEVER PAYS
"ROLL ON THE BOAT" A COMMON PHRASE
I'LL SAY NO MORE IN ALL MY DAYS.

                    PoW 1944

23

Gefangenenschaft.

BEHIND BARBED WIRE A WORLD IS KNOWN
COMPRISED OF MEN WHO ONCE HAD FLOWN
WHERE TALES ARE TOLD OF COURAGE RARE
HEROIC DEEDS DONE IN THE AIR.

MEN WHO HAVE LIVED AND FOUGHT FOR OTHERS
HERDED TOGETHER CLOSER THAN BROTHERS
STRUGGLING ALONG ON DEUTCH BROWN BREAD
AS TOUGH AS TEAK AND AS HEAVY AS LEAD.

NEVER A MAIL DAY BUT COMES THE NEWS
THAT PUTS A FELLOW DEEP IN THE BLUES
A LOVED ONE MARRIED A YANK OR WORSE
OR BACK PAY GOING IN THE WIFES OWN PURSE.

THE WORTHY HOST A JOVIAL BRUTE.
TAKES OUR KIT AND CALLS IT LOOT
STOPS OUR FOOD AT THE LEAST PRETEXT
ONE WONDERS WHAT OR WHO IS NEXT.

BUT ALL IS NOT LOST FOR THESE SALVAGED WRECKS
WHO DREAM OF BACK PAY, BOOZE, AND SEX
SOON THEY'LL FIND THEIR EGO INCREASED
WHEN THEY SAIL THE SKIES OF THE FAR FAR EAST.

                    1944

Trust in a heavenly body – the Navigator's prayer, from my father's diary.

"... TRUST IN A HEAVENLY BODY."

A Roberts - 44

"I don't want WAR!....."

Talented artists in the camp.

The men who did not come home.

Above left: 1219595 Sgt Gordon S. Bowles – Rheinberg CWGC Plot 2. F. 10.

Above right: 127296 F/O John Baxter (Bomb Aimer) – Rheinberg CWGC Plot 2.F.09.

Above left: 1092623 Sgt William B.J. Happold (Pilot) – Rheinberg CWGC Plot 2.F.08.

Above right: 1602585 Sgt Duncan R. McGregor (Air Gunner) – Rheinberg CWGC Plot 2. F. 11.

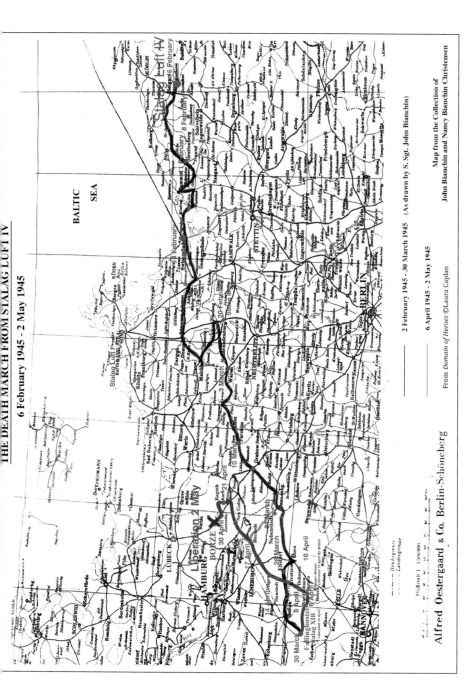

The long, hard road to liberation, 1945.

The Bomber Command Memorial, Green Park, London.

Chapter 8

Missing

They say there's a Halifax leaving the Ruhr
Bound for old Blighty's shore,
Heavily laden with petrified men,
Prostrate and prone on the floor

– Aircrew song

The afternoon of Monday, 26 April 1943.

Bernard Happold and his crew, minus my father, checked the ops board and they were once again assigned H-Harry as part of twelve 102 Squadron Halifaxes detailed to raid Duisberg. They were assigned the young Canadian John Dartry Erzinger as a temporary replacement navigator to cover for the absence of my father. In Flying Officer Erzinger,[1] they had a highly competent and experienced navigator and he was readily accepted by the crew. After the briefings were completed the seven men had climbed aboard H-Harry and run through the usual start up procedures prior to take off. Bomber crews were well-known not only for their highly superstitious nature but also for their general dislike of changes of personnel or routine. Anything that disrupted the unity of the crew was particularly unwelcome. My father and the pilot Bernard Happold had been together since December 1942 at RAF Lossiemouth (20 Operational Training Unit) where they trained together on Wellingtons and were then posted to 1652 Heavy Conversion Unit at Marston Moor, where they had their first taste of the Halifax, and it must have been unsettling to lose their mate and navigator, even for a short period.

At 00:37hrs the wheels of H-Harry left the ground and the crew settled in for their long flight to the target. That night 561 aircraft had been assembled to attack Duisburg, a mix of Lancasters, Halifaxes, Wellingtons and Stirlings together with a few Mosquitos. Although target marking by the Pathfinders was claimed as accurate, much of the bombloads appeared to have fallen to the North East of Duisberg but Bernard Happold's crew reported that they had observed encouraging results:

> *Attacked primary target at 16,000 feet heading 210°M 220 IAS. Smoke haze on ground. Centre of cluster of six red T.I markers in bomb sights. Numerous good fires burning in broad strip running NE to SW. No ground detail could be seen but the area attacked was well alight.*[2]

Bernard Happold's crew, once again aboard H-Harry, was in action the following night (27 April) as part of a formation of six squadron Halifaxes detailed for Gardening operations (minelaying). H-Harry was in the air again the next night, this time with a different crew, under the command of Flying Officer H.S. Hartley, on Gardening duties, dropping mines from 5,000 feet on a DR (Dead Reckoning) fix from the onboard navigator Sergeant W.H. Hughes.

Three days later, on the last day of April, Bernard and his crew (again with John Ezinger as Navigator) climbed aboard H-Harry, now their regular aircraft, as one of twelve tasked to attack Essen. This time 305 aircraft were detailed as part of the attack and although heavy cloud was reported the Oboe equipped Pathfinder Mosquitos were able to mark the target well and final raid analysis showed that 189 buildings were destroyed and 237 severely damaged. For the crew of H-Harry however it would be another frustrating night as the heavily laden aircraft taxied into an unlit Wireless Transmission Van parked near the runway which damaged the airframe sufficiently for it to need repairs.[3]

Shortly afterwards on Saturday 1 May my father was discharged from hospital having had a few days recuperation from his stomach operation and immediately returned to Pocklington to re-join his crew and resume flying duties. His replacement John Erzinger had been an excellent stand-in and was a first-class navigator; he had ensured the crew had reached the target and got safely back again, and my father and must have been relieved to get back to his own crew and find that they were all safe.

Tuesday, 4 May 1943.

The morning had been a cloudy, overcast affair and the accompanying chilly breeze in the afternoon provided a suitable backdrop for what was to prove to be a difficult night for 4 Group. Here and there the distant sound of groundcrew whistling, of tractors towing trolleys on their way to the bomb dump and vehicles driving around the airfield could be heard. Now and again a Rolls-Royce Merlin engine was being coaxed noisily into life by one of the ground crew. The aircraft were kept in their perpetual state of readiness for the night's ops by a dedicated body of mechanics, fitters and armourers who worked all hours (and in all weathers) to ensure their crews had serviceable aircraft. It was to be a momentous night for Bomber Command as the raid would be undertaken by the largest four-engine bomber force sent to bomb Germany up until that date.

For my father and the crew of JB869 H-Harry it would however prove to be momentous for an altogether different reason. As the day wore on the crews began to make their way to the usual briefings – pilots and navigators first for their initial briefing as always. A murmur of apprehension rippled through the assembly of both as they sat huddled together in rows in the briefing room at RAF Pocklington, eyes fixed on the large wall map hidden by blackout curtains at the front of the room. As with all wartime stations on ops that night the airfield was again in lockdown with RAF Police posted on guard duty outside the briefing room, locking the men inside and ensuring no-one went in or out. At the allotted time, and as one body of men, the assembled aircrew rose to their feet once 102's formidable Commanding Officer, (later Air Chief Marshal) Gus Walker GCB, CBE, DSO, DFC, AFC strode purposefully to the front of the room. The CO would lead the primary navigation briefing flanked by his flight commanders including 'A' flight's Squadron Leader F.R.C. 'Chick' Fowle.

Bidding the crews be seated, the black drapes hiding the target map were pulled back disclosing the target for the night's operation.

'Gentlemen, your target for tonight is Dortmund.'

The sound of whistles, and a few groans filled the room. So, it was to be Dortmund – a target known to be heavily defended by flak and one of the key targets in the Ruhr Valley, or 'Happy Valley', as the crews' gallows humour termed it. For others however it would become their graveyard. It would eventually transpire that the night's raid, codenamed Operation Sprat,[4] was to be the largest four-engine bomber raid of the war (up to that point at least) and the first major attack on Dortmund itself. Almost 600 aircraft were destined to be involved in the raid, mostly Lancasters and Halifaxes supported by Wellingtons and the more vulnerable Stirlings. In addition, ten OBOE-equipped Pathfinder Mosquitos were detailed to drop yellow TIs (target indicator flares) on the flight path to the target and then Green TIs at the aiming point. Seventeen Halifaxes from 102 Squadron had been detailed to take part in the raid.

With the navigation briefing well underway the Commanding Officer handed over to his flight commanders and then to the 'Met' (meteorological) men and other assorted specialists. Along with his fellow navigators my father took copious notes during the session, making neat, careful pencil annotations taking in crucial information concerning flight times, chart plots and positions for course changes as well as known locations of flak batteries and searchlights. The outward leg of the trip would take them north of the flak battery at Texel on the Dutch coast and then down to Dortmund.[5]

Following the main briefing pilots and navigators were then joined by the rest of their crew for a secondary briefing on the raid. This would also be the first outing for the crew in H-Harry since the abortive night of the Essen raid on 30 April when the aircraft had taxied into an unlit signals van as the crew were about to take-off. Deemed category A/FA[6] the aircraft was swiftly repaired on site and was ready for operational flying.

Donning their flying kit, the seven men had climbed aboard H-Harry in the afternoon to carry out their usual air tests and ensure that she was fully serviceable for the night's operation. All was well and she was declared fit for the trip. As the crew disembarked, they exchanged smiles, some lit cigarettes and they strolled back to the crew room to change. For many crews the time waiting around before going on ops was the worst, most just wanted to get in the air and get on with the job but with all preparations complete there was little to be done except kill time and, as with previous raids, crews would do so as best they could, either taking time to sleep (if they could) to read, play cards or perhaps write letters home to their wives, sweethearts or parents.

For Duncan McGregor, at just nineteen the youngest member of the crew, his thoughts must at some point have returned to the birthday tea that he had treated his young sister Helen to in Uxbridge a few days ago on leave before re-joining his squadron. Speaking to her at her home in Hillingdon in 1997 she recalled the day with great clarity, how smart he looked in his uniform and how he had promised her he would take her out again soon:

> *He was such a handsome boy, so full of life and hope.*
> *I waved him off at the station, but it was the last I saw*
> *him and then days later he was killed, it was just so sad.'*[7]

For the other members of his crew – in fact for all the crews dotted across the bomber bases in Yorkshire, Lincolnshire and beyond – all they could do was wait. Some preferred to talk, share a joke and a cigarette while others chose to be alone with their thoughts. Fear was, for all, ever-present but had to be choked down lest it be seen by others. As the losses mounted in 1943 and the missing crews and empty tables in the mess hall could no longer be disguised, many crews had started to become increasingly fatalistic.

Max Hastings describes a much-liked officer in 67 Squadron who, after a few ops, decided that he would not survive for much longer: and that he would soon go.[8]

Most men seemed to cope well with any doubts and worries they had about operational flying but those for whom fear took a hold could expect little in the way of sympathy from the RAF. At the first sign of any issues almost all were quickly removed from their crews lest the 'contagion' spread and had their service records stamped LMF (Lacking Moral Fibre). Some were banished from the stations entirely; others were humiliated on parade in front of the entire squadron, stripped of their rank and posted to the worst type of ground duties as a warning of what others might expect. Men did their best to hide whatever fears or misgivings they had and sometimes reasons were given for crews' abortive trips or early returns that masked the problem – engine problems, u/s compass or magneto drop and the like. Of course, many were genuine problems, but all were investigated thoroughly by ground crews who were under strict orders to report anything that looked remotely suspicious when a crew returned home early.

Sometimes reminders of the nightly dangers they faced were starkly evident, especially when rear gunners in their turrets had been unlucky enough to be on the receiving end of flak bursts or attention from German night-fighters, and some unfortunate crewmen walked past a member of the ground crew swilling out the rear gun turret and what was left of the unfortunate gunner after being hit by 20mm canon fire or a flak burst.[9]

Though all men on ops felt fear, relatively few of them actually cracked. Some broke down while in the air and were quickly removed from the station on their return, not to be seen again. Others who did so received a reprieve of sorts. In that respect the case of Arthur Smith, as related in James Taylor and Martin Davidson's excellent *Bomber Crew*[10] is not atypical. Smith, a bomb aimer on Halifaxes, was on his twentieth operation when the strain finally became too much and on the way over the coast he became paralysed by fear and unable to function. The aircraft had no choice other than to turn back. Once on the ground Smith was berated by his CO and taken to see an RAF psychiatrist where it was explained that he would be stripped of his rank, everybody would know he was LMF (including his family) and he would never see his crew again.

The alternative, it was explained to him, was to ask if his crew would have him back so that he could continue flying. They did so without hesitation and Smith completed the rest of his tour of thirty ops. Every man that took part in operational flying at that time, particularly in Bomber Command, possessed courage – but for those men like Arthur Smith who went back into the air to complete their tours after experiencing what was clearly a mental breakdown, that courage is even more remarkable.

The 'tally-ho', 'wizard prang', jovial RAF stereotypes seen in wartime propaganda films and post-war movies, with cheery gait and pipe clenched firmly between teeth, bore little relation to the true reality of life in Bomber Command in 1943. Many of the aircrew I met while researching for this book were dismissive of this rather patronising image of them, my father among them. Speaking to him in the 1980s I asked him about fear and combat flying and whether he was ever scared in the air. His response was short and to the point:

We were all shit-scared and anyone who says he wasn't was a bloody liar. But you didn't dare show it. You didn't want to let your mates down or let them see it. You couldn't. We all had a job to do, and we relied on each other.

As the clock ticked down to their appointed take-off time the crews would assemble, draw their flying kit and parachutes, and prepare themselves accordingly. A last cigarette and then they would climb into the trucks to take them to their aircraft, which could be up to a mile or two away, such was the wide pattern of aircraft dispersal at a wartime bomber station. On arrival at the hardstanding Skipper Bernard Happold and Flight Engineer Gordon Bowles walked around their old favourite H-Harry to check the control surfaces and that the all-important pitot tube cover had been removed. Duly satisfied the pilot signed the Form 700 to take charge of the aircraft. Looking at the bombed-up Halifax the crew sensed the size of what was to come – for the Dortmund raid the aircraft was laden with 2 × 1,000lb MC (general purpose) bombs and sticks of 7×9 XLL and 6×8×30 Incendiary bombs,[11] designed to cause maximum damage and to start a series of fires on the ground.

Bernard Happold gave the order to go, and the crew clambered into their aircraft. Welshman Tommy Jones scrambled along the rear of the fuselage into the cramped rear turret that would be his home for the next few hours. At the other end of the huge bomber Sergeant Happold lifted himself into his seat, strapped himself in and, looking out of the side Perspex window at one of the ground crew indicating which engine to start, he and his flight engineer started the engines in a well-rehearsed, pre-ordained order.

'Contact port outer'
'Contact port inner'
'Contact starboard inner'
'Contact starboard outer'

One by one the huge Merlins exploded into life, flames licking from their exhaust ports. Flight Engineer Gordon Bowles' eyes flicked over the faint glow of his control panel for signs of any problems as the mighty Halifax's engines were run up. Once happy that all was well, he and Bernard Happold then started the tricky process of keeping her moving on the concrete as the huge aircraft taxied slowly to the main runway, pilot and flight engineer struggling to control her using the brakes, the rudders and through shorts bursts of throttle on the port and starboard outers. One slip off the taxiway now with such a heavy bombload and she would quickly sink in the soft ground and wreck the carefully planned take-off schedule for the squadrons' aircraft. Under enforced radio silence and already sweating under their heavy flying suits both men eventually lined the bomber up at the start of the runway ready for their appointed take-off slot and waited for the Aldis lamp signal to take off.

At 22:41hrs Bernard Happold pushed the control column and throttle levers forward, released the brakes and felt the fully laden bomber slowly creep forward on the runway. As she picked up speed Gordon Bowles remained braced next to his skipper ready to hold the throttles forward to ensure maximum power at take-off, any problems at this stage or the loss of an engine could spell certain catastrophe for both aircraft and the crew. Slowly her tail wheel came up and then H-Harry groaned into the air.

For three of her crew, it would be the last they were to see of England for two years. For JB869 herself and her other four crew – Bernard Happold, Gordon Bowles, John Baxter and Duncan McGregor – they would never see it again.

Immediately they were in the air the intercom cracked as my father called out the course for the outward leg. Slowly the crew settled into the long flight ahead of them as the throng of aircraft headed out over the North Sea, on a course for the dogleg north of the small island of Texel and then on to Germany. As they neared the Dutch coast, they saw the first bursts of flak in the distance, illuminating the night skies. Traversing their turrets Tommy Jones and the mid-upper gunner Duncan McGregor swept the dark skies for night fighters. The night was cloudless but also moonless making it favourable for any that would be on the prowl. The intercom crackled twice more as the navigator gave the new course to his pilot and then Bernard Happold made sure his gunners were alert:

Enemy Coast Ahead Skipper.
Okay nav – you gunners, make sure you keep your eyes open.

The bomber slowly rolled to starboard to join the burgeoning bomber stream heading for the Ruhr Valley and on to Dortmund. Flying over enemy territory for hours at a time required maximum concentration from each member of the crew and the need to be alert to everything around them. Gunners peered into the black night, eyes constantly searching, searching, searching for the presence of enemy fighters. For my father his time was spent sitting at the navigator's table in the front section of the aircraft, hunched over his maps checking courses and keeping the pilot advised of any course corrections. Apart from the deafening roar of the four Merlin engines, flying at altitude and at night during wartime exposed the crews to bitterly cold temperatures and while some had electrically heated suits, for the most part the crews wore sweaters under their flying clothes and then sheepskin lined Irvin leather flying jackets, fur-lined flying boots, thick gauntlets and silk undergloves.

With aircraft potentially in the air for many hours toileting was also an issue – standard issue on aircraft was the Elsan chemical toilet – essentially a bucket with a lid. Difficult to use and with a tendency to leak, few crews wanted to take the risk of using it especially anywhere near the target and most who needed to would urinate in a beer bottle or use the flare chute and do their other business (for those that needed to) in a cardboard box and throw it from the aircraft.[12]

The aircraft flew deeper into the heart of Germany, north of the Ruhr and they began to pick up the stream of Target Indicator flares dropped by the Pathfinder force. As they approached the target, they could see the vast bright glow from the extensive fires that raged across Dortmund and the surrounding area, illuminating the night sky. When they closed in for their bombing run the aircraft shook and rattled as flak burst all around them and the stench of cordite hung in the air. Staying straight and level for a few minutes over the target was the most nerve-jangling time for many crews and it was when they were most vulnerable. Pressing the button on the bomb release control Glaswegian John Baxter finally yelled down the intercom: 'Bombs gone'.

Relief. Job done. The crew braced as the now much lighter Halifax lurched upwards, her bombload hurtling down towards the industrial heart of Dortmund. The damage inflicted on the town below was terrible. Although some of the Target Indicators dropped earlier in the night were inaccurate, and diversion fires had been lit, it is generally estimated that around

45–50 per cent of the aircraft that reached the target that night managed to drop their bombs within three miles of the aiming point. Forty-five acres of the industrial centre of the town was destroyed, including 28 factories and 693 people on the ground were killed in the attack as incendiaries were dropped to devastating effect. In excess of 4,000 fires blazed all night across the town and surrounding area and 320 were classed as *Grossbrande* (big fires) by contemporary German reports.[13]

Such was the intensity of the firestorm that many crews, amongst them JB853 DY A-Apple and DT743 DY O-Orange from 102 Squadron, reported in their post-op debriefing that the glow from the fires was visible even when they crossed the Dutch coast on the way home and even from the Zuider Zee.[14]

Meanwhile aboard H-Harry, having done their bit, the crew focused on getting away from the target and heading for home. Bernard Happold clicked his microphone on: 'Right – let's get the hell out of it – give me a course for home please, navigator.'

As the bombers swung for home, their bellies bathed in an orange and red glow from the town beneath, the various crews knew that they would have to run the gauntlet once more of ferocious anti-aircraft fire from the numerous flak batteries, as well as the ever-present threat of night fighters and the possibility of being picked off as they made their way home, now that the defenders knew they were here.

Immediately after dropping their bomb load another of 102's Halifaxes, JB864 DY B-Bertie, which had taken off from Pocklington only a minute after H-Harry, was picked up in a searchlight and Sergeant D.W. Ward – her pilot – threw the aircraft into a corkscrew dive from 20,000 to 11,000 feet in a desperate bid to escape being coned and managed to throw the beam off.[15] They were lucky as it was estimated that over 200 searchlights were believed to be operating around Dortmund at that time.[16]

Others were not to be so lucky as Sergeant Powell, the Wireless Op on DT743 DY O-Orange recounts seeing aircraft coned by lights and then exploding.[17] At around the time that B Bertie had run into trouble, W7820 DY V-Victor was hit by heavy flak and lost an engine over the target, losing a second engine over the North Sea before eventually ditching some 75 miles off Flamborough Head. Happily the entire crew were successfully retrieved from their raft by the Air Sea Rescue service as their aircraft sank into the depths and, as an interesting footnote, were pictured with (and being congratulated by) the C-in-C Air Chief Marshal Sir A.T. Harris during his visit to Pocklington on 5 May.[18]

Through their Perspex windows and canopies the crew of H-Harry could see the arcs of tracer fire coming up at them and the meandering searchlights suddenly sweeping across the sky. In his dark, curtained navigator's compartment my father must have cursed as the airframe bucked and rolled, the smell of cordite and the percussive 'whump' of anti-aircraft fire continued for what seemed like an eternity and then the jolting stopped, and the aircraft flew on in the night, the relentless roar of the engines the only other constant sound.

For the crew of H-Harry their thoughts must have started to turn towards home. They had successfully evaded the high concentrations of flak and the attentions of the searchlights around Dortmund and were now well into their homeward journey, heading northeast over the district of Kevelaer and only a few minutes flying time from the Dutch border. The gunners kept their eyes focused on the dark skies outside, straining for the sight of a night-fighter and the tell-tale light from exhaust flames that would alert them to their presence. Inevitably fatigue would creep into weary crews heading for home as over six hours in the air – three of them over Germany – would take its toll, not to mention the surge of adrenaline while over the target area itself. For many the combination of the soporific drone of the engines, the euphoria of having added another raid to their tally of ops and the relief that they were heading home could lead to loss of concentration in the air – for many crews there would be a particularly rude awakening.

Tonight, it would be H-Harry's turn.

The deafening blast shook the airframe violently and threw my father from his seat onto the floor and in the process striking his head against one of the fuselage support spars above him, which rendered him briefly unconscious. As he came to, he could feel the blood trickle from a cut near his left eye and could see the port wing of H-Harry searing like a blow torch with both engines alight. He groped groggily for his parachute, stowed behind him, and with help from John Brownlie, the wireless operator, he managed to secure the locking mechanism of the parachute harness, his head still spinning, the roar of the engines increasing in pitch. Knowing the aircraft was doomed pilot Bernard Happold wrenched the control column up to gain as much height as he could and gave the order to jump:

We've had it – Bale out, bale out.

In the rear gun turret Tommy Jones cranked the hand wheel to rotate his turret, opened the doors and dropped out backwards into the night sky, catching sight of H-Harry, long tails of flame licking across her port wing engulfing the engines. On board it was a desperate struggle for life as John Brownlie and my father struggled to open the escape hatch below the navigator's seat while the aircraft bucked and turned. Flight Engineer Gordon Bowles and Mid-Upper gunner Duncan McGregor were, most likely, already dead as they both failed to respond to the order to abandon the aircraft, leaving just the pilot battling to keep the crippled bomber in the air. Finally, with a wrench, the escape hatch opened – Sergeant Brownie spoke once more to the pilot over the intercom:

'Are you going Skip'?

Bernard Happold screamed back: 'Christ…Jock? Where are you? Get out, get out for God's sake JUMP!'[19]

My father and Sergeant Brownlie tumbled through the hatch into the blackness, a combination of the jerk of his 'chute deploying and the slipstream tearing off the latter's flying boots and the scarf from his neck as the night air filled his lungs. Still on board Bernard Happold was fighting a losing battle, drenched in sweat, and using every ounce of his strength to maintain level flight while his crew baled out, he would have known that the spreading fire would soon either ignite the fuel tanks or burn through the wing. At some point John Baxter the bomb aimer managed to exit the burning aircraft (that much is now known)[20] but seconds later he was seen by one of the others to have been caught in the blast when H-Harry exploded in mid-air, and he was most likely killed instantly.

For the three who got out – my father, John Brownlie and Tommy Jones – there was nothing they could do but watch as the fragments of the burning aircraft spiralled downwards, the shattered pieces coming to rest in the fields south of Frau Verhaag's Farm, Keylaer 67, Kevelaer.[21] For the men who had survived, the shock of being shot down was slowly turning to apprehension about what kind of reception committee they would soon face on the ground, given the levels of destruction that their coming was now causing across the length of Germany.

Speaking in 1988 shortly before his death, my father, in one of his rare discussions about the night he was shot down, told me what he could recall of the moments immediately after he had jumped:

I think I was probably concussed from banging my head when we were hit. The pilot told us to get out and I remember feeling sick and a colossal pain in my head on the way down. I had no idea where we were going to come to earth or even how high we were when we jumped, but then I felt searing pain in my ankles and back as I crashed through the branches of what I realised was a tree. I crossed my arms and put them over my face to protect my eyes and then I came to rest amongst the branches as my parachute ripped and then snagged. The pain in my legs and ankles was excruciating but I was conscious of not wanting to attract attention or call out so tried to keep as quiet and still as possible. I was worried about falling further down as I had no idea how high up I was and I knew I'd done some damage to my feet so thought it best to just stay still.

In fact, my father had broken one ankle, badly sprained the other and cracked vertebrae in his back as he crashed through the trees. Almost forty-five years later in 1988 the consultant treating my father for his cancer asked me if I knew how he had received such damage to his back and ankles as evidenced in his X-rays.[22] When I explained the likely circumstances, he expressed surprise that he had managed to lead such an active life after the war given the extent of what he had seen in his X-rays.

John Brownlie had met with a similar fate on the way down. All three men had landed in woodland and at least two had crashed down through trees and suffered accordingly with damaged shoulders, ankles, knees and various cuts and bruises as evidence of a particularly hard landing. But they were, at least, alive.

At that point the three survivors were unaware that on farmland nearby their three comrades John Baxter, Duncan McGregor and Gordon Bowles lay dead, the wreckage of JB869 still smouldering around them. Bernard Happold's body was the fourth and last body to be found in what remained of the Halifax's cockpit section. The occupants of a farmhouse came out and covered the dead with blankets. Perhaps somewhat unsurprisingly given the night's heavy raid, it was to be several hours and almost dawn before a mix of Luftwaffe soldiers from nearby Krefeld airfield, alerted by the fires, arrived at the crash site and, counting the number of crew lying dead, immediately began a search for the missing three amongst the fields and trees. According to reports my father was freed by two local men, Herr Angenendt and Herr Brauer using a ladder and a rope to lower him down.

My father takes up the story again:

> *I saw several soldiers with rifles and was a bit anxious as I knew I was in a state and didn't know what they were going to be like. They stole my boots, flying jacket, cigarette case and my gold watch but otherwise I was treated okay. I saw that they had caught the wireless operator too but at that point didn't see anyone else. I was driven under guard to a small local hospital and then later to a larger one, which I later found out was Dusseldorf. I had no idea what had become of the others at that point.*

Whether it was anti-aircraft fire from the ground or a night fighter that brought them down is still open to conjecture. We shall probably never know for sure as no claims were ever made for the aircraft from either flak battery crews on the ground or *Nachtjagd* pilots in the air.[23]

Whatever it was I do know from a discussion with my father and contemporary, albeit brief, written accounts from the other crew who survived, that it was extremely sudden and the aircraft was set on fire almost immediately. For many years it was assumed that it had crashed 'somewhere in the region of Monchengladbach', but no further information was known. Sergeant Happold, McGregor, Bowles and Flying Officer Baxter were certainly buried there, interred side by side at the Stadtfriedhof[24] where they lay until 2 August 1946 when their remains were exhumed and reburied at Rheinberg Cemetery.[25]

However, in 2006, while investigating likely crash sites for JB869, the author was put in contact with Steve Heppenstall, a researcher and former serviceman with a specific interest in locating crash sites for aircraft lost over Germany in the Second World War. We corresponded frequently over the years, assisted by the late Tom Wingham, secretary of the 102 Squadron Association who first put me in touch with him. After some early dead-ends I received an email from him in January 2020 confirming that he had located the crash site of JB869 and that it had come down in an area northwest of the town of Kevelaer.

Steve had consulted local archive records and contemporary reports of the time. One such report[26] noted that on the night of the raid a four-engine bomber had crashed in the vicinity of Verhaag Farm, Keylar 67 and that four crew were dead with three held as prisoners. One crew member was injured and was taken to nearby Kevelaer hospital for treatment and then on to Dusseldorf. Steve also found the names of the two German civilians that freed my father from the tree and forwarded them to me.

The final piece of the jigsaw slotted into place when a colleague of Steve's, working for a museum in the locality of Kevelaer, had an eye witness relate to him that one of the dead crewman of the 'British Bomber' near Frau Verhaag's Farm was either an 'L or a J Baxter'.[27] Only two aircrew with the surname of Baxter were shot down on the Dortmund raid that night – one of them, Sergeant J.R. Baxter from a Wellington belonging to 466 Squadron baled out and became a PoW[28] which meant without doubt that the wrecked Halifax at the farm was, indeed, JB869.

And so began almost two years of captivity as a prisoner of war for the three survivors of H-Harry. My father had escaped the burning aircraft, bailing out where others had not and had avoided, for now, the ill-treatment of downed airmen that was becoming increasingly commonplace at that time.

Had he known what was to follow at the hands of his captors he would perhaps have realised that the easy part was over and that his ordeal was only beginning.

Chapter 9

Heart, Nerve and Sinew

If you can force your heart and nerve and sinew
To serve your turn long after they are gone,
And so hold on when there is nothing in you
Except the Will which says to them: 'Hold on!'

Kipling

omber Command lost a total of 31 aircraft on the
Dortmund raid; a mix of Halifaxes, Lancasters,
Stirlings and Wellingtons, plus a further eight aircraft
that crashed in the UK on their return. That night 150 airmen
were killed with an additional 67 ending up as PoWs.[1]

102 Squadron lost three aircraft: JB869 DY-H Harry, HR
667 DY-O Orange which came down in Holland[2] and W7820
DY- V Victor, which ended up ditching in the North Sea off
Flamborough Head. Along with countless other squadron
commanders that day the OC of 102 Squadron spent the morning
communicating casualties to the Air Ministry, detailing the men
who had failed to return from the previous night's operations.
From there, telegrams were sent to the nearest Post Office to
the recorded next of kin of aircrew believed missing or killed
and the Telegram boys would deliver the telegrams in a plain
brown envelope.

At 14.15hrs on 5 May the telegram machine clattered into life at Hednesford Post Office. Writing the words down carefully in pencil the telegram clerk handed the enveloped message to the telegram boy who set off on his bicycle. At No.8 Anglesey Street, Hednesford it was like most other days. The house was quiet – my grandfather was underground at the colliery, six of my father's seven sisters were either at school, or work, and my grandmother was preparing food in the kitchen. Only Gladys, the seventh sister, remained in the house. Through the gap in the curtains my grandmother could see the comings and goings of people in the street.

Her eyes focused on the familiar figure of the telegram boy, black uniform and pillbox cap, on his bike, looking for a particular house. She watched him as he cycled past and went back to her cooking. Then she heard the rap of knuckles on the door. Gladys heard it too.

No-one answered.

Again, the rap of knuckles but this time followed by the sound of my grandmother's shoes on the floor. Wiping her hands on her apron as she unlatched the door there was a brief, mumbled exchange, the tearing of paper. For an instant there was an eerie silence and then: 'NO, NO, NO! Not my boy, not my boy!'

The telegram would be read and re-read by the family in the days that followed:

Priority Mr J. Barratt, 8 Anglesey Street, Hednesford, Staffs

Regret to inform you that your son 657168 J H Barratt
is missing as the result of air operations on night of 4/5
May 1943. Letter follows. Any further information will
be immediately communicated to you.

O.C 102 Squadron[3]

The same scene would be repeated throughout the length and breadth of the country. For many it would be the start of weeks, sometimes months (and in some cases even years) of waiting to find out whether sons, brothers, husbands, fathers had perished or been one of the lucky few to have survived as prisoners.

Hours later, at Pocklington Airfield in Yorkshire, home of 102 Squadron, Gus Walker was waiting to greet Bomber Command's Commander-in-Chief Air Chief Marshal Sir Arthur 'Bomber' Harris who was paying a surprise visit to the station. Harris was an extraordinary but also deeply divisive figure – he was loved by his crews (his 'old lags' as he termed them) but was regarded as abrasive and obstinate by his political masters. As we have seen earlier in this book, Harris fully embraced the concept of Strategic Area Bombing and was convinced that Germany could be brought to her knees with a concerted and sustained effort – the British by night and the Americans by day.

Visiting the station, he was introduced to the crew of V-Victor who had been successfully plucked from the sea by the Air Sea Rescue launch and had even made the newspaper headlines[4] as a welcome boost to wartime propaganda. A fortnight or so later Harris would be visiting another Bomber Command

Squadron, this time at Scampton in Lincolnshire where he would meet Wing Commander Guy Gibson and the surviving crews from 617 Squadron who, on 16/17 May carried out the audacious raids on the Moehne, Sorpe and Eder Dams – the Dambusters. Fifty-six men were lost on the raid, drawn from some of Bomber Commands finest crews; three of them would survive bailing out to become prisoners and by a quirk of fate my father would eventually end up in the same hut as one of them, Sergeant Frederick Tees, the rear gunner of Lancaster ED910 AJ- C-Charlie.[5] My father and Sergeant Tees would remain friends through the camps, the forced marches across Germany in the winter of 1944 and for a lengthy period after the war until they lost touch sometime in the early nineteen sixties.

Meanwhile, in Kevelaer town hospital, the morning after the raid, my father was being treated for his injuries, kept in a side room – a guard at the door – away from prying eyes. His broken ankle was reset, his wounds dressed and his back braced and stabilised. At that point my father could speak no German and the nurses, orderlies and doctors very little English, but he remarked to my mother years after that he had only experienced kindness from all the medical staff that he came into contact (with the camp guards, however, it was to be a completely different matter). After treatment he was loaded aboard a truck on a stretcher and driven to the much larger and better equipped hospital at Düsseldorf for further treatment. On arrival at the hospital he would have ended up in a ward room, presumably with other wounded airmen and possibly even with crewmate John Brownlie.

At this point my father, like many other downed airmen, would have been unaware of the fate of the rest of his crew but would have suspected the worst. He knew that John Brownlie had managed to get out as they had both exited the aircraft within seconds of each other, and it's likely that he had witnessed the explosion that killed John Baxter and seen the glow from the shattered remains of JB869, lying in surrounding fields, but he was unaware that the other four crew members had died.

As well as thinking about the fate of his crew my father would also have been acutely aware of the official telegram that would have arrived back home on the morning after he was shot down; in particular the effect receiving it would have on his family, especially his mother, and he would have been keen to send word home that he was alive. After a short stay of 7-10 days in the hospital he was deemed fit enough to be discharged ready for the train journey to Oberusel and to Dulag Luft for interrogation prior to a permanent camp. Though mobile on his crutches he was still largely incapacitated. He was supplied with a pair of plain shoes to replace the flying boots that had been taken from him when he was cut down from Frau Verhaags's tree and was dressed in what remained of his flying kit – blue trousers, shirt and battledress jacket. His Irvin flying jacket had gone the same way as his boots and his other possession. PoWs were usually heavily guarded, but given my father's injuries and the fact that he was on crutches, he was obviously regarded as low risk in terms of potential escapees and was placed in the care of an elderly Feldwebel:

They handed me over to this old Corporal, he had a rifle, but it looked pretty unused really. I somehow doubt it was even loaded but then again, I wasn't exactly going anywhere, was I? They loaded me into a car, and we were driven to the station to wait for the train.

At the rail station the two men made for the platform that would take them to Barth, almost 400 miles to the north-east and the start of prison camp life. In essence it was a nondescript wartime railway station like any other at that time, with a mix of civilians and military personnel going about their business across the Reich – only the bomb damaged and shrapnel scarred buildings provided a clue as to the increasing spread of the aerial bombardment now facing Germany. Nevertheless, the German party newspapers were full of reports of the bombing raids across the Ruhr and Göebbels' propaganda machine lost no time in whipping up the civilian population with reports of casualties caused by the *Terrorflieger und Luftgangsters* (Terrorfliers and Air Gangsters) from the RAF, RCAF and the USAF that was raining down destruction on German towns and cities. Increasingly downed aircrew could expect harsh treatment should they fall into German hands and what follows is a detailed and factual account of what almost happened to my father, exactly as he described it to me.

As we will see his experience was sadly not altogether uncommon.

At the railway station I was attracting a lot of unwanted attention – I was still in my flying kit, on crutches and with an elderly guard next to me. I couldn't really hear or understand what the people milling about were saying but they were obviously hostile and so I kept my eyes fixed on the tracks. The old boy with me must have sensed it too as he kept nudging me and motioned me to move further down the platform, which I did but it was a bloody effort on crutches! It was this point that I saw one of the mob was holding a rope. Still the crowd moved nearer and this time I could pick out a few words 'Englander' and the like. The old boy looked a bit panicked and he kept telling me to move down the platform 'Schnell, macht schnell' (quickly, hurry up). We had moved almost to the end of the platform, the pain from my back and ankles was murder and I was sweating under the effort of it all. I looked at the guard and he looked petrified. I remember thinking 'You'll be bugger all use if anything happens'. Sure enough when I turned to look at him again he'd disappeared – I was on my own. I tried to move a bit further but I was in too much pain to move. They were pretty close by this time. I thought, this is it, and I've had it.

At that point salvation came from the unlikeliest of sources;

I braced for what was coming and just hoped it would be over pretty quick but almost at the last possible minute a young German soldier suddenly emerged from a room on my left, possibly a waiting room or something like that, and stood between me and the mob. It happened really quickly but he was armed and levelled his machine gun at them, he yelled at them in German and they stopped, but there was still a lot of shouting and pointing. It seemed

*to go on for ages but then I heard him cock his gun ready
to fire and he yelled at them again. They must have
though he meant business as this time they cleared off
and that was that. He was only a young bloke, late teens
to early twenties I'd say and he was in the uniform of
the Afrika Korps. God knows what he was doing there
but if it hadn't been for him they'd have lynched me, of
that I'm sure. The old boy with the rifle then reappeared
and the two exchanged words. We got on the train when
it came and the young soldier sat with us. He gave me
a cigarette and shared some chocolate – it was a long
journey and he got off somewhere along the way, can't
remember what the place was called, but he saved my life
that day, absolutely no question of that. I'd have been
done for were it not for him.*

My father was very lucky indeed to have escaped what would
have most likely have been a brutal end had the mob managed
to get their hands on him. Other airmen were not so lucky.
Oliver Clutton-Brock's excellent book *Footprints On The Sands
of Time*[6] devotes two chapters to the subject of war crimes by
German soldiers and civilians carried out against allied aircrew,
some proven, some not, during the war years. Be warned, it
makes for particularly grim reading and details numerous cases
of captured airmen being appallingly mistreated at the hands of
their captors. Cases ranged from downed airmen being beaten
and kicked to death when they landed to summary executions
by Police, SS men, Hitler Youth and even regular soldiers,
shooting their captives in the back of the head at point blank

range. Worse still lynching by enraged civilians, such as nearly
happened to my father, were increasingly commonplace. What
happened to one American airman who bailed out over Lubeck
in 1944 was not uncommon.[7]

He had landed safely in a field next to a highway near
Lübeck-Siems, Germany, fourteen miles from the Baltic Sea,
and German soldiers immediately captured him. In addition to
landing safely, being in the custody of soldiers must have offered
an initial sense of relief for the flyer, since rumours among
airmen described German security forces, Party officials,
and especially civilians as likely to be more hostile to downed
airmen than soldiers. Downed flyers who evaded capture and
returned to England with the aid of resistance fighters, as well as
prisoners of war who had returned through medical exchanges,
all bolstered these rumours with personal accounts of seeing
Allied flyers hanged from lamp posts in bombed-out cities or
from beams at train stations. Yet as the soldiers escorted the
flyer along the highway towards the city of Lübeck, his sense
of relief quickly turned to fear. An angry mob incensed by the
aerial attacks (made up mainly of civilians, two SS soldiers, and
the local block leader) encircled him.

The block leader, a low-level Nazi Party official responsible
for neighbourhood supervision, told the two soldiers guarding
the flyer to 'leave him to us so that we can have some sport with
him.' After SS and Party officials questioned the airman about
his nationality, the mob (including women) beat him mercilessly
with farm tools, steel helmets, and anything they had at hand.
The terrified flyer bled profusely as they ruthlessly directed
blows at his head. The injuries quickly took their toll on the

airman, who collapsed from the pain and shock, but the crowd did not stop after they rendered him unconscious. They beat him until his face was unrecognizable then dragged his lifeless body back into the cornfield, where the block leader shot him eight times in the back and the head. The perpetrators then threw his body in the trunk of a nearby vehicle and buried his remains in an unmarked grave.

Other documented examples, where injured airmen were picked up and thrown back into the flames of their burning aircraft to burn to death are frankly too horrific to be related here. On arrival at Oberusel my father was taken the short distance to the interrogation centre at Dulag Luft,stripped and his clothes searched on arrival. From there confinement was in a smallish cell where he would receive regular visits from an interrogator. Captured airmen were asked to complete a report form with the usual name, rank, serial number info followed by questions about next of kin, life at home, then service details including squadron and aircraft details. All allied aircrew received training on what they would face if captured and they were wise to the questioning.

Some communal areas where they were allowed to mix were very obviously 'listening areas' that were bugged with microphones and prisoners either said nothing at all or the more confident among them would utter fanciful gibberish to feed the Germans 'duff gen'. Even at these transit camps prisoners minds were always alert to the idea of escape – two famous would-be escapers were Spitfire pilot Roger Bushell (who went on to lead the famous 'Great Escape' of 76 prisoners from Stalag Luft III, memorably played in the film of the same name by Sir Richard Attenborough) and future Carry-On film star Peter Butterworth, who after being initially captured by a member of the Hitler Youth remarked that he would 'never work with children again'.

Those recaptured from the escape attempt in 1941 were, allegedly, given a case of champagne with the words 'Better luck next time, even if I'm not supposed to say so,' by the Kommandant Major Rumpel. It is most likely an apocryphal story but if it is even partly true then attitudes to escapers would harden considerably within three short years, as the fifty men executed by the Gestapo in the aftermath of the Great Escape provide grim testimony.

After a brief interrogation in Oberusel my father was transferred out, again on crutches, for the train journey from Frankfurt and then by truck to Stalag Luft 1, located two miles northwest of the town of Barth on the Baltic Coast. The camp had been opened in July 1940 and was the archetypal PoW camp of rough-sawn wooden barracks, raised slightly on posted stilts (so that the guards could check under the huts) and surrounded by high barbed wire fences, with wooden lookout posts staffed by sentries armed with MG42 heavy calibre machine guns dotted along the perimeter. Ten feet or so in from the perimeter fence was the infamous 'warning wire', usually a single or double flexed strand of barbed wire. Crossing it would mean being shot without warning.

Once settled in his wooden bunk in the barrack hut he was allocated my father wasted no time in writing a brief *Postkarte* (Postcard) dated 19 May 1943 to send home via the German

Kriegsgefangegenepost (Prisoner of War Post) network and let his parents know he was safe:

> *Dear Mother & Dad. You have probably heard by now that I am quite safe and in good health but I thought I would drop you a line to tell you not to worry unduly. I'm being treated fairly well but am naturally anxious to be home again. Will write a letter as soon as I'm settled. Love Harold xxxxxx*

Such was the delay in transit that it would be almost another month before my grandparents would receive news that my father was safe. My grandmother wrote to the British Red Cross in Belgrave Square London in early June for any news of him and received a reply dated 15 June stating that they had no news, but that the Air Ministry had confirmed that the rear gunner, Sergeant T.H. Jones, had been officially reported as a Prisoner of War. Official Air Ministry confirmation that her son was indeed a prisoner was finally received by my grandmother a few days later on the morning of 19 June when another handwritten telegram would arrive at No.8 Anglesey Street, Hednesford:

> *J. Barratt, 8 Anglesey Street, Hednesford, Staffs*

> *Information received through the Red Cross states that your son, Sgt Joseph Harold Barratt, is a prisoner of war wounded in German hands. Stop. Letter confirming this telegram follows.*

> *Air Ministry London*

Wireless Op John Brownlie wrote to his parents on 16 June from Barth and he was keen to find out what had happened to the other four members of the crew:

I lost my flying boots on the way down but I think I'll be kitted out at the other camp, also I want to know what happened to the rest of the crew as it happened so quickly and I only saw the navigator bale out in front of me. I hope they are all okay but will let you know when I can.[8]

In a subsequent letter written from Stalag Luft 1 John Brownlie confirmed that he was bunked in the same room as my father and also Tommy Jones, the rear gunner, by which time I suspect that he would have known the fate of the other four members of his crew. On 6 July my grandmother wrote to Mrs Brownlie and by that stage the fate of the rest of the crew was clearly known by their next of kin.

Dear Mrs Brownlie,

I am so very pleased to hear that you have had news that your son is safe, it is grand. I do wish they could all have been saved, it is terrible to hear that four out of seven have lost their lives, it is a very sad loss. I have not heard any news from my son since receiving his card but a letter from the British Red Cross Society says he is a prisoner of war, wounded, in German hands.

Yours sincerely E. Barratt

As a prisoner of war, newly 'in the bag', my father along with other new arrivals would start the long process of getting used to a life of incarceration that in his case would last almost two years. Initially, he would no doubt have felt some sense of relief at having survived being shot down and bailing out. Perhaps he may also have allowed himself the feeling that the inherent dangers of combat flying were behind him and survival was more assured. Equally, his thoughts may have been tempered by so-called survivors' guilt that so many PoWs experienced and, for some, the imagined (but misplaced) shame and humiliation of being captured and feeling that they had somehow 'let the side down', which of course was nonsense. Over time these feelings would be replaced by frustration at the soul-destroying grind and routine of prison camp life and then, in turn, to fear given the increasingly brutal treatment he received. Finally, when the end of the war and liberation seemed within touching distance, he would experience the cruellest of depravations and the despair of watching men die around him during the forced marches through the bitter winter of 1944/45.

At Barth, camp life was reasonably comfortable for the recent influx of RAF men who found themselves unwilling guests in the care of the Reich and, for many of the men, it would be positively five-star accommodation compared to the future horrors that they would experience at Heydekrug and Gross Tychow. For active young men, used to the adrenaline rush of operational flying, the sedentary life of a prisoner would prove to be a very different (and difficult) proposition and the initial relief at their own survival from being shot down would increasingly give way to annoyance and frustration at being held. Nevertheless, they were there and had to make the best of it. Physical education provided a way of keeping men fit and active, as were sports, particularly football, with men grouping into sides representing the famous teams of the day and knockout tournaments being held. In one of his letters home on 18 July (prisoners were only allowed to write two letters and four postcards a month) my father gives an early insight into camp life, ruefully mentioning the football (as he couldn't join in) and also hints at what was to become one of the bugbears of all captives – the lack of news coming in from home and the need to kill time:

Dear Mother Dad and all at home

It's getting monotonous, writing letters and not getting replies to them, but I suppose when they do start coming I shall be getting them regularly. We had a bit of a gala day last Saturday with sports lasting all day and a football match. We were also supplied with beer, but it was beer in name only, I could only tackle ½ cup of it and my ankles prevented me entering into any of the sports. Things here are much the same, although, we are all eager for news so naturally we get plenty of rumours but they all turn out to be what someone has made up. I wouldn't attempt to send me any news though, because the censors would never pass anyhow. I trust you are all keeping well.[9]

Love Harold

My father had written four postcards and three letters before the three letters written by his mother reached him around 21 August. Of course, what he didn't realise at the time was that the Prisoner of War mail (*Kriegsgefangenenpost*) was intolerably slow and both mail going in to and out of Barth first had to go via Stalag Luft 3 (Sagan) where each letter was read and censored by hand. As a result mail and parcels could take many weeks, if not months, before they arrived, but as the war went on he finally realised that the delays were down to the process and not due to my grandparents and his seven sisters ignoring him.

And so, like all of the 10,000 RAF prisoners held in camps during the Second World War he proceeded to try and make his stay as tolerable as he could while he slowly recovered from the injuries to his back and ankles that he had received when bailing out. The camp at Barth had, by all accounts, a good library of general titles and reference books that were sent over from England to the various prisoners and my father was soon able to reignite his love of books and learning. He also applied himself, like many prisoners, to mastering a few words of German and practised some of his new-found skills with those guards who were reasonably receptive to the odd phrase being uttered, although fraternisation on either side, was discouraged for obvious reasons.

As time went on he became more confident and his understanding of the language, and his vocabulary, grew. The Germans were no doubt amused that their captives were trying to learn Deutsch (which was also explained by the prisoners to their captors as 'something to do to kill the time' or to 'make themselves more easily understood'). Of course, application to the task of learning to become reasonably fluent in German was for an altogether different ulterior motive, knowing that if they were to stand a reasonable chance of escape, at some point they would almost certainly need to be able to pass themselves off as natives of the land and not allied airmen.

Escape activities in the camp were properly coordinated and invariably tunnelling was seen as one of the best and safest ways of getting men out, although by its very nature it took time and if the efforts were discovered months of hard work had effectively been for nothing – one of the biggest issues, as in all camps, was that the soil they were constructed on was deliberately sandy to discourage tunnelling. Wood (usually bed boards) was always needed to shore up the insides of the tunnel walls and ceiling to prevent them collapsing. Tunnelling was a dirty, dangerous and back-breaking job for those men who were doing the actual digging underground, but the success of the entire operation also hinged on the other members of the escape committee doing their 'part' of the role they had been assigned to from forgers, tailors, scroungers and lookouts through to inventors and 'fixers'.

The ingenuity of the men in the camps and the quite extraordinary things they managed to build and concoct from the most rudimentary things was truly remarkable. In the early years lack of credible news of the progress of the war outside of the confines of the camp made things very hard, but this was eventually eased by the building of a crude but working radio receiver set that not only gave the prisoners a heads-up, but also survived numerous attempts by the Germans to find it (they never did and the PoWs even managed to smuggle it from camp to camp).

For my father, still unable to do much physical work at this stage due to the problems with his back and lower legs, his mobility was still very limited and any chance of escape at this point was out of the question – for the time being at least. Nevertheless, he was able to play a part and he helped as a 'stooge' – one of a number of prisoners strategically placed around the camp to keep an eye open for approaching guards or sentries that may come too close to tunnelling or associated escape-related activity.

An elaborate set of visual and audible warnings was devised that could be swiftly communicated from man to man so that any suspicious activity was long stopped (or disguised) before the guard strayed too close for comfort. It could be a cough, a sneeze, a scratch of an ear, a pipe being 'emptied' by being tapped against a wooden post with a quick 'rat-a-tat-tat' noise. All were seemingly innocent to the uninformed onlooker but slickly rehearsed to shut down anything within moments. It was an impressive set-up and also allowed each man to contribute something and helped many over the feelings of helplessness about being prisoners.

This was a way that they could 'get one over' on their captors, doing something under their noses to show that even as men of the air grounded for the duration they still possessed the ability to outwit and outfox their captors and to participate in something that may even lead to escape from the camp and the chance to get home again. All prisoners had the same choice to make once they were in German hands – to either calmly sit back and accept a life of captivity or to resist. Like many men my father chose the latter, to at least try. It is important to state that this is not to cast judgement on those men who didn't, for whatever reason, choose to attempt escape, for who knows what individual traumas each man had been through before their feet finally landed on German soil. The fact that they were there at all already meant their personal bravery was beyond question.

Although the men in the camps tried hard to keep themselves fit and occupied inevitably their minds would, at some stage, reflect on the circumstances that led them to end up in captivity and to the members of their crew (and others) who had not managed to make it to the ground alive. In his last letter from Barth, dated 28 August my father mentions the contacts that my grandmother made with the relatives of members of his own crew. She had written to John Brownlie's parents in Scotland, to Tommy Jones's in Wales (both men were in the same hut as my father in Barth) and to Bernard Happold's parents.

Dear Mother Dad and all at home

So far I have had 3 letters, two from you and one from Middlesboro'. It has certainly taken a weight off my mind to know that you are all O.K and are not worrying unduly. I hear you've been doing quite a bit of letter writing. We've just got word through that you've written to Wales. By the way you asked me to write to Mr & Mrs Happold but you forgot to send their address. Perhaps you'll send it in your next letter. Time seems to pass fairly quickly here and we can always find something to do. I've baked two cakes so far but they were both unsuccessful, needless to say they were both eaten but we suffered after!

Love Harold xxxxxxx

Though understandably sporadic during the period of his incarceration it was the start of a regular correspondence that my father would have with the parents of Bernard Happold that lasted until they both passed away. Every year my father would send flowers to the house on 5 May, the anniversary of the raid that had claimed their son's life as a result of the action he took that saved my father, Tommy Jones and John Brownlie. My father would never discuss it directly but my mother always said that it affected and troubled him to the extent that she believed he never truly came to terms with it.

After the war, on their return to the UK, the loss cards for each Bomber Command aircraft lost on operations were updated with comments from the shot down crews. John Brownlie's comments are noted thus:

> *W/Op Brownlie cannot give details of how pilot died. 'He gave the rest a chance to get out while having practically no chance himself. Germans said he was buried at Moenchengladbach with the three others.*[10]

As autumn slowly turned into the winter of 1943, almost a thousand men, my father among them, were to be informed in November that they were to be moved to a new camp. They were headed for Matzicken in German occupied Lithuania and leaving the relative comfort of Stalag Luft 1 Barth for the far less hospitable Stalag Luft VI.

Chapter 10

Gefangenschaft

The worthy host a jovial brute
Takes our kit and calls it loot
Stops our food at the least pretext
One wonders what or who is next

J. H. Barratt PoW No 1168

Packing up whatever kit they had with them, the thousand or so RAF prisoners marched into the compound of Barth for Appell (roll call) one last time and were herded into trucks and driven to the railway station. On arrival, after being roughly sorted into groups and under the pretext of taking precautions against their escape, they were forced at gunpoint to remove their boots, braces and belts for collection when they reached the camp. The men were loaded into what were essentially cattle wagons and told to sit in silence. More and more men were loaded but despite the increasing protestations from those already inside that the wagons were full, the remaining men were pushed and prodded in, with the occasional encouragement from a rifle butt to the ribs for those who were deemed not to be moving quickly enough.

Finally, after what seemed like an age, the heavy doors of each carriage were slammed shut and the men inside heard the scraping of the locking bar being heaved into position and then locked ready for the journey. It took a while for their eyes to grow accustomed to the dim light in each compartment, only broken by the thin shafts of light that came through the gaps in the wooden slats and small ventilation grille that cast a comforting sliver of light here and there. Not knowing how long they would be in there the men tried to make themselves as comfortable as they could, the only noises being the occasional guttural shout or laughter of the guards outside and then finally the dull scrape of a shovel, and what they could make out as the clanging of boiler doors being closed as the locomotive at the head of the line was coaxed into life with a whoosh of steam, the pressure building before the train jolted out of the station.

The journey to the new camp at Heydekrug was supposed to take around three days and the men made themselves as comfortable as possible in their temporary accommodation, squatting down and trying to give the fellow next to them some room. The arrangements for personal needs came in the form of an empty oil drum, sited in the centre of each cattle truck and whose foul-smelling contents would eventually slop and spill around the floor with the lurching of the train carriages. By the time the evening came around men retched with the suffocating stench and pleaded for the doors to be opened so that they could obtain some relief from the rank air. Some were already falling ill with gastric complaints that would only worsen with the already deplorable conditions, but their protestations would go unheeded, and they had to cope as best they could.

Hunger and thirst were the immediate problem as neither food nor water were distributed on that first day. However, true to form, in one of the other carriages early attempts were already being made at an escape by a small group of prisoners who had somehow managed to hide amongst their persons the remains of a broken off hacksaw blade and, taking it in turns, they were making admirable efforts to get through the iron bars of the carriage despite the effort required with such a tool and the constant danger of being heard above the clanging and rattling of the train. Incredibly, they succeeded in making the opening wide enough to get out and several managed to squeeze out of the carriage, including one of my father's friends Percy Wilson Carruthers. They planned to make for an airfield and steal an aircraft. Despite their valiant efforts, covering almost 100 miles on foot, the would-be escapees would be recaptured after a week at large.

Meanwhile, on the train bound to the camp at Heydekrug, the situation of the men who remained incarcerated in the foul-smelling cattle wagons was about to take a turn for the worse. Realising that some men were missing, the Germans had stopped the train in a siding and forced the men out of the carriages for a headcount to be taken. Being taken outside bought some relief in the form of fresh air but the annoyance of the guards that some of their charges had dared to escape was there for all to see. Men were sworn at and some ended up bloodied by the liberal application of the butt end of that perennial German soldier's favourite – the Mauser Kar 98k rifle.[1]

The prospect of food was also denied as a further form of punishment and after a time they were forced back into the carriages to continue their journey onward after first being warned of the consequences for them all should there be any further attempts to escape. Finally, after many more hours of being confined in a jolting, stinking train snaking its way across Germany the train arrived at its destination and the men were roughly unloaded into trucks to be taken to the camp.

Stalag Luft VI Heydekrug had started life as Stalag 331 in 1939 and was originally used for Polish prisoners of war, followed by French and Belgians. Redesignated Luft VI it would house British, Canadian and later American, Australian and Kiwi prisoners as the camp expanded.[2] Located just outside of the medieval town from which it had taken its name, the camp at Heydekrug was remote, located as it was in a cold, bleak and desolate part of Lithuania and the conditions outside of the camp effectively mirrored that on the inside. The construction of the camp was roughly similar to the one at Barth and the arrivals gradually settled down to their new surroundings and to the immediate necessities in hand – claiming bunks, finding out who was to be housed with them, plus sounding out any new men for their 'technical skills' that may prove helpful in the overall escape effort. The journey to the camp had been grim, but the immediate thoughts of the majority of prisoners were to notify their families at home of their new locations and instructions for sending any parcels. My father wrote home on 9 November:

Dear Mother & Dad.

As you will notice from the address, I have been moved. It was a bit of a bind, but I am once again settling down.

*The address for letters is STALAG LUFT 3; LAGER
K and for parcels is STALAG LUFT 6, so in future
send your mail to these addresses. From what I can see we
shan't have so much work to do here, we don't have to cook
as its communal messing. I have not received any parcels
yet, but do not under any circumstances send any more
clothing parcels, I don't really need them. You can send
cigarette parcels if you wish to. I hope you are all keeping
well and perhaps you will endeavour to give me the 'gen'
I've asked for. Hoping to see you all again very soon.*

Love Harold xxx

The attentions of the ever-present *Kriegsgefangenenpost*
censors, plus his desire not to worry his parents and sisters
unduly, would preclude any attempt to describe the true nature
of the horrendous conditions and treatment he and others had
endured en-route to the camp, but the rest of his letter provides
some interesting clues. Cigarettes, and not clothing, were (and
to some extent remain) the universal currency of all prison
life, both for personal use, for cards and gambling and most
importantly for the bribing of persuadable guards (along with
good chocolate, a luxury in wartime).

As with Luft I at Barth the airman in charge (camp leader)
of the British PoWs at Luft VI Heydekrug was the inimitable
James Alexander Graham Deans. Known by the men as 'Dixie'
Deans, he was a sergeant bomber pilot with 77 Squadron who
had been shot down in 1940 and soon became camp leader.
Trusted, admired and respected by the body of prisoners,

Deans was ideal for the task in hand. He had many qualities, a born leader, he was thoughtful, diplomatic and quick-thinking and is widely credited with having saved the lives of many thousands of airmen, including eventually leading the march of 2,000 men (one of them my father) to safety across Poland and Germany at the end of the war.[3]

Deans also spoke fluent German and was able to negotiate, placate and sometimes directly influence his captors during particularly difficult times. His cool-headedness was to prove vital in maintaining discipline and ensuring the safety of his men, especially during the final months of captivity when tensions within the camps resulted in a powder keg environment that threatened to ignite at the slightest pretext, with potentially catastrophic consequences. The rough treatment that the men had encountered on their way to Luft VI had made many resentful and bitter and, for the most part, as they adjusted to life in the new camp they took any opportunity to wind up the Germans. The guards viewed the prisoners as non-combatants with no honour; the prisoners viewed the guards equally harshly, as men who had not even been up to fighting in the first place and by definition were 'second-rate'.

Gefangenenschaft

Behind barbed wire a world is known
Comprised of men who once had flown
Where tales are told of courage rare
Heroic deeds done in the air

Men who have lived and fought for others
Herded together closer than brothers
Struggling along on Deutsch Brown Bread
As tough as teak and as heavy as lead

Never a mail day but comes the news
That puts a fellow deep in the blues
A loved one married a yank or worse
Or back-pay going in the wife's own purse

The worthy host a jovial brute
Takes our kit and calls it loot
Stops our food at the least pretext
One wonders what or who is next

But all is not lost for these salvaged wrecks
Who dream of back pay, booze and sex
Soon they'll find their ego increased
When they sail the skies of the far, far, east.

Joseph Barratt 1944

Appell (roll-call) was a particular favourite where men meandered about and generally frustrated any attempts by the Germans to count them accurately, resulting in much mirth from the captured and much irritation for the captors! With nothing much else to do the prisoners enjoyed wasting as much of the guards' time as possible and winding them up – 'goon-baiting' as it was called. Finally, and after a prolonged period of confusion where several 'totals' were reached by increasingly exasperated guards the men were brought to attention by the 'man of confidence' and a German guard would begin the roll call anew.

Percy Carruthers describes one particularly memorable occasion where a group of prisoners, threatened with time in the 'cooler' (solitary confinement cell), took things to a new level and gave various made-up names to cause further confusion.[4] The protocol was to give first name and surname to the German guard, spell it out slowly then shout it out for the benefit of the guard. I will leave the reader to paint a mental picture for themselves of the ensuing hilarity resulting from one airman who identified himself to the guard as 'Yura Koont'!

While amusing and perfectly understandable, goon-baiting had to be regularly tempered by the camp leader, as if they pushed it too far the safety catches would click off the rifles and the bullets would start to fly – often men were merely warned by bullets flicking the sand around them, but some men were wounded and on a few tragic occasions, killed. Camp leader 'Dixie' Deans and his appointed man Vic Clarke, who was in charge of K Lager where my father was held, were both instrumental in making sure that things never got too feisty for too long. As the weeks ticked by my father had developed a routine of walking around the perimeter of the huts in the camp, or 'doing circuits' as he termed it. His crutches were gone but he used an impromptu 'stick'. The guards regarded him with mild curiosity and the occasional eye-rolling gesture and derisive comment to a fellow guard as he slowly made his way around the well-trodden path. They thought he was determined, perhaps even a little eccentric, if harmless, but the stick was a ploy:

I knew I was getting stronger, and my ankles were much better – daily exercise strengthened the muscles in my legs that had been weakened for such a long time. I didn't really need the stick but I realised that they wouldn't pay much heed to a bloke they thought of as being crippled, so I thought 'bugger it' and I used it, all the time I was getting stronger.[5]

Writing another letter home just before Christmas he seems to have been in particularly good spirits, no doubt boosted by receiving a Red Cross parcel, and in his letter he hints at a feeling that he may soon be home:

3 December 1943

Dear Mother & Dad and all at home.

I have just received my first clothing parcel, and I might say I'm very pleased with it. I suppose the second one is already on its way but if you haven't already done so I wouldn't send any more because I don't really need them. You might thank Mrs Pritchard for the pipe and tell her it smokes a treat – I've just tried it out. I suppose Christmas will be over by the time you get this and I hope you all really enjoyed yourselves and trust Dad didn't get too drunk. I have no idea what sort of Christmas we are likely to get here, but in any case, I'm not really worried because I'll make up for it when I get home, which won't be long now. Was Sheila pleased with her Christmas presents? Tell her I'm sorry I couldn't get her and Betty anything in time, but I'll try to bring something on my way back.

Love Harold

Two months after arriving, and feeling himself fit enough, he began to think seriously about the possibility of escape. Members of the Escape Committee in the camp made it their business to study, to the minute, the behaviours of camp life. When roll calls were taken, when guards were changed, which guards were changed (and where), how long they took to reach a certain point. All of these details were recorded in records disguised as everyday writing, sports day results, time taken for men to run the camp perimeters etc., but in reality recorded to help work out any blind spots in the camp and how long they would have to create diversions or for men to get themselves into positions that may present useful opportunities.

Part of this process also saw the men note all the comings and goings to the camp including the regular deliveries of food and general supplies – trucks going into the camp and out again would obviously catch the eye as it meant a potential means of escape. Also, they were not guarded and so only had a driver. Once on 'the other side of the wire' each man would be on his own – but when in the camp they worked as a team and each man did his bit to help.

Men hiding under the axles of lorries had been tried before (and had worked on occasion) but many were easily picked up at the final search before driving through the main gates to the camp, either from the dogs scenting them or from a guard searching. However, the men noticed that the guards were none too interested in the mix of wooden and metal containers loaded and unloaded onto the trucks from the kitchens. Though infrequent there was a pattern to the trucks' arrival at the camp. Mostly, the prisoners assumed, they delivered supplies but, on the way out, some waste and other detritus was known to be loaded. Some reasoned that it may provide a way out – provided they could sneak someone in unnoticed and disguise his presence.

My father volunteered to try it, his German being 'good enough' for a few relevant phrases and his health sufficiently recovered that he would be relatively easily mobile. The plans were laid and everything carefully planned so that when the trucks were due to collect again from the kitchens the attempt would be made. He never outlined the detail of how he got into the truck (in fairness I don't think I asked him), but I do recall him mentioning that there was a rumpus which distracted the guards and he secreted himself away and covered himself up. He did however mention the appalling smell from the back of the vehicle and also that it took an age for it to move, during which time he was absolutely certain he would be discovered at any moment.

Once inside and hidden, the plan was to wait until he was well outside the camp, ease himself out and then slip away at the first opportunity. Eventually he felt the lorry judder into life as it made its way out of the camp. When the truck stopped, he would have known that they were at the main gate – hearing the voices of the guards carrying out their usual searches he knew that this was the time of greatest risk. He heard the voice of a guard getting nearer, he couldn't understand that much of what he was saying but this was it – if they poked about too much it would be over.

He told me jokingly that 'that the stench alone' probably dissuaded the hapless guard from venturing into the back of the vehicle and the truck juddered back into life and drove on through the gates and out of the camp. He was out, all that he had to do now was wait until he was sure that he was far enough away from the camp to risk making an appearance without being seen and then he would make his escape. 'Just a few more minutes, be patient,' he told himself – from where he was he could see the tops of the surrounding trees and knew they must be a reasonable distance away from the confines of the camp by now.

Suddenly he was aware that the truck was slowing and he felt it pulling over to the left. His heart rate quickened and his mind raced. What was it? A checkpoint? Mechanical trouble? He hadn't expected the truck to stop so soon into its journey. The vehicle stopped and the engine was switched off, he heard the squeak of the hinges as the cab door opened briefly and closed again as the driver got out. Straining to hear he could just about make out the crunch of his boots on the gravel, but he seemed to be going away – perhaps he just needed a leak? Yes, that was it, nothing to worry about – just keep calm and he'll be back. Then he heard the crunch of gravel again, only this time much heavier and this time several voices, getting louder and coming closer. He hardly dared breath as the boots stopped at the back of the truck and he heard the tail first being unlatched and then dropping down.

A lone voice spoke: 'Raus' (Out)
He kept perfectly still and tried to work out what to do.
'HERAUSKOMMEN' (COME OUT!)

This time the voice was more insistent and carried a degree of irritation. But who were they? Civilians, workers or soldiers? Clearly, they suspected something. Should he try and sit tight and take the risk that at any minute he could be dealing with a jab from a bayonet or perhaps something very much worse. Deciding that discretion was the better part of valour he slowly raised himself with his hands in the air. As he stood up, he glimpsed the tops of the familiar dark grey steel helmets – soldiers. Ordered out of the truck the soldiers motioned for him to put his hands on top of his head while they shoved him to the front of the truck and carried out a cursory search:

There were two of them plus a bloke in civvies (civilian clothes) smoking and eying me with a mix of curiosity and annoyance. I guessed that he must have been the truck driver. The two soldiers didn't seem very happy and were a bit aggressive really. I must have stunk to high heaven so I wasn't surprised.

The search over he was taken back to the camp to begin the obligatory time in solitary confinement – aka 'the cooler' (so beloved of Steve McQueen's character in The Great Escape). Prisoners caught escaping and returned to camp could expect, at that time at least, a lengthy stay – often weeks – in a small cell with a hard wooden bed base, a bucket in the corner and a window set high up so all they had to do was sit and stare at four walls all day every day until such time as they were allowed back out. For my father he must have spent the first few hours, if not the first few days, wondered what went wrong. How had they suspected someone was in there? Had he been seen getting into the truck, had someone talked and grassed him up, had he been missed in the camp or at an impromptu Appell, or was it simply bad luck and it had just been a routine search?

Whatever it was they had him and he would now have a time on his own with his thoughts to contemplate not only what may have gone awry but to think about what could be done next time around and how he could improve the chances of getting out. As it transpired it would be a few months in early 1944 before he would have another opportunity to attempt an escape and, again, he would choose to try the same means to get out by stowing away in transport out of the camp, figuring that 'they would not expect the same trick again'.

As before he managed to get through the main gate and told me that he half-expected at some stage for the vehicle to slow down for a repeat of last time's disappointment. He must have been on tenterhooks for most of that early journey but as the truck lurched through the gears and continued on its way, his confidence must have started to slowly increase.

As the light began to fade he prepared to make his exit. Again, it would be another nerve-jangling moment of the would-be escape as he needed to slip out without being seen by the driver, but equally he couldn't afford to stay in too long and risk discovery by an overly-inquisitive guard should they reach a check point, which would happen sooner or later. As the lorry began to travel through a wooded area the twist and turns of the road gave him the opportunity he had been waiting for and he carefully clambered onto the back of the tailgate, at a suitable left-hand bend he flung himself down onto the verge and into a mix of scrub that disguised a shallow ditch. He kept perfectly still and waited for the sound of the truck skidding to a halt, but all he heard was the reassuring sound of it continuing on its onward journey at the same pace. He waited until the sound of the truck finally disappeared into the distance until he could hear it no more then, slowly, lifted his head to check that there was no-one about and that the road was clear.

Eventually he began to move off slowly, into the relative safety and cover of the trees where he would spend his first night on the move. As the temperature began to drop he wrapped the clothing he had around him as best he could. Progress was slow on a moonless night. He was conscious of the ever-present risk of stumbling into something, or someone. He was also acutely aware of the need to take extra care when moving around the uneven woodlands at night – turning an ankle, especially given that he had only recently recovered from the injuries received to them when he bailed out, would have proved disastrous. This was not the place to have to start hobbling around! But at least he was out, beyond the confines of the camp, beyond the guards, beyond the wire. Now it was up to him, but to successfully evade he would have to move carefully, think ahead, and plan each step from here.

Reasoning that it would be far safer to move by night as there was less chance of being seen or running into anyone who may ask awkward questions, he laid low during the day sheltering in wooded areas and under whatever natural cover was available. He moved around as little as possible to conserve energy and to avoid drawing attention to himself, vigilant for any noises of people who may be out looking for him. Back at the camp they would be aware by now he was missing and would soon be out looking for him and others would know he was loose. At night he moved as quietly and stealthily as possible and told me that he would always try and stay parallel to one of the main roads but far enough away so as not to risk being seen.

Although he was only able to cover a reasonably short distance each night the cautious approach seemed to be paying off – on a few occasions when he heard voices, the occasional dog barking, or other signs of habitation from within and without the various farmhouses and shacks, he would quietly double back the way he came in a wide arc. He recalled that the nights were bitterly cold, even though he was moving which helped him stay warm, but as he entered into the early hours of the third day the biggest problem was his supplies of food and water were running desperately low. He knew that he would, at some stage, need to find enough of both and that would mean having to venture further out from the safety of the wooded areas and would also have to be moving partly during the day which would bring its own risks.

After weighing up the risks he decided to take a chance and walk out onto the edge of the woodland and make his way along. He figured that, given the length of the road and the remoteness of the landscape the chances of meeting anyone on foot would be slim and anyone in the area would most likely be driving, in which case he would have enough time to react and melt back into the trees – at least that was the theory.

My father takes up the story:

> *The whole area was pretty barren and I didn't see anyone in the time since I got out of the camp, it was so remote and so I thought it worth the risk. I was careful and walked along the treeline so I was pretty confident I could get out of sight quickly at the first sign of any real trouble.*

He made his way along in that fashion for some time, occasionally ducking back into the trees when he needed a rest or fancied that he had heard something approaching on the road. By now his hunger was becoming more pressing – as was the need to find water and he was hoping to come across somewhere suitable where he could take advantage of whatever was lying around. At that point he decided to fully step out and walk along the road and it was to prove a fateful decision. Rounding a long, sweeping bend he thought that he had caught sight of something – or someone – on the opposite site of the road in the distance. He couldn't be sure but if it was a person, they would almost certainly have seen him so he dare not risk ducking out of sight as it would look too obvious. Cursing his luck he continued walking, straining his eyes for a clue as to the nature of the blurry figure that he could just make out in the distance. The figure seemed to be wandering somewhat haphazardly between the road surface and the knotty scrubland between it and the treeline.

A dog! My father heard the bark of a dog and could make out the much smaller shape moving next to the figure in the distance who now seemed to have something slung over his shoulder. A forester perhaps, out with his dog or maybe someone out hunting – he narrowed his eyes to try and make out more detail – anything to provide a clue as to who or what the solitary figure moving towards him was. Then, as the figure loomed further into view, he could slowly make out the forage cap, boots and the unmistakable *feld grau* (field grey) of a military uniform and what looked like a rifle slung over his shoulder. His heart leapt into his mouth. He was a soldier. A soldier with a dog. Were they looking for him? Were there others nearby? Cursing again under his breath my father decided that he had to just try and bluff it out – it was too late to do anything else. He tried to look as relaxed and nonchalant as possible as the two men got closer, he had a forged identity card – an *Ausweis* – and was mentally going through what he was going to say with his stock of German phrases if challenged. His German was good enough for a few short phrases and greetings but certainly not conversational by any stretch.

As the soldier approached, my father glanced over to briefly to size him up. He was youngish, not quite mid-twenties my father reckoned, slim build – a *Lanzenkorporal* (Lance Corporal) indicated by the black and white chevron on the upper arm of his uniform. The two men were only about ten or fifteen yards apart by this stage, the soldier had not even glanced up and was busy looking ahead and seemingly more focused on his dog rooting around ahead of him. As the men grew level the soldier then briefly looked up and my father smiled and greeted him with a cheerful 'Morgen' (Morning).

The soldier looked over briefly then looked away, muttering a return greeting before turning his attention back to his dog. My father remarked to me,

> *He didn't seem in the least bit interested in me – far from it, he was more interested in his dog and I thought Christ, I'm going to get away with this.*

The two men carried on walking and were about sixty or so yards apart at a point when the road was just beginning its sweeping left curve when my father suddenly heard a voice from behind him: *'Hey, wohin gehst du'*? (Hey, where are you going?)

He wasn't confident to answer fully in German and didn't want to invite a conversation, so my father pretended not to hear and carried on walking trying to look as relaxed as possible.

'HEY!, ich rede mit dir, halt!' (HEY, I'm talking to you, stop!)

Still, he carried on walking, only this time he raised his right arm, bent at the elbow, and waved his hand as if in informal acknowledgment. Moments later he was aware of the presence of the dog running close to him. The soldier had unleashed his dog and the Alsatian was paying particular attention to the scent from my father's legs.

My father takes up the story again:

> *He shouted out 'Ich sagte stehe still'* (I said stand still*).
> The German solider that I had passed yelled out to me
> again to stand still. His dog was the trouble, the bloody
> thing wouldn't leave me alone. I kept walking and as
> I approached a bend in the road, I had decided that I was
> going to make a run for the trees. It was then I heard the
> sound of a rifle bolt being drawn and so I put my hands
> up and turned round. He was aiming his rifle at me. That
> was it, they had me again.*

He must have been devastated to have been caught again, especially as he thought that the soldier was 'the only other bugger I saw all the time I was out'. I heard my father repeat the circumstances of this attempted escape a few times to various people and he was always utterly convinced that he was only caught because of that dog. It wasn't aggressive towards him but it was inquisitive and would not leave him alone, sniffing around his legs. He had a theory that the soap given to PoWs in the camps to wash their clothes was either a special brand of soap, only given to 'Kriegies' or it was normal soap laced with something, so that the soldiers knew if the keen noses of their dogs took an interest then there was something about the man wearing the clothes that was worthy of investigation.

Whatever it was he was 'in the bag' again and though he didn't tell me the details I'm sure he would have been cooling his heels in solitary confinement again for some time. He did tell me that he was directly warned about the consequences of any future escape attempt from the camp: *'They told me that if I was caught out again then I would be shot.'*

That warning would prove grimly prophetic for a number of RAF prisoners in the months that followed as the Reich's attitude to escapers, and to airman of all nationalities (but particularly RAF men) was to harden considerably, with truly appalling consequences.

Chapter 11

Hard Road Ahead

In days to come when I am free
In looking back I'll sometime see
The Insterburg by Memel Quay
Which borders on the Baltic sea.

Luft IV 1944

In early April 1944, the 10,000 or so allied airmen men held in camps across Europe were called out for a special Appell. Something was very clearly amiss; the atmosphere was charged and the prisoners noticed that there were significantly more guards on parade than usual. Many of them had clearly been brought in at short notice on the expectation of trouble.

In Stalag Luft VI at Heydekrug it was the body language of the guards that caused most concern amongst the men assembled. The former were on their knees, machine guns levelled at the men gathered. Most stared at the prisoners, showing no emotion, their teeth set and their legs fixed and unmoving. Others, particularly those camp guards who were known to the prisoners and who were also known to be of a less aggressive nature, looked somehow uncomfortable and awkward. Few, if any, would make eye contact with the body of men that they guarded. Finally, 'Dixie' Deans called the men smartly to attention.

Those readers who have watched the movie *The Great Escape* or read Paul Brickhill's book of the same name,[1] at any point in their lives will be familiar with the backstory to what follows. A German officer, Major Heinrich, stepped forward, cleared his throat and in a loud, steady voice that echoed around a camp stilled into eerie silence, made a short announcement in German. An interpreter then repeated the message in English. Seventy-six men had escaped from Stalag Luft III at Sagan in March 1944. Fifty had been shot while 'resisting arrest' after recapture. At first there was silence, men struggled to process what they had just been told, some looked around at each other not knowing how to react, others shuffled uneasily and looked about to gauge the reaction of their comrades. The initial murmuring from within the ranks of prisoners slowly grew in volume as the news finally sank in and the enormity of the mass murder (for that's what it was) hit home.

A lone British voice from somewhere within the ranks broke the silence: 'You bastards.'

At this the clamour grew and more angry voices started to vent against the German officer and his men. The guards tensed and cocked their weapons, an action which only served to enrage the men further. The steady lines of prisoners began to waver and threatened to break altogether. At that point another solitary British voice broke through the clamour with clarion resonance:

'STAND FAST!'
It was 'Dixie' Deans' voice and the men slowly fell back into order.
'YOU WILL STAND FAST!'

This time his voice was louder but still unwavering and clear and it diffused the situation, for the time being at least. Wasting no time Deans promptly dismissed the parade and ordered all men to go back to their barracks and wait:

'No-one is to do anything – nothing at all. You are to take no action of any kind, go back to your huts and stay there.'

His actions that day undoubtedly saved many lives and it is testament to the regard in which he was held that, though inwardly seething, to a man the ranks of prisoners did exactly as he had asked and returned to their individual huts. Outrage and anger at what had happened slowly gave way to a growing realisation of what their captors were increasingly capable of and, more chillingly perhaps, that the SS and the Gestapo were becoming ever-more involved in both the management and the fate of aircrew prisoners. Life under the current regime had been no walk in the park, but at least they were still in the (relatively) safe administrative hands of the Luftwaffe.

For my father and many others, the dreadful events at Sagan had been something of a wakeup call. He had been committed to trying to get out, to get home and to carry on the struggle – solitary confinement had not bothered him unduly, he had used the time in that dingy, dank cell to exercise; a daily routine of press-ups and squats, to keep fit and to continue to build the strength in his limbs. More than that he had used that time to close his eyes and envisage life 'beyond the wire', what he would do with his life when he got home, what he would cook for himself on his first day back and the things he would do, the boat he would buy and the life he would build for himself. But for now, he had to survive.

The repercussions of the events of Sagan weighed heavily on his mind. He had escaped twice, the last time he had gone further than he ever had before and had deemed himself somewhat unlucky in running into what was probably the only soldier for miles. But this was different, being brought sheepishly back to camp for a spell in solitary was one thing, but ending up with a bullet in the back of the head in a ditch was something altogether different and – like many – he now began to reason that it was now about biding his time and making sure he survived a war that was surely about to end.

The summer of 1944 would be momentous for all allied prisoners for many reasons. The long-awaited invasion on 6 June had, of course, finally materialised on the beaches of Normandy with allied troops pouring ashore in their thousands, supported by airborne troops, to fight their way through murderous German defences, push out into the interior of France and head for the Rhine. The British, Americans and other allies were pushing from the West and the Russians from the East – for Hitler and the Third Reich it was the beginning of the end. The British were sending coded messages to the senior men in camps to the effect that escaping should now be discouraged altogether, the risk to life was deemed to be unnecessary now that the end was very much in sight.

Meanwhile, in Luft VI, 'Dixie' Deans was concerned about men reacting too quickly – not to mention too vocally – to news that the invasion had started. It would be blatantly obvious to the Germans that the men had access to a radio receiver,[2] and so they had to try and play down the news accordingly and overly exuberant celebrations were discouraged. Many secretly hoped that liberation would follow relatively quickly and envisaged a short trip back home, to freedom, to their families and to an end to a war that was now in its sixth long year. For these men however, the summer and autumn of 1944 would see their misery prolonged for almost another year as the Germans had already been busily making plans to move them further inland and away from the advancing forces and liberation.

Rumours spread around the camp like wildfire that they were to be moved and Heydekrug would indeed be the first PoW camp to be abandoned, away from rapidly advancing Russian forces, with prisoners being moved out in groups. Thursday 13 July saw one of the first of these contingents moved out. Hundreds of men, my father amongst them, would be destined to take the so-called 'Baltic Cruise', confinement in the filthy hold of a cramped, decaying coal ship en route to their new prisoner accommodation at Stalag Luft IV (Gross Tychow) in North-Western Poland.

The camp itself would become notorious, a byword for cruelty and ill-treatment and their journey there eventually led to allegations of atrocity and war crimes against those who perpetrated it. What happened to these men over the next seven to ten days is well-known in ex-PoW circles and there are several highly detailed accounts already in existence written by the men who took part. I warn you, what follows is harrowing and many will find the next few pages a very hard read. I am well acquainted with the story through my years of research, but even now the sheer barbarity and levels of cruelty inflicted never fail to shock. To know that my father was one of the men who went through it makes it all the more affecting. What I am about to describe here is recorded fact, there is no embellishment of any kind. The details are based on the testimonies of many who were there, including my father, and it happened as it is described.

Those prisoners 'selected' for the trip were instructed to be ready to move at short notice and to take with them only what they could carry in their backpacks, everything else was to be left behind. The body of men were then marched to the local railway station to be once again crammed into the same type of cattle wagons that they had previously had to endure on their journey from Barth all those months ago. As before the men were driven into the wagons and packed in like sardines, protestations to the guards that there was no more room were either ignored or answered by a swift crack to the head from a rifle butt. It is generally reckoned that up to eighty men were held in each carriage.

The ensuing train ride was horrendous, men had to stand as there was no room to sit, taking a leak (or worse) was done where one stood. Despite the conditions and the putrid, foul air within each wooden wagon the guards refused to stop to open the doors and allow the men a chance to stretch their legs or to snatch some clean air, so they had to cope as best they could and try and hold each other upright and avoid a crush as the train lurched its way to its new destination. It was early evening by the time the train with its unhappy human cargo finally drew into a rail siding near Memel in what used to be East Prussia. With a scraping thud the heavy bolts on the doors of the wagons were finally drawn back and the men hastily unloaded with much shouting and cajoling by the guards who had also dismounted from their positions on the train. Thirsty, hungry, sore and with many suffering from the hours of confinement on the train, the prisoners were in a rough state and tried to take breaths of the sea air as they were quickly formed into a queue by the guards who screamed abuse at any men who, for whatever reason, were slow off the mark to get in line. After over an hour of being pushed, shoved and often clubbed into line the men were ready to move out.

Finally, in the early hours of the morning of 16 July they were marched onto the quayside and confronted with the silhouette of a decrepit old cargo ship, the SS *Insterburg*. Built in 1919 the *Insterburg* had started life as a Swedish registered ship the SS *Olof Brodin* and passed through various hands until being captured by the Germans and renamed in 1941. Her most recent use had been to transport thousands of tonnes of coal in her two holds.[3] Tonight she would hold a very different cargo down in the bilges. The men were marched up the gangplank and onto the deck of the ship, ordered to remove their packs and leave them on deck, they were forced at gunpoint down the thin ladder into the dark, filthy holds. By the time she was fully loaded over 900 men were crammed in, stumbling and tripping in the darkness and sitting as best they could, knees drawn up.

With the final numbers either pushed below into the hold or handcuffed on deck the hatches were slammed shut and the men left in darkness 30 feet below, afraid and alone with only the stench from the bilge pumps and the hammering vibration from the engine to break the silence. There was no ventilation in the hold, no port holes and – unlike on the cattle wagons – no oil drum in which to carry out the normal bodily functions.

They would be at sea for three days on the *Insterburg* and, at first, the Germans refused to allow men on deck and sanitation needs were catered for by a bucket lowered on a rope into the hold for men to fill. With the pitch and yaw of the ship at sea much of the contents would soak the men sitting in darkness in the process of it being drawn up to the surface. The same bucket would then be sluiced with seawater by the guard, filled with drinking water and lowered down for the men to drink.

Unsurprisingly, many already sick from the train journey to Memel were suffering the beginnings of dysentery and the U-shaped channels at the bottom of the hold, in parallel with the keel, ran with a nauseating cocktail of urine, vomit and bloodied gastric motions. The stench was appalling. After two days at sea some men had become delirious due to the stifling conditions in the hold, lack of water, dysentery and the baking heat of the next day.

At some point Vic Clarke, 'Dixie' Deans' right hand man, had managed to negotiate with the Germans for small groups of men to go on deck to get some air and relieve themselves and so a few at a time managed to scale the thin ladder to breathe in fresh salty air, crawl to the side of the ship and vomit, breathe, vomit again and urinate over the side before being forced down into the hold once more. On the third day the ship rolled and heaved due to bad weather and by now almost all of the 900 held in the hold were ill to varying degrees.

Another of my father's poems in his PoW book, topped by his own pencil sketch of the *Insterburg*, provides an insight from one who was there:

> *In days to come when I am free*
> *In looking back I'll sometime see*
> *The* Insterburg *by Memel Quay*
> *Which borders on the Baltic sea.*
>
> *I'll smell again that stifling hold*
> *Where near a thousand prisoners bold*
> *Were stowed as slaves in days of old*
> *In transport to another fold.*
>
> *Three nights I spent there sick and sore*
> *Huddling round the dirty floor*
> *Wondering if I evermore*
> *Would see old England's shore.*
>
> *But such is life in many ways*
> *Tempt not the fates it never pays*
> *'Roll on the boat' a common phrase*
> *I'll say no more in all my days.*[4]

Eventually, the coaler with its fetid and sickening cargo came slowly into the port of Swinemunde and as the engine stopped they knew that, for now at least, this part of the journey was over. After some time the men were off-loaded, staggering down the gangplank, squinting after three days and nights with no light and, glad to be released from the foul air, they sank to their knees and retched, only to be brought back to their feet by the furious shouts of the guards who rained blows down on them with rifles and anything else that came to hand. Two prisoners, almost certainly delirious through a toxic mix of chronic thirst, hunger and the dysentery that wracked them, broke from the line and attempted to run across the quay, both were immediately cut down in a hail of machinegun fire and their bodies, oozing blood, were left where they fell as a warning to others not to try the same. According to contemporary reports many of the guards laughed and joked at the fate of the two men.

Once unloaded, the prisoners were ordered to remove their boots, belts and to give up anything else that the guards regarded as material to be confiscated. They were roughly shackled together, the handcuffs soon chafed on the wrists of men who in reality were already hardly more than skin and bone and the resultant sores would soon become infected. With little time to rest the men who had survived the horrific conditions on the dilapidated coaler now found themselves once more driven on to the familiar and detested cattle wagons to be moved onward. The wagons had been out in the morning sun, doors tight shut and were like ovens, but as their captors drove them into the wagons suddenly a new threat loomed – the air raid sirens blared and the men, locked in the carriages, were left to their own devices to face the wrath from the allied bombers that many of them had crewed only months before. Helpless, they would have no choice other than to sit it out and hope that the falling sticks of bombs would miss them. Those men not yet in the wagon were told to take cover under it.

Fortunately, it turned out not to be a full-scale raid but just a handful of aircraft. When the air raid started the guards had scattered, some took shelter under the carriages with the prisoners and could be seen crawling on the track, accompanied by much jeering from the men locked in the carriages who saw them through the cracks in the floor. When the raid had passed the guards emerged from cover and the loading process carried on until all the prisoners were finally on the train. The heavy doors were slammed shut and the train slowly jolted its way along the track and out of Swinemunde for the next stage of an already arduous journey. The journey by train was to last several more hours, once again with no food or water, no ventilation, no sanitation and the pleas of the men inside for the guards to open the doors to let some air in fell on deaf ears once more.

By now some of the men were in a very bad way and when the train arrived at Kiefheide[5] more vocal protestations were made to at least allow those worst affected to get some air and preferably to be carried out of the wagon so that they could be properly revived.

Unfortunately for the prisoners the guards were having none of it and the men in the cattle wagons, who had already endured so much, would be destined to spend the night locked in with their chronically sick comrades, without food, with little water and unable to escape the fetid air that hung heavy in the carriage. More concerning was the knowledge that the guards who had made the train journey with them from Swinemunde had all gone, replaced by Kriegsmarine – marine cadets from the Hitler

Youth – who were young, fanatical and had been brought in for a purpose. All were armed with rifles and had fixed bayonets. Many had spent the night hours sharpening those blades, the harsh note of grinding stone against metal providing an ominous note of preparation of which the prisoners were only too aware. Those German speakers amongst the PoWs could also hear the young Kriegsmarines laughing and joking about how they would be sure that the *Terrorfliegers* would 'get what they deserved' in the morning.

Few in the cattle wagons slept that night – morning would provide a relief of sorts as they would surely, finally, open the doors to move the prisoners on – but on to what? Some men had a growing sense of unease at what was waiting for them outside. Others felt that they would rather take their chances out in the open than stay any longer in the suffocating heat of the wagons; unable to move, to urinate or defecate or to lie down, many had reached the end of their endurance.

As the temperatures started to climb on the morning of Wednesday 19 July, another hot summer day, the conditions inside the closed wagons were now bordering on the unsurvivable. The men inside who could still muster the strength once more implored the guards to open the doors – shouting in German and in English – but the young Kriegsmarine just laughed and ignored them, occasionally one smashed his rifle butt against imploring fingers poking out from the wooden sides of the wagons. The morning hours ticked by, the heat rose steadily and inside the oven-like conditions of the wagons an increasing number of men collapsed and sank to their knees – so tightly were they packed in that it was impossible for the others to hold them up and those who fell were trampled on, there was no alternative. There was simply no room.

Just after 13:00hrs the doors to the wagons were finally pulled open and the human cargo spilled out onto the ground, the men at the front gasping for air and those behind, still handcuffed, doing their best to drag the sick and the lifeless out of the wagon and lay them on the ground in the fresh air in an attempt to revive them. Men vomited, others – already suffering from dysentery – did their best to clean heavily soiled clothing with tufts of grass; all dropped to their knees or attempted to lie down. Almost immediately the mass of young Kriegsmarines punched, kicked and cajoled them back on their feet – none were allowed to sit, all had to retrieve their backpacks and wear them. Those men who stumbled were viciously beaten until they staggered to their feet.

The bedraggled prisoners were sorted into two lines and made to head out onto the road outside the station, shackled as they were in pairs. As they stumbled out they could see more of the young Kriegsmarines in their white uniforms waiting for them either side of the road, all armed and with bayonets drawn, some with machine guns and here and there handlers with packs of large, snarling Alsatians – barking and snapping at the prisoners and being egged on by their handlers. As the men lined up, all now weak through lack of food and water, they realised that there would be no transport to take them to the camp. They would walk there, but no-one knew how far and how long their journey would be. The guards formed up either side of the road and the long columns of prisoners was halted – they could see that the road ahead was long and bordered on either side by pine trees.

While the men were standing still a German Kubelwagon (a type of jeep) rolled into view; in it was Hauptmann Walter Pickhardt ('The Butcher of Berlin'). Exiting the vehicle, he wasted no time at all in revealing the reason for his presence – screaming with rage he proceeded to whip up the Kriegsmarines with emotive language about the nature of the ragged band of prisoners that were in shackles in front of them. He screeched that they were the *Luftgangsters*, little more than 'common criminals' who had been bombing German cities, indiscriminately killing men women and children in German towns and that they needed to be punished.[6]

With a dramatic wave of his arms he screamed at the band of young soldiers: *'Alles laufen, alles laufen'* ('all must run, all must run')

The groups of prisoners, shackled in pairs, at first resisted the attempts to get them to break into a run by simply quickening their pace, but then they began to be screamed at and abused, punched, kicked and struck across the head and back with rifle butts. Dambuster Fred Tees and the man shackled to him, Bob Bell, two of my father's friends, did their best to resist the cajoling, but soon all of the shackled men would have no choice other than to break into a trot and then a run. Those soldiers with dogs lengthened their leashes so that the dogs could attack the prisoners and those on the outside were worst affected with dogs lunging at them and biting fingers, hands, arms, legs, anything they could get hold of. Soon the dogs were in a frenzy whipped up by the smell of fresh blood and the raucous goading from their handlers. Here and there men – already exhausted from the journey the night before, thirsty and hungry – stumbled and fell and were immediately met with a brutal mix of kicks and blows from rifle butts and at least two were torn into by the Alsatians that continued snapping and biting.

All the while Pickhardt was alongside his young Kriegsmarines, leaning out of his vehicle and egging them on, screaming out the names of German cities that had been devastated in the bombing offensive and encouraging the young soldiers to commit even greater acts of monstrous violence. Some began to use their bayonets, driving them indiscriminately into the mass of prisoners running past and arms, legs, buttocks, shoulders and backs were pierced by the razor-sharp blades.

As the men staggered onward the assaults grew in intensity until they were a column of bloodied, bruised and battered men. In the midst of such appalling treatment there were individual acts of defiance and heroism, men stopped to help comrades who had fallen, receiving a cascade of blows raining down on them for their pains. One Canadian airmen was hit so hard by the butt end of a rifle that the wooden stock actually splintered into fragments leaving a deep wound in his scalp, yet he carried on half-carrying a fellow prisoner despite the blood pouring down his face into his eyes. Another prisoner, standing still with exhaustion, looked round to see a guard unleash his Alsatian towards him. As the dog gained on him, he waited until the last moment then aimed a kick at its head felling the animal and stunning it. The guard was enraged and the prisoner immediately started running again, stamping down hard on the unfortunate dog's throat as he passed it and ultimately, he hoped, killing it. Elsewhere the mayhem continued and if one man went down the man he was shackled to invariably

tried to help him to his feet, drawing the wrath of the marines
– often both went down under the sustained violence being
perpetrated on them, surrounded by marines stabbing, kicking
and screaming at them in an orgy of violence.

Meanwhile at the head of the column men had already started
to shed their packs and they in turn presented an extra unwanted
obstacle in the road for the men following, many tripping
and stumbling over them. The savagery from the guards had
intensified further, Pickhardt was firing off rounds into the air,
red-faced and still screaming, urging his soldiers on:

'Lauf, Lauf deine Englischen Schweine!'
(Run, run you English swine!!)

Driven on by the actions of their officer the marines now began
firing off rounds from their rifles – it was a tinder box that only
need a spark to set off what could be a massacre. Vic Clarke
was at the head of the column and along with others glanced
to the edge of the road and with a sense of foreboding noticed
that the Germans had set up heavy machine guns on tripods on
the edges of the treeline set well back from the road. Realising
what this meant he shouted instructions that were to be quickly
passed back down the line imploring his men to keep order and
not break ranks.

The instructions were repeated endlessly to make sure
everyone kept driving forward and didn't veer off the path.
The physical onslaught against the men still shackled together
continued and, if anything, increased still further in intensity.

The dogs were now snapping at anything and everything, causing terrible injuries. Some of the men up front with Vic Clarke noticed more heavy machine guns set even further back in the forest in hastily cleared areas and then, chillingly, he noticed cameras set up on tripods. His suspicions grew – why were they there, was this to record 'evidence' should the column scatter and the cameras record men being mown down by machinegun fire in the process of 'attempting to escape'? The cameras would only record men fleeing and not the reason for the 'break' and so would be effective 'propaganda'.

Realising this, Clarke repeated his orders to be passed down the line with renewed urgency: that no-one should break rank – no matter what the provocation, no matter what happened. Still the beating of the prisoners continued, many had by now lost their packs altogether either willingly or cut from their backs by marines with bayonets. The blows from rifles continued to rain down on them as they did their best to try and dodge the blows and the lunging jaws of the snarling, foaming dogs. Eventually, after a 'run' of almost two miles the battered and bloodied column of prisoners arrived at what passed for the gates of Stalag Luft IV, Gross Tychow, in reality just large fence posts and wire driven into the ground.

The beatings subsided as Pickhardt barked out orders to his men. The column of prisoners was held at a standstill, some barely able to stand, others doing their best to stem the flow of blood from the multitude of lacerations, stab wounds and dog bites that covered much of their bodies. They had, at least, made it.

Hauptmann Pickhardt, however, had other ideas and one last surprise for his captives.

Once the back of the column had caught up with the front he ordered his men to form into two lines outside the main gates, facing each other, to create a macabre *garde d'honneur* for the prisoners, some twenty yards long. Each line was comprised of marines with fixed bayonets on their rifles. The exhausted prisoners were to be put through one final act of brutalisation before passing through the gates of the camp. Running through in pairs they did their best to avoid the thrusting bayonets of the baying Kriegsmarine but inevitably some received more stab wounds, lacerations and blows from rifle butts. It should be acknowledged that not all the guards participated in or approved of what was being perpetrated – generally they were the older, regular soldiers, not the younger fanatics of the Hitler Youth and Kriegsmarine.

There are several documented accounts of some of the older guards attempting to help fallen airmen and also helping some who were still running and on their feet to stay that way. With the last of the men through the gate they were lined up to be counted and made to stand while the slow, laborious process took place. After the count they were strip searched and made to lie face down on the grass in silence, warned by the guards that they would be shot if they dared look up or speak. They were to be kept like that for several hours, the groans of the wounded the only sound heard. There was no water, there was no food. Meanwhile the young Kriegsmarines sat down outside the camp and noisily and joyfully tucked into the food and treats that had been looted from the Red Cross parcels in the prisoners' backpacks.

It was a clear attempt to brutalise, dehumanise and humiliate a body of men; to rob them of their dignity, to push them to the limit and then to try and break them. Accounts of how many were injured that day differ and range from 70 to over 150 men receiving bayonet wounds, bites from dogs and blows from fists and rifle butts. One man was seen to have over 50 bayonet wounds to his body, but he survived to tell the tale, others were not so lucky and there were fatalities.[7] A German doctor was present and was called upon by Vic Clarke to inspect his men and detail the wounds they had received – what words passed between them are unrecorded but several accounts observe that the doctor's reaction on inspecting the mass of beaten, cut and bruised bodies was one of amusement and he was seen to laugh openly on seeing the worst of the dreadful injuries that had been caused.

The prisoners spent their first night at the new camp shivering out in the open as the camp barracks had not yet been made ready and were under construction by Russian prisoner labour. At last a few buckets of water were distributed so at least the men could slake what was by now an almost insatiable thirst and the most severely injured men could have their wounds cleaned if not properly dressed. For the next few nights, the men would be housed in what Percy Carruthers describes as prefabricated wooden 'dog kennels' measuring 14ft by 8ft by 4ft high and each was supposed to accommodate ten men and would be their 'home' until the traditional barrack blocks in the main camp were finished.

The collective ordeal that the prisoners went through during July 1944 cannot be understated; the train journey from Heydekrug to Memel, incarceration on the *Insterburg*, endless hours spent crammed into cattle wagons in the searing heat without food, water or adequate sanitation and then the infamous 'Run up the Road' drove men to the very limits of human endurance. Few men actually broke down but they would all carry the scars – mental as well as physical – for the rest of their lives. My father was one of them.

They had survived thus far but had witnessed first-hand what their captors were now truly capable of and conditions in the new camp would turn out to be much worse than at Heydekrug. Stalag Luft IV Gross Tychow was to become notorious for cruelty, ill-treatment and for the appalling subsistence provision by the Germans that would see many men exist on little more than a starvation diet. The conditions they were housed in, and the treatment they would receive, would become increasingly challenging as the incarcerated prisoners suffered beatings and degradation on an almost daily level.

Chapter 12

The Greatest Escape

On 23 July 1944 a formal notice, in black and red text, was posted up in every Prisoner of War Camp in the Reich, which warned of dire consequences for anyone caught beyond the perimeter without permission.

To all Prisoners of War
The escape from a Prison Camp is no longer a sport!
Germany has always kept up to the Hague Convention,
and only punished
recaptured PoWs with minor disciplinary punishment.
Germany will still maintain these Principles of International
Law, but England has, besides fighting at the front in an
honest manner, instigated an illegal warfare in non-combatant
zones in the form of Gangster Commandos, Terror Bandits
and Sabotage Troops, even up to the frontiers of Germany.
They say in a captured secret and confidential English
Military Pamphlet

'The Handbook of Modern Irregular Warfare:
'The days when we should practice the rules of
sportsmanship are over. For the time being every soldier
must be a potential Gangster, and must be prepared to adopt
their methods where ever possible. The sphere of operations

should always include the enemy's own country and occupied territory and in certain circumstances neutral countries he is using as a source of supply.'

England has, with these instructions opened up a non-military form of gangster war.

Germany is determined to safeguard her homeland, and especially her War Industry and Provision Centres for the fighting fronts. Therefore, it has become necessary to create strictly forbidden zones, called Death Zones, in which all unauthorised trespassers will be immediately shot on sight.

Escaping PoWs on entering these zones will certainly lose their lives. They are in constant danger of being mistaken for enemy agents or sabotage groups.

Urgent warning is given about making future escapes.

In plain English stay in camp and you will be safe.

Breaking out of it is a damned dangerous act.

The chances of preserving your life are almost nil.

All police and military guards have been given the most strict orders, to shoot on sight all suspected persons.

Escaping from camp has ceased to be a sport!

In times past the reaction of most prisoners to such an edict would probably have been largely contemptuous amusement mixed with a feeling that they must really be getting under the skin of their captors for them to post such material. Yet with the recent terrible events at Sagan, the murder of fifty recaptured prisoners by the Gestapo and the appalling treatment they themselves had experienced first-hand, it was clear that things had entered a new, and very dangerous phase and there was little ongoing appetite to escape. Already weakened by ill-treatment and hunger many men felt that with the end of the war seemingly so close the imperative had switched from escape to survival. Having gone through so much it was now all about staying alive so that they could once again see home.

So, for the time being life would consist of the daily struggle just to stay alive, to stay in one piece and to keep going while the Allied and Russian forces inched closer onto the heartland of Germany following the invasion of Normandy and the Russian Army pushing through from the East.

Life in the prefabricated 'dog kennels' that the PoWs were forced to live in until their barracks were ready was made even more miserable by the weather and the violent and fierce thunderstorms of 29 July which saw ball lightning claim several lives including Sergeant Roy Stevens, RAF, who was killed after being struck by lightning. In his first letter home after moving to the new camp my father references the incident directly:

August 1944

Dear Mother & Dad and all at home

By the time you get this you will be wondering what has become of me. I never had the opportunity of writing my last month's letter cards, we have recently arrived at a new camp and I possess exactly what I stand up in but whatever you do don't send any more parcels, clothing or cigs. It's been some time since I had any mail so I'm not at all up on home news. The weather here is still quite warm but the great trouble is the flies, they are fairly big and I'm sure they bite. We had a thunderstorm a day or so ago, and it came on very sudden, and very heavy. The lightning struck one of the huts, and one of our boys was killed, and three or four more suffered from shock or burns. I trust you are all well and I'm looking forward to the next letter from you, it seems ages since I had the last one. I guess that's all for now.

Love Harold xxx

Years later my father once described to me that he had seen the phenomenon of ball lightning in the flesh after someone on a television programme said that they doubted its existence – this must surely be the occasion to which he was referring. Sadly, four men lost their lives that night[1] and they were buried unceremoniously in sacks. One of those injured swallowed his tongue in the process of being struck and, as the Germans refused to allow any treatment, choked to death in front of the other prisoners. What strikes me most about reading my father's letter is how matter of fact he is, having only recently survived the appalling mistreatment described in the previous chapter. Naturally he would have known that the wartime censors would not have permitted any reference to the atrocities that had been perpetrated on him and his fellow 'Kriegies' so it would have been pointless attempting it, and he would not have wanted to have alarmed his mother, but the reference to not sending any more parcels would be clear – all would invariably be 'looted' by the Germans and so it was far better nothing was sent at all than allow it to fall into their hands.

Eventually the new barrack huts were ready and the men assigned accordingly. My father was to occupy a bunk in Barrack Hut 1 Room 10 along with Fred Tees, Bob Bell, Bill Ashley, Ross Elford, Dennis Emes and Leofric 'Lofty' Stift,[2] among others whom he would become firm friends with. He told me that when they moved in they were visited by some of the Russian prisoners who had built the barracks. At first they couldn't understand what they were trying to warn them about but eventually it became clear. They were trying to warn them about certain aspects of the barracks that they had constructed. As my father explains:

> They had assumed they were building the barracks for German soldiers, and not for us, and so there were all sorts of things wrong with them, floor joists missing and some partially cut through, sharp nails and even fragments of razor blades and broken glass hidden in wooden door frames and edges that could slice your hand open. When they realised what they were building was for us lot they wanted to make sure we knew where the various 'traps' were hidden so we could put them right or were at least aware of them.

Camp life at Tychow continued in some sort of normality, or a version of it at least, but many of the things that made life bearable at Heydekrug were not to be found here. Conditions in the camp were a good deal more harsh and the camp Kommandant

Oberleutnant Aribert Bombach, an active supporter of the Nazi party, positively encouraged ill-treatment and ensured that the men were given no quarter. Regular, unannounced searches were commonplace where prisoners would be roughly turned out into the yard outside the huts and made to stand at attention for hours while the searches took place – bunks would be ransacked and possessions thrown around, confiscated, stolen or destroyed as part of the process of simply not allowing them to settle and denying them even the most basic of possessions.

Accompanying the new regime was the presence of a new type of guard who found themselves posted to the cold, dank and inhospitable place that was Luft IV Gross Tychow. These men were little more than sadists, misfits who took personal pleasure in making the lives of the men in captivity as miserable as possible. Beatings were commonplace, usually for the smallest of infractions and often they were as entirely unprovoked as they were vicious and sustained. The worst of the type was undoubtedly the infamous Feldwebel (Sergeant) Hans Schmidt. Nicknamed 'Big Stoop' by the prisoners due to his large build and awkward gait, he appeared to have resembled something of an early 'Shrek'.

He was reckoned by the prisoners to be aged around fifty, 6ft 7ins tall, oafish and thick set, he had what many described as unusually large, spade-like hands. His reputation within the camp for brutality was well-known and most men knew to give him a wide berth and certainly not to catch his eye or to attract his attention. Nevertheless Schmidt would often launch sudden unprovoked attacks on prisoners for no other reason than he didn't like the way they looked at him, didn't move fast enough when called to Appell or simply because he felt like it. When he targeted a man he would beat him to the floor with a large, smooth wooden club that he used to carry with him and continue to kick and stamp on the unfortunate victim when he was down until the man was eventually rendered unconscious. He was also known to carry a whip that he showed on frequent occasions he was more than ready to use.

One of the prisoner's post-war accounts relate the details of how 'Big Stoop' once beat a man viciously with a belt and that the buckle opened up lacerations on the victims' scalp so deep that his skull was exposed. His favourite method of amusing himself was to walk up behind a prisoner and, with a purposely cuffed hand, deliver an almighty cuffing blow to the side of the man's head, often bursting their eardrum and sending them to their knees in searing pain where a sustained beating would often follow. Schmidt was also known to help himself to prisoners' belongings, reading their mail and rifling through their occasional Red Cross parcels. He was universally loathed by the men in the camp and many made him a leading target for collective revenge once liberation finally came.

One of the worst aspects of life in the new camp would be the ongoing issues with food. Camp rations consisted of Deutsch brown bread and coffee in the morning, a kind of thin watery soup for lunch and then bread and what passed for jam in the evenings[3] – as the war started to enter its final phase the frequency, quantity and quality of even this meagre offering worsened as the priorities of the Reich were now concerned with homeland defence and repelling the invaders, not feeding

PoWs who were increasingly seen as a liability. As the food situation deteriorated, men began to lose body weight and muscle mass rapidly. Red Cross parcels, when they did arrive, were systematically looted by the guards and many prisoners made sure that once the official post service for the camp was set up and running they were able to write home and instruct their loved ones not to send any further parcels or clothing. Soon new arrivals would begin pouring into the camp, a mix of nationalities including Americans, British, Poles, Czechs, Australians, New Zealanders and South Africans.

My father's next letter home and could only hint at conditions within the camp;

30th September 1944

Dear Mother & Dad and all at home

I've just received your letter dated 17/7/44 and you tell me that you've seen my photo in a group, it's quite possible but if it is then it would be the only one I had taken, so you'd better keep it. I've just finished washing, and it's not good drying weather so I guess I'll have to stay in bed or at least inside until they dry.

Love Harold xxxxxxx

In reality, washing facilities within Luft IV were virtually non-existent and coupled with the poor sanitation and overcrowding, many of the prisoners now found themselves infested with lice.

There are essentially three types of lice that can infest the human body – head lice, pubic lice and body lice – and the prisoners at Tychow found themselves unwilling hosts to all three varieties of these most unpleasant parasites. Discomfort aside, caused by the terrible itching that these three visitors bring, body lice can also harbour and transmit disease such as typhus, trench fever and louse-borne relapsing fever. The Germans refused to provide the men with delousing powder so the only way they could even attempt to rid themselves of the problem was through vigorous personal washing and washing their clothes regularly in boiling water, neither of which was a particularly viable option given the inadequate facilities in camp. All these factors combined meant that transmission of parasites between groups of men was almost inevitable and men were constantly re-infected to the point where any meaningful attempts to contain the spread were virtually abandoned and they just had to put up with it.

As the camp numbers swelled with new arrivals throughout the latter months of the year it was noticeable that more and more Americans were flooding through the gates. Initially they would mix with the English contingent but eventually it became apparent that they would need their own compound to be housed in and after some discussion the Camp Kommandant eventually conceded the point and the American prisoners were housed separately.

The winter of 1944/45 would turn out to be one of the coldest on record and as the colder months arrived keeping warm in the camp, as well as having enough food to eat, became a preoccupation for all prisoners. They had little in the way of extra clothing and the meagre fuel ration provided for the stoves that sat in the middle of the huts was rarely enough to provide even a basic level of heating. Men woke up in the morning hungry and went to bed in the evening hungry, the nagging dull ache in their stomachs a constant reminder that the sustenance that they were receiving was in reality little more than a starvation diet and with no means of getting additional food, over and above the haphazard delivery of the Red Cross parcels, there was little hope of the situation improving.

It would steadily get worse, much worse. For many, staying in their hut in bed was the best way to conserve energy as well as keeping warm.

Conditions at Luft IV were arguably among the worst of any that had been experienced among the main PoW camps and the uncertainties of the post-D-Day landscape would also prey on the prisoners' minds. The majority coped as best they could and tried to keep busy and vigilant as they believed that liberation must surely come soon. Many presumed that the attitudes of the guards would most likely soften as they would not want to do anything that could leave them open to harsh treatment from liberating troops if they were identified as particularly cruel or brutal. Others however believed the exact opposite and feared that when the end of the war was close they would either be used as some form of human shield or perhaps just executed en masse when their captors had no further use for them.

While the morale of the camp guards also ebbed and flowed with the progress of the war beyond the camp, there seemed little evidence that attitudes to the men they guarded within were changing. Certainly for men like Feldwebel Schmidt – the Big Stoop – it appears to have been very much business as usual and his penchant for casual cruelty continued unabated and sometimes was supplemented by something altogether more sinister as related to me here:

> *One morning, before the end of the 7am curfew forbidding men to leave their huts, the early morning quiet was rudely broken by the sound of many boots pounding on the compound. At least twenty German soldiers surrounded one of the huts, where the men suspected that it was yet another tiresome search where they would be ordered out into the courtyard while the hut was ransacked, and their belongings pillaged. Usually, the guards would burst in without ceremony and turf the prisoners out with plenty of shoving and the odd crack from Schmidt's large baton. But today was something different.*[4]

Looking out the men saw the familiar bulk of 'Big Stoop' and also an officer organising their men. The guards stood, or knelt, with their machine pistols drawn and aimed at the hut. One of the men, an officer, stepped forward and shouted in stilted English to the men in the hut: 'Bring out the Jew Boy.'

Laughter from the ring of soldiers. Silence from the hut.
'I said – bring out the Jew Boy. Bring out Joseph, send him out.'

Again, more laughter and catcalls from the assembled guards. Again, silence from within the hut. David Joseph, a Jewish airman, was in room four of hut ten and the prisoners realised what would most likely happen if he went outside. They had no intention of letting him walk out alone. Still, none of them spoke a word. Outside in the yard the German officer was becoming more restless and this time his tone was one of irritation rather than confidence:

'This is the last time I will ask – send the Jew boy out now.'

This time a solitary, clear voice from within the hut answered: 'Fuck Off'.

The laughter among the guards stopped and the mood suddenly darkened. The officer, whoever he was, looked around as if suddenly no longer sure of himself or how to proceed. He had not expected to meet resistance to his simple request. He tried again;

'Your last warning – send out the Jew or we come in.'

A long silence ensued before, once more, a solitary voice came from the hut, rang out, this time accompanied by a few other voices shouting obscenities while anything to hand was piled up against the hut door:

'Try and take him.'

The situation was now somewhat of a Mexican stand off and one where clearly neither party wanted to escalate the situation, but also neither could afford to lose face. Suddenly, as quickly as they had arrived, the guards shouldered their weapons and were gone. It was never fully understood what caused the abrupt about-turn – perhaps the officer had been acting on his own initiative and defused it of his own accord when he realised that it could escalate into something that he may not have been expecting – perhaps he was ordered to disperse? Whatever the reason there was an uneasy and charged atmosphere around the huts and few men ventured out of their own accord unless absolutely necessary. Trigger happy guards in the watchtowers, armed with MG42 heavy machine guns took great delight in strafing the compound from time to time to 'test their guns' and if a prisoner happened to be hit? Well, that was seen as '*Sehr shade*' ('too bad').

On 10 November 1944 my father wrote the last of his letters from the camp at Tychow:

Dear Mother & Sisters.

You must be getting some optimistic news over there as most of the letters say it will be over before Xmas! I only hope you're not handing out duff gen, as I take it to mean this Xmas. The latest letter I've received from you is dated 14th Sept. I was pleased to know that my W/O (Warrant Officer) has come through though you didn't give any details and my curiosity gets the better of me.

*I'd like to know if I was paid for 12 months as a Flt/Sgt
(Flight Sergeant) and if you're getting the increased pay
for W/O. I trust you are all keeping well and not working
too hard it is not worth the risk, as for myself I am quite
well and fit although I would be much better if I had more
to eat. Still, it won't be much longer. (How I detest that
phrase).*

So a Merry Xmas to all – Love Harold x

'Over by Christmas' – one can only imagine how loathsome
that phrase must have been for prisoners of war (and serving
men and women) all over the world. For the ten thousand or
so allied airman held as PoWs in the camps it would mean yet
another Christmas away from their mothers, wives, girlfriends,
children, brothers and sisters and friends as hope of liberation
and salvation dwindled away with the start of another year.
None of the men in Luft IV would have any idea that the war
was set to drag on for another five months and that for the last
three of those months many of them would experience the most
perilous conditions since they had first arrived on German soil.
A great number would not survive.

January 1945 saw the snow piled deep around the huts of the
compound at Tychow, food was scarce, fuel for the stove was
scarce (many had already resorted to burning furniture and
whatever they could lay their hands on) and there were numerous
unsavoury rumours flying around the camp. The Germans had
been organising the digging of a very large, deep trench outside

the perimeter of the camp. When questioned they had explained that it was for burying potatoes to preserve them for food stocks – some men suspected they were preparing mass graves but when they started to hear the rumours that they were be to be marched away from the oncoming Russians and the camp abandoned they reasoned that the Germans had been telling the truth and that they had been for potatoes all along.[5]

On 5 February 1945, with the sound of Russian artillery clearly audible in the far distance the men were told that they were being evacuated and would leave the following morning. They would only be allowed to carry what they could in their packs and everything else was to be left at the camp.

Men packed what they could along with what scant clothing they possessed and the following morning, Tuesday, 6 February 1945 they were marched out of Luft IV to begin the long march away from the advancing Russians. Ex-Gulf War Tornado Pilot John Nichol and Tony Rennell in their book *The Last Escape* described the subsequent forced march from Gross Tychow as an of act of bravery which, though unrecognised, was one of the most significant of the Second World War.[6]

The march – later known as the Death March or the Black March – would last almost three months and would see the body of men march over hundreds of miles lasting up to 86 days (for some) across frozen wasteland, unprovisioned, with no winter clothing and in one of the coldest winters in living memory. Along the way they would suffer brutality from the guards, frostbite, starvation, thirst, crippling blisters and severe gastric complaints. Some men drank from ditches that others had used as latrines, food and protein was taken wherever it could be found, from the Red Cross parcels that they managed to take with them and when they ran out some would dig up vegetables from the side of the road and eat them soil and all, some men ate rats, raw and uncooked, some even ate grass such was their desperation.

For those men who could no longer go on and who had dropped exhausted and sometimes doubled up in pain by the roadside, despite the best efforts of their fellow prisoners to help them, the outcome would always be the same. The column of men would keep moving in the bitter, blizzard-like conditions and they would see a guard running back to where the stricken man lay slumped. They would hear the echo of a single shot ring out in the distance and after a few minutes the guard would return and trudge past them, rifle slung back over his shoulder. The German plan was to get the men across the Oder River before the Russians could cut them off and so the pace of the march was brisk and the men were often expected to cover great distances each day, often up to 20 miles. The roads were icy and snowbound, sometimes the men were taken across fields, ridged hard with frozen ground which twisted ankles, jarred backs and burst blisters; at other times they pounded down roads and tracks driven ever onwards by the guards with the odd clout from the butt of a rifle as encouragement and sometimes through snow knee-deep.

At night sometimes they had the luxury of a farmer's barn to sleep in and the men would pull straw around themselves for warmth, at other times they would be forced to sleep in the open, in the driving rain, sleet and snow, huddled together for warmth as best they could. On more than one occasion men awoke to find that the man next to them had frozen to death during the night. There was no time to bury them, only to snap their dog tag in half and retain it so as to one day advise the loss – and then remove whatever clothing could be useful, including boots – and get ready to move once again.

As they passed through German villages and hamlets the reception varied greatly – in some place they could trade cigarettes, rings and chocolate for scraps of food from civilians by the side of the road, some civilians even handed out bread and hot coffee to the men feeling sorry for them – in others they were spat at, punched and abused, the guards uninterested in making any attempt to intervene.

The unrelenting pace of the march was now taking its toll on many of the men after a full thirty days on the road. A number were suffering with burst blisters that were starting to become infected, their boots and socks were permanently sodden resulting in trench foot-like symptoms which was making walking painful. Men like my father, who had suffered with injuries to their feet, ankles and back when bailing out, were starting to struggle – many were reluctant to take their boots off at night for fear that they would either be stolen or that they would simply not be able to get them on again if their feet started to swell. No boots meant no walking, no walking meant a bullet in the back of the head. Every morning the exhausted men would drag themselves back to their feet and in line, three abreast, to continue the march, but by now the column was sickening rapidly and the ranks of prisoners were suffering from a range of health problems.

With no way to wash, no water, rampant seething lice and no proper sanitation, dysentery was again rife and men stopped frequently to ease themselves, the snow either side of the column flecked with bloody stools, watery excrement and littered with soiled and discarded underclothes. Some of the healthier men implored their captors to slow the pace or to at least provide longer breaks so that the men might recover somewhat, but all complaints landed on deaf ears. The Germans were determined to drive the men onwards, fearful of the Russian advance and men were coerced and cajoled by the liberal use of blows from rifles if required.

Just outside Swinemunde, as night was falling, the exhausted prisoners were told that they would again be sleeping in the fields as there were no barns. Cecil Room (who was to write a detailed account of the march on scraps of paper, card, anything he could get) estimated that the temperature that night was minus nineteen degrees. Most tried to stay awake, fearing to go to sleep in case they never woke up, and in the morning the frost crackled over their bodies as they were relieved to find they were still alive.

The march continued with distances of anywhere between 10 and 20 miles covered in a day – dead horses and animals lying by the roadside would have slivers cut from them by prisoners stooping and slicing with a knife or anything that they could fashion into a blade. Eating presented its own problem due to the insanitary filth they were forced to exist in. Their stomachs cried out for food but at least the horrendous diarrhoea had stopped as there was nothing left to eject. When they ate the scraps of meat it was invariably too much for their recovering systems to take and the soiling process started all over again – degrading and humiliating and there seemed no end in sight.

Lack of water also made the symptoms of dysentery worse, and dehydration would have been a major issue in itself were it not for the fact that prisoners could gain some relief by eating fresh snow and drinking from whatever standing water was around, including breaking the ice on puddles – they had long since ceased to care about whether it was sufficiently clean to drink safely.

As the snaking column of prisoners moved ever westward in the rain and snow for weeks on end each man did what he could to keep his spirits up, to think of home, to think of seeing those most precious to them again, to think of every foot forward being one more step towards freedom, one more day was another to strike off the calendar towards home. Counterbalancing that was the rapidly deteriorating health of the men. Blisters turned to abscesses, infected and untreatable, frostbite to gangrene and some had already lost fingers and toes. Still they keep marching through the clawing mud and the snow. At the back of everyone's minds though was the realisation that they were, as a group of men, getting sicker, weaker, slower, more spread out and becoming more of a burden to the guards. None would voice it publicly but privately to trusted comrades their shared their innermost thoughts and concerns.

'Why are they keeping us? What happens when we can't go any further? When will they decide it's all over and dispose of us rather than leave evidence?'

The murders of the fifty at Sagan had already shown what the Germans were capable of, why should they expect to be treated any differently?

February had come and gone, March was almost over and the harsh winter months had begun to soften, temperatures were slowly lifting, nights were less cold and word filtered round the column on the road that they were headed for a new camp. The issue of a Red Cross parcel lifted spirits beyond measure and those that were able enjoyed the sparse treats within. By this stage they had covered some 215 miles or so since leaving Luft IV behind in early February. My father's ankles had made it almost impossible to walk and those that could took turns to help both him and others keep moving, 'at all costs you had to keep moving to stay alive'.

Finally, the shattered ranks of men arrived at Ebsdorf railway station and they were loaded into the obligatory cattle wagons that they had all become so acquainted with during their time in Germany. Exhausted and packed in as before they at least had some relief from the marching, from the snow and the driving rain. This time, mercifully, there would be no two or three day ordeal. After a journey of a couple of hours the men pulled into Stalag XIb at Fallingbostel. As before the Germans kept them in the cattle trucks overnight and the doors were not finally pulled open until midday the following day – some had not made it; despite coming so far their bodies could stand no more and they had passed away at some point during the night, their bodies unloaded, anything of use stripped from the corpse which was then covered with filthy scraps of whatever could be brought to hand.

Conditions at Fallingbostel were horrendous, worse even than Tychow, and the men looked on in mute horror at the scene that greeted them, Russian prisoners barely more than skin and bone fought for meagre scraps of food that were thrown onto the ground, fighting like animals to secure a mouthful. Here and there dead bodies lay amongst the discarded possessions and detritus of the camp – the worst affected from the march, my father among them, were carried to a hut that was designated by the Germans as a 'sick bay'. There were no beds, only a few tattered and filthy blankets on the floor stained with a pungent mixture of dried vomit, human excrement and sometimes blood. The huts had been occupied formerly by Russian prisoners, every scrap of furniture had been burned in an attempt to keep warm in the winter months, the blankets on the floor seethed with lice yet the men shared them to cover themselves as best they could.

For some men the ordeal of the march would not end there, Fallingbostel would be a temporary respite and after ten days 'rest' those who could were marched out to continue the march away from advancing liberators where their ordeal would continue until they were finally liberated around 2 May.

For my father, and dozens like him, Fallingbostel was to be his journey's end. Unable to walk due to grotesquely swollen ankles, blistered and scarred feet, doubled over with dysentery and unable to move, the RAF men strewn over the floor in one of the lice-ridden, bare, draughty stinking huts accepted that this would be their end, they simply had nothing left to give, nothing left to offer. Australian soldiers held at the camp, seeing their fate, brought them their share of the weak potato soup that someone had made in a huge pot boiling in the compound from the rotten and decaying vegetables found in the stores and made sure the RAF men lying on the floor received what little food they could bring or spare.

Most men feared the worst, that the end would come as a bullet or – worse – consumed by fire as the remaining guards had been stockpiling jerry cans of fuel by the gates (in actual fact it was to replenish their vehicles for them to flee). Some were so far gone they no longer cared what was to become of them.

Then one morning they awoke to men running into their room and announcing breathlessly that the German guards had gone. All of them – gone, not a single guard left, they had abandoned the camp altogether and left the men to fend for themselves. On 16 April 1945 the advancing units of the 8th and 11th Hussars reached Fallingbostel and liberated the camp. Appalled at the conditions of the men they found there they quickly tried to establish food and medicine regimes to help those worst affected. Stalag XI B was the first PoW camp to be liberated by advancing forces and word was passed back to their command post at what they were finding. All over Germany camps were being discovered in similar appalling conditions, not only for the incarceration of prisoners but also work camps *arbeitslager* for a range of 'non desirables' of the Reich, including Jewish people, homosexuals, political prisoners, Roma gypsies and the disabled – Concentration Camps.

Only the day before British forces had liberated Bergen-Belsen concentration camp and a week after the PoWs at XI B were themselves freed American forces would liberate Dachau concentration camp and discover the decomposed, fly-blown, emaciated corpses piled into cattle wagons that the fleeing German guards had not had time to incinerate.

For the allied airmen held in the camps the initial feelings were of euphoria, relief and a numbing realisation that it was finally all over. For some it would take days for it to come out – for others it would take years, even decades – and then it was as if the floodgates had opened.

After liberation however, came retribution and vengeance. The guards at Fallingbostel had long gone but all over Germany the soldiers who had meted out such brutality in the camps suddenly found the roles reversed and it was a time for the settling of old scores. In the case of Heydekrug and Gross Tychow some of the more sadistic German guards were singled out – Hauptmann Pickhardt, the maniacal ranting figure that had overseen the 'Run up the Road' when the men first arrived at Tychow from Heydekrug, was reportedly shot on the spot by Russian soldiers once he had been pointed out to the soldiers by a few prisoners. Elsewhere prisoners were invited to identify any German guards who had treated them particularly badly and those identified were dragged to a patch of land and summarily executed – there are even credible reports that some airmen were handed loaded weapons by liberated allied troops and invited to finish the job themselves.

On 5 May 1945 at Dachau, opened in 1933 by Hitler's regime as the first of the concentration camps, around fifty to sixty German SS soldiers and the dogs that they had used to terrorise the camp inmates were lined up against a wall and machine gunned by outraged men of the US 157th Infantry division.[7]

For 'Big Stoop', the sadistic camp guard with the oversized hands who liked to inflict pain and beat men to within an inch of their lives, there would also be a brutal reckoning. Reports as to how he met his end vary – some describe him lying spread-eagled outside Luft VII at Moosberg with a pickaxe driven through his skull, others record that his headless body was seen lying outside the camp gates and that two prisoners were later observed gleefully wandering around the camp with a bloodied basket containing his severed head. Conceivably both versions could be true, but whatever the actual version no-one shed any tears that the oafish tyrant had 'got what was coming to him'. No-one particularly cared how it had come to pass, only that he was dead.

With the torment of almost two years of brutalising captivity over, my father's last remaining challenge was to get fit enough to get back home. He had lost around 35 per cent of his body weight since landing in Germany and a muscular boxer's physique was now reduced to little more than skin and bone – he was emaciated, suffering badly from dysentery and riddled with lice. What was left of his clothing hung around him in rags. As it turned out my father was one of the first to be repatriated and as well as basic sustenance, he received immediate medical attention for his ankles and feet and, after a short period, had rallied enough to be deemed fit enough to withstand the rigours of the journey back to England.

Barely able to stand he found himself on crutches again to help take the weight off his ankles and he made some attempts to get around but as he was to later confess:

I didn't really have the strength to do anything but sit around and listen to the news that the boys who liberated us had to tell. We wanted to know everything. We wouldn't believe it was finally over.

In a week, he would be flying home to family, friends and to a country that at times he believed he would never live to see again.

Chapter 13

The Long Way Home

Lives of great men all remind us
We can make our lives sublime,
And, departing, leave behind us
Footprints on the sands of time.

Longfellow

With the end of the war now only a matter of weeks away the RAF put into operation the long-prepared plans to repatriate the estimated 354,000 ex-PoWs who were still in Germany. Operation Exodus began on 2 April and saw a vast fleet of aircraft – mainly Lancasters, Dakotas, and Halifaxes – sent over to Germany to collect the ex-prisoners and bring them home as quickly as possible.[1] In total, Bomber Command would fly over 3,500 sorties bringing men home to specially set up reception centres across the county to help process the returning ex-prisoners. The poor state of many of them would shock the reception staff and would also see the beginning of the collection of evidence for war crimes prosecutions.

My father found himself in a long line of PoWs who were waiting to board one of the Douglas C-47 Dakotas that would be taking them home. He was still on crutches and as he struggled to mount the steps and stood at the door cut into the fuselage he paused and take a last wistful look back. His eyes scanned the snaking lines of gaunt, hollow-cheeked and dishevelled PoWs, all queuing patiently and shuffling forward to board the banks of aircraft dotted around the airfield that would be taking the men out of Germany and back home. It had been almost two full years since he had last flown, the memories of the night that he was shot down now replaying in his mind – he thought about the men who wouldn't be coming home – of Bernard Happold, Gordon Bowles, John Baxter and of young Duncan McGregor. A flurry of images flicked through his mind, of the near lynching, the terrible journeys on those heaving cattle wagons, of the *Insterburg*, the brutality of Luft IV Gross Tychow, the hunger, the ill-treatment, the men shot in front of him and the horrors of that final March to Fallingbostel.

'Come on then chum, let's go shall we?'

Glancing up he saw the smiling face of an airman looking down at him from within the aircraft. Taking the outstretched hand offered he pulled himself into the Dak and found a space on the floor to sit as the aircraft was slowly filled with men ready to fly home. Once airborne all were left alone with their thoughts with only the steady thrum of the engines as a backdrop. Some men laughed and joked, others quietly wept as they realised their ordeal was finally over but, as my father recalled, most just sat in silence and inwardly ruminated, trying to process their time in captivity.

They had survived, they had come through it all and were going back home – but back home to what and to whom? How on earth could they just pick up the threads of lives that would forever be so far removed from the horrors of what they had all endured during their period of captivity. How could they explain to the people who weren't there just what it was like to starve, to see men beaten to death on a whim, to be filthy and lice-ridden with no proper food for weeks on end and to be forced to march in sub-zero temperatures and witness acts of unimaginable brutality? The men who survived and were flying home all counted themselves as the lucky ones next to 'the boys who didn't come back' but they would all be very much changed from the fun-loving, fresh-faced young men of only a few years before. Many would experience severe psychological problems long, long after their physical scars had healed. Some men would never fully recover and they would be tormented for the rest of their lives by the experiences they had endured as prisoners of the Reich – a few, tragically, would take their own lives in the years that followed.

As the wheels of the Dakota carrying my father touched down at one of the RAF receiving centres in Buckinghamshire a cheer erupted among the animated prisoners, they were back on English soil and, for the time being at least, the slick and well-oiled military processes of the RAF would form a protective shield around these men and take care of its own. As the aircraft taxied to its stand the men huddled round the small square windows on either side of the fuselage and strained for a view of what was outside. When the prop blades slowly stopped the men were held for a few moments and then ushered down the steps onto the hardstanding. Here and there men knelt and kissed the ground, others embraced and drew in huge deep lungfuls of English air and stood for a few moments to take in the lush green spaces around them. Waiting for them were a selected team of RAF men and WAAFs as part of the reception committee. Once unloaded the ex-prisoners boarded a train bound for RAF Cosford, just outside Wolverhampton. Located there was 106 PRC (Personnel Reception Centre) where they would undergo an initial medical examination and an assessment to establish their condition and any urgent medical needs.

Unsurprisingly the men were, for the most part, filthy, unkempt and many were still lice-ridden. A high number were suffering from chronic stomach conditions including diarrhoea and some were still suffering the lasting effects and indignities of dysentery. The worst affected were immediately hospitalised and all were relieved of their tattered and dirty uniforms and clothing, which were incinerated while the men washed and were deloused before being given new uniforms. They were then processed and debriefed in one of the huge aircraft hangers that had been specially prepared for the job before being seated down in the mess hall to eat. The process of feeding them was problematic in itself as for many their stomachs were by now too shrunken to accept anything approaching regular food and they were unable to digest the (comparative) richness of the meal offered compared to what they had been forced to subsist on – many were placed on special diets, my father among them.

Malnutrition was a major issue amongst the returning ex-prisoners and was clearly evidenced by the shockingly poor physical condition of the men and the associated problems that came with it. Sallow skin and skin lesions, hair loss, problems with eyesight and water retention issues were by no means uncommon. A number of men displayed symptoms of possible psychological and neurological problems with episodic anxiety and depression – many had understandably lost a degree of interest in life and were suffering from low self-esteem and confidence, something that would take considerable time to restore. Many just wanted to be left alone and were distant and withdrawn.

My father, a Warrant Officer since his promotion in June 1944, was to be housed in the Fulton Block at Cosford along with all other officers – more junior ranks once more found themselves in the ubiquitous Nissen huts that were dotted around the airfield, as they were across so many of the other operational airfields up and down the country. During his time at Cosford he received treatment for the problems with his ankles and the problems that dysentery had caused – as with so many men putting on weight was now the main priority. Men who were deemed fit enough were, after a short stay at 106 PRC, sent home on an extended twenty-eight day leave pass in order to see their families. Others were kept at Cosford to ensure that their ongoing medical needs were properly met and to make sure that they were continuing to gain weight sustainably and to get their strength back before going home.

My father's recollections of that time were numerous and positive:

We were really treated with kid gloves. We had slow and steady exercise and special meals that they give us, small portions but fairly frequent to help us get used to food again. We had as many smokes as we wanted given to us as like everyone else I smoked in those days and we could pretty much do what we liked. I had a beard, moustache and my hair was over my collar, but I couldn't be bothered to get it cut. An MP (Military Policeman) said a couple of times for me to try and get my hair cut but they had been told not to bother or annoy us in any way, so I just used to tell them I'd get it done when I felt like it and to leave me alone.

My father was to stay at RAF Cosford for some time before he was deemed fit enough to return home. At some stage he would have arrived at Hednesford Railway station and then prepared himself for the short walk to No.8 Anglesey Street and to the reunion with his family. One can only imagine what that was like, especially seeing his mother for the first time in over two years – she absolutely idolised him and I'm certain that he would have been mobbed by the whole family and his especially his sisters who doted on him. However, they too would notice the change in him and, as my mother recalled once in a telling anecdote, mealtimes could be problematic:

The family used to eat together in what was, as you know, a small house and your grandmother told me that at first when your dad was served his meal he would immediately pick up his plate and stand or sit in the corner of the room with one arm around the edge of the plate almost as if he thought someone was going to take it off him. He didn't

like eating in front of others. Your gran immediately
shoo'd everyone else out and after that your dad was fed
on his own in the back room and no-one was allowed in
until he had finished. She did this for some time I believe.[2]

Shortly after his leave, on 24 April 1945 he would report to
112 PC (Personnel Centre – Refresher) at RAF Church Fenton
near Tadcaster in North Yorkshire, now a civilian airfield
known as Leeds East Airport. The Refresher Centres were
devised by the RAF to help returning ex-prisoners prepare for
their lives ahead by bringing them up to speed with events
that happened while they had been prisoners and had been
deprived of news. The updates were supplemented by lectures
on various subjects, covering both civilian and military topics,
and as Oliver Clutton-Brock notes in his superb *Footprints on
the Sands of Time*[3] many ex-prisoners were resentful of having
to spend time attending (attendance at which was compulsory
as they were still serving airmen).

However, as far as I can establish my father was a willing
participant and at one point was considering staying in the
RAF and so he was sent to 1 (0) AFU (Advanced Flying Unit)
at Wigtown around 28 June – he knew the location well as
this was where he had last been in August 1942 training as a
navigator on Avro Ansons. Presumably he was there to brush
up on his navigation skills and also to become acquainted with
the newer navigational aids that had been introduced since he
was a PoW. He remained at Wigtown for some weeks, leaving
for Church Fenton on 8 August and thence on to a period of
extended home leave.

In the intervening period he began to think about what he wanted to do with the rest of his life and, for whatever reason, decided that the RAF was no longer for him and he advised them that he wanted to leave the service. On 19 January 1946 he was officially released from service at 100 PDC (Personnel Dispersal Centre) at RAF Uxbridge and then boarded the train to return to the family home at No.8 Anglesey Street, Hednesford.

Once demobbed my father would also go through a period of 'letting off steam'. He used his considerable back pay and also the money that my grandmother had carefully saved up for him during the time he was a prisoner, to take time out to enjoy his new-found freedom. She had taken a part time job at the local munitions factory packing high explosive shells to help the war effort. The money she received from this was intended for my father to help him get started again after he got back from Germany and perhaps to allow him to start a small venture, or at least to sustain him while he worked out what he wanted to do in life.

Invariably after his demob and having been denied access to all the creature comforts we take for granted, my father seemed determined to make up for lost time and for much of the remainder of 1946 he spent most of his life in various pubs and bars and, shall we say, re-establishing relations with the fairer sex. Much of the time he could be found in the saloon bar of the Anglesey Hotel at the bottom of Anglesey Street in Hednesford, drinking and chatting with his friends. In between times he would top up his funds with a flutter on the horses.

He studied the flat racing and the formbooks religiously and by all accounts managed to subsidise a reasonable living out of it through a betting system that he devised.

At some point it is known that my father got together with Tommy Jones and John Brownlie and they decided to visit the relatives of Bernard Happold, John Baxter, Duncan McGregor and Gordon Bowles to try and relate what they knew about the night that their sons, husbands and relatives had lost their lives. By and large the meetings went very well and my father seems to have had a particularly strong bond with Bernard Happold's parents, William and Clara. Every year on the anniversary of JB869 being shot down, my father would send flowers to Clara Happold and did so right up until she passed away. One meeting did not go so well and a distraught mother, naturally still grieving for her son, refused to receive my father:*'Why are you still here and not my boy?'*

Despite the gentle remonstrations of her husband I understand that she slammed the door in my father's face and although he tried they never communicated again. By all accounts it affected him for many years and from the discussion that I have had with my mother and other family members it's clear that he suffered from what is now called 'survivors guilt'. My mother said that he never really got over the loss of his friend and pilot Bernard Happold but, although he resolutely refused to discuss it, she could see it tormented him. It would do so at various points for the rest of his life. Apparently, my grandmother and my mother discussed it often – my father suffered from nightmares for many years but would not get help or open up about it.

At home, free and with money in his pocket, my father, like so many servicemen returning from that terrible war 'wanted to make up for lost time' as he had once written in a letter. My grandmother saw the money that she had saved for him being frittered away and she very much disapproved of his drinking and his lifestyle, particularly with a string of different women on his arm. He would not discuss the ordeal that he had been through as a prisoner within the family but she realised from his mood swings that he had obviously suffered a great deal and that he needed to get it all out of his system. For a man who had regularly faced, and saw first-hand, so much death it's no wonder that he was determined to enjoy the very things that reminded him he was free and that he was alive.

As the months passed his reliance on alcohol would grow and it had started to become a real problem for him – a way of letting his hair down but also, perhaps, a way of self-medicating to blot out some of the painful memories that would play on his mind for the rest of his life. From what I gather through discussions with my mother, my grandmother was very patient, tolerant and understanding with him but, with his drinking becoming heavier and his reluctance to give thought to what he might do with the rest of his life, a crisis was looming and she felt that she would need to act.

My mother told me that eventually it came to a head after another night of his returning from the Anglesey after a skinful, lying in bed until midday with a hangover, ready to do it all again. Apparently, my grandmother went upstairs into his cabin-like room, quietly closed the door behind her and spent some considerable time talking to him and telling him it was now time to stop, that he had to start to make something of his life and not waste the opportunities he had been given. She spoke of the work that she had done to earn money that was meant to give him a start and how worried she was about him.

Whatever words passed between them in that room seemed to result in something of an epiphany for him – the heavy drinking stopped almost immediately, and he began work for a local construction company, Parkfield Concrete. After a period at Parkfield he decided to apply for a position with a much larger company – Tarmac Construction in Wolverhampton. Arriving for his interview in a suit with his RAF macintosh over the top he introduced himself to one of the secretaries who settled him with a cup of tea and then came back into the main office – my mother takes up the story;

> *One of the other secretaries, came in and said: 'Marjorie, have you seen that handsome chap outside in his RAF Mac? He's here for an interview for the vacant Manager's job – you'd be his secretary wouldn't you – look well if you married him!! Well, I couldn't believe it, I said that I didn't even know him – what a thing to say to me honestly! Anyway, I went to meet him and took him into the interview room and left him to it.'*

Not only did the 22-year-old local girl Marjorie May Corson become his secretary, but she did indeed become his wife and they married in Wolverhampton on 2 June 1948. My mother's friend, the secretary, reminded them of the accuracy of her prediction on their big day, much to everyone's amusement. My parents would be married for just under forty years.

John Brownlie, the wireless operator from H-Harry, who had been through so much with my father, kept in touch and was also a guest at my parents' wedding. Returning to Scotland he began the process of readjustment to civilian life. Like so many he suffered due to the deficiencies of the diet he was forced to endure during those terrible years and he passed away long before his time in 1967. Tommy Jones returned to his family in South Wales and, very sadly for a man who had endured so much, lost his beloved wife shortly after he returned home, leaving him to raise his two young sons on his own. Like John Brownlie the depravations he suffered in the camps took their toll and I understand that he too passed away in the late nineteen-sixties.[4]

My father worked for Tarmac Construction for many years and specialised in the area of pre-stressed concrete – he was heavily involved in overseeing the construction of motorway bridges and causeways. In 1955 my parents bought a plot of land in Foley Avenue, Tettenhall Wood and built the bungalow that would be my childhood home. The bungalow is there to this day and still owned by the same family who bought it from my parents when they moved to Hampshire with me in 1971.

As I wrote in the introduction to this book my father rarely spoke of the darker episodes of those days, but he would often open up with anecdotes about events that were amusing or that he thought I would find funny. He eschewed veterans associations and didn't even apply for the medals that were due for his war service (I did so in 1996 and have them in my possession). Like so many ex-Bomber Command servicemen he quietly resented the appalling lack of recognition that their service received after the war and subsequent vilification at the hands of armchair historians that sought to denigrate the achievements of Bomber Command. One thing I do recall is his complete lack of animosity towards Germany as a nation and whenever we were on holiday he was engaged and friendly towards German youth.

However, with German men of a similar age to him, who most likely saw war service, it could be a very different story. In 1978 on that previously mentioned family holiday to Dubrovnik, Yugoslavia with friends, this became very much apparent. One of the excursions was to an island by boat where the crew who took us there would catch and cook mackerel for us to eat. Seated a few tables away were a collection of German men, their wives sat together on a table behind them. The men were, at a guess, all in their fifties and they swayed from side to side, banging their pint glasses together while singing. I remember thinking it was funny seeing these old guys swaying from side to side in harmony and shouting in German. My father, however, was very obviously far less amused and I saw him sitting red faced, glowering at them, his knuckles growing white as he clenched the handle of his beer.

Without warning he suddenly rose to his feet and strode over to the table and, stopping a few feet short, he unleashed a shouted barrage in fluent German (I had never heard him speak a word in that tongue before) and whatever he said caused consternation as the choreographed swaying of the Germans

abruptly stopped. Some of the German men rose to their feet
and there was much shouting and finger pointing. I remember
my father shoving a couple of the German contingent (hard)
before people intervened and my mother implored him: 'Harry,
Harry, please sit down. Please. Please Harry.'

All I recall is how unafraid he was, as he stood there, veins
on his temple bulging, legs planted, pointing and shouting at
them. At my father's wake in 1988 I reminded the family friend
who was with us on that holiday of the story and he laughed as
he remembered that day before explaining what had happened:

> Did your dad never tell you then? They were clearly old
> soldiers, singing Nazi marching songs and stuff like that.
> Your dad went over and told them to 'Shut their effing
> mouths' and that 'No-one wants to hear that rubbish'
> and they took exception to it. Your mum was worried but
> your dad was more than ready to start throwing punches
> I think.

I also recall attending a function with my parents where we were
next to a table of mature gents accompanied by their wives, all
smartly dressed in their blazers and ties. My father seemed
bored and distant for much of the evening but at some point
I recall the discussion amongst the men moved on to war service
and one of the guys mentioned that he had been a rear gunner
on Lancasters in Bomber Command and was shot down and
spent time as a Prisoner of War. I remember my father's eyes
lighting up and I remember seeing the pair of them at the bar

chatting away, laughing and knocking back whisky as if they'd been pals for years. They seemed pretty much inseparable for the evening and I don't ever recall seeing my father so animated as they were obviously reliving old times.

Like many veterans he generally chose to keep his war service to himself – only in the last few years did I find out from a very good friend of mine, Simon Robinson, with whom I was at school, that the reason for his own father's disability was down to the wounds he had received (shot through the legs) as a young Royal Marine Commando at the Battle of Walcheren in 1944. As young boys of twelve and thirteen Simon and I watched war films avidly on television (as most young boys did in those days) but we perhaps never fully appreciated the real-life part that our own fathers played in events that seemed a lifetime away from our own experiences and the silver screen.

Invariably the dynamic between fathers and their sons shifts several times at various points in their life and there were times that my father and I were very close and times when we were light years apart. I vividly recall one such instance when we were arguing about some subject or other and I remember – in the arrogance of youth – trotting out a remark that was a conversation stopper:

Dad – what have you ever done eh? Where have you ever been? What do you know, you have seen and experienced nothing – ever.

Even now, decades later, I recall the look on his face. What we were discussing has long ago faded from memory but that look on his face I can still see clearly to this day. The confrontation stopped abruptly, and I remember him standing very upright, looking at me and holding my gaze for a few moments then his eyes flickered down and he walked away. In the arrogance of youth I remember feeling pleased and emboldened that I had put my point across and in my naivety I had interpreted his abrupt withdrawal as somehow proof of my 'winning the argument' – knowing what I now know of what he went through I cringe at the memory of that discussion and wonder what thoughts must have gone through his mind.

My memory of my father as I became a youth was of a man who had a natural aversion to authority and resented any attempt to frustrate or interfere in any way with his life. He ran a successful business with my mother, enjoyed his golf, enjoyed his whisky, enjoyed his Jaguars and we were fortunate in being able to go on numerous foreign holidays and experience countries and cultures that I feel blessed to have visited and which have helped shape my world view. My mother told me that when they were younger he had said that there were times he thought he would not survive the war and so intended to enjoy each day to the full.

In July 1986 sitting in the back seat of my father's car, driving back from my university graduation, I noticed a golf-ball sized lump at the base of my father's neck. Typically, when I quizzed him about it, he dismissed it as nothing and said it was 'swollen glands'. Throughout 1987 he continued working and playing his beloved golf. In October that year my parents finally sold their business and retired, renting a house in Church Crookham near

Fleet in Hampshire while they planned where they would spend their retirement – my father wanted to retire to the coast, learn to sail and buy a boat. He also wanted to paint seascapes and to fly again, to take lessons and perhaps purchase his own aircraft. I moved with them and it was lovely to see them relaxed, free of the stresses of running a business and he looked more relaxed and content than I had seen him in many years, my mother too.

Meanwhile I watched the weight continue to drop off him and I made several attempts to try and find out what was going on as his once muscular frame began to wither. He would, of course, greet such questions with a dismissive wave of the hand and suggest a trip to the golf course or the pub. Finally, he confided to my mother and I that he had Hodgkin's Lymphoma but insisted that it was easily treatable and that 'he was fine'.

A few days before Christmas 1987 he bowled through the front door of the house in Tudor Way making my mother and I jump with a start – a broad grin on his face, he emerged with armfuls of goodies that he had bought from Waitrose. My mother and I looked at each other and laughed – neither of us had ever seen him strike out on a trip to the supermarket on his own – that event alone caused us both great amusement, and then when we saw the bottles of Möet & Chandon champagne, smoked salmon, caviar, fine wines and other luxuries that he had been out buying we looked at each other, each pulling a quizzical face and laughed again. My father was in the very best of moods and the fine goods kept coming as I went out and helped unpack the boot of his car. Once all the goodies were safely in the fridge and the cupboards he turned to us and smiled before announcing:

I have been to the doctors today and they have given me a
complete clean bill of health, they're very pleased with me
and we're going to have the best Christmas ever.

With that he popped the cork on the first bottle of Möet and the champagne flowed that day as it did all over that wonderful Christmas. I remember he bought me an expensive CD player, he was – as ever – generous to a tee. He cooked the turkey, he cooked the Christmas pudding, he prepared the vegetables, he wouldn't let my mother do a thing in the kitchen. We watched films, we played games, we made plans, he laughed, he joked, and we had a truly fantastic Christmas. However, between Christmas and New Year he suddenly started to go to bed early in the evening and my mother and I assumed he had just overindulged and needed to catch up on sleep.

A few days after New Year my mother was out shopping and I returned early from work. I found my father lying on the floor of their bedroom, barely conscious. At first I thought he had suffered a heart attack and went to call the ambulance but he recovered slightly and insisted that he was okay and that I was not to call for help as 'it will only worry your mother'.

I remember he was quite adamant about it, but I crept out and called the family doctor at the local surgery who came out to see him. By this time my mother was there and my father had once more slipped out of consciousness. After a brief examination the doctor turned to my mother and told us to prepare for the worst and that this had been 'expected'. The stunned looks on our faces must have prompted his taking us into another room after his having called an ambulance. We related the announcement that my father had made before Christmas when walking in with that beaming smile and bottles of Möet & Chandon. The doctor looked pained and broke it to us gently that there had indeed been a meeting involving my father, only with his oncologist and not with himself. The result of the meeting was that my father had been told that his cancer was advanced, aggressive and that nothing more could be done for him. Rather than the clean bill of health that he had professed to us he had, in fact, been sent home to die. The act that he had so skilfully put on for the benefit of my mother and I was flawless, not once did he ever let the mask slip, not once was there even a whiff of what the true dreadful picture was. Stoic to the end he had coped over Christmas until the cancer had overwhelmed him.

He remained in hospital for close to twelve weeks between January and March 1988 where he clung to life as the disease took him apart. In the last few days he asked for whisky – the nurses refused. I decided to ignore them and sneaked in a bottle of his favourite – Johnnie Walker's Black Label. I poured a couple of fingers into a glass and held it for him while he sipped it through a straw, his eyes an almost preternatural shade of blue as he looked at me, and then he managed the faintest of smiles. His consultant told me he could have whatever he liked, as much as he liked, at any time he liked.

On a bright Saturday morning, somewhere around 9am on 12 March, my father quietly slipped away. Free at long last. He was 71.

A fortnight or so later he was cremated at Aldershot Crematorium but I remember virtually nothing of the actual service, only the wake. I just remember feeling numb, angry and cheated. Today his ashes lie in the well-tended grounds of Bushbury Crematorium, Wolverhampton. At the age of twenty-three I was asked by my mother if I would like to choose the epitaph for my father's headstone. There was only ever one inscription in my mind, the Latin motto of The Royal Air Force:

Per Ardua Ad Astra (Through Hardship to the Stars)

Thirty-four years later, approaching my sixties, I can still think of no better words to describe the life of a man who was no stranger to adversity, practically from birth, but for whom hardship and suffering were duly met at every turn with defiance, courage and the indomitable will to survive and then to thrive. Almost all of the veterans of Bomber Command have left us now, but they leave behind their stories, their memories, their letters and their logbooks. For the men who came back many would go on to live fulfilled, successful lives – personally and professionally – to marry, to have children, grandchildren and even great-grandchildren and so their legacy carries on through story and memory. For those men who didn't make it back, especially those from H-Harry, memoirs and written narratives such as this book are a way of making sure they too are heard and remembered, for the men they were and for the contemplation of what might have been had they lived.

The events of almost eighty years ago and the millions of deaths, the misery and the suffering caused by one man's misguided and murderous ideology scarred a global generation, several generations actually. It is too much to hope that we have forever escaped the tyrants of history, for it is happening again under our very noses even as I write this in 2022. Now, as then, all we can do is ensure that those who survive tell their stories to give a voice to those forcibly rendered mute, to keep alive the testaments of courage, integrity and of defiance and to pass them on to those who come after us. In that respect The Greatest Escape is ongoing, for it is to ensure we always keep a few steps ahead of those who would try to dictate how we think, how we look, what we read, and how we live our lives alongside the others who share this fleetingly short ride with us.

Eternal vigilance is the price of liberty
Wendell Phillips.[5]

Postscript

This book is the culmination of almost a quarter of century of research and during that time there were periods of great activity, followed by the inevitable lulls (and a few dead ends), before another surge of desk research as new leads started to come in. I realise that there may be some readers who are either already involved in, or are contemplating, a similar project concerning their own relative's war service. It's a fascinating project to become involved in and I would urge anyone with an interest to pursue it. To that end I would like to share some learnings that I discovered during my journey that may help in your research.

The first thing that I would say to anyone undertaking a similar project is that it is most definitely a marathon and not a sprint and even with the vast array of information sources and assets that are out there a certain amount of patience is required when trying to uncover specific details of a given individual, crew or series of events.

In 1996 when I first started this project, online resources were fairly minimal and much of the information I extracted was gleaned from newspaper articles, visits to museums, airfields and libraries, as well as extensive letter-writing to various individuals and organisations. I generated a significant amount of paperwork which, at the time, yielded little but over the years it has paid dividends as others have subsequently come across my letters and articles which prompted them to get in touch with me.

Of course, I was lucky in that many of the veterans were still living at the time and I was able to correspond with them, to talk to them for hours over the telephone and also to visit some of them in their homes. It was, I have to say, a great privilege to meet these men and I am very grateful for the time that I spent with each of them. They were, to a man, incredibly gracious and giving and went to a great deal of trouble to provide information and contacts and help me establish a sequence of events and, in some cases, talk to me about their personal recollections of my father when they knew him in the respective PoW camps in which they were incarcerated together. Their memories were pin-sharp and even with the passing of the years men were able to recall, with incredible clarity, events that had happened so many decades ago and that was an invaluable help. I would urge anyone with an interest to read the first-hand accounts of these men, either regarding their time in Bomber Command and/or their experiences as PoWs as many men are name-checked in the books themselves which often leads on to other avenues of research. Some of their books are included in the bibliography at the back of this book and I thoroughly recommend them.

In 1996 when I first decided that I wanted to find out about my father's military story and to piece together the fragments of the anecdotes and family history about him that I had heard over the years, I realised that I needed to understand the journey that he had been through and to start with the basic framework of facts.

My first port of call was the RAF Personnel Centre at Innsworth in Gloucestershire in order to get hold of a copy of my father's war record. I think the fee was around £30 from memory and I needed his official next of kin at that time (then my mother) to grant permission. The photocopied two page record I received from Innsworth has been invaluable in understanding the chronology of my father's movements and postings in the services, both when in the Royal Artillery and the Royal Air Force, and about what happened to him when he was flown home from Germany after liberation form Fallingbostel in April 1945.

Be warned that the records contain a large number of abbreviations for units and postings and the nomenclature can take some working out, but any of the internet search engines and/or specialist online groups will be able to help in that respect. The RAF 'AIR' series of records held by the PRO (Public Records Office) are also invaluable and the Squadron Operations Records Books (summary and detail) can provide information on aircraft, serial numbers, crew lists assigned to each aircraft and also debrief information given by the crews returning from the raid. In the 1990s these records existed only on microfiche and an appointment had to be made to attend in person, request records and then obtain photocopies. PRO staff were very helpful but it was a slow and laborious process – now they are available online and can be downloaded from the comfort of one's own armchair or study.

These records gave me the names of my father's crew and I was then keen to look into the individual histories of each of the crew members. However, I knew nothing about them and had no idea which part of the country they came from. Writing back to the RAF I asked if it was possible to be put in contact with the next of kin, naturally they could not send me their details as the info was confidential, but Innsworth suggested I write a letter to the relative explaining why I was making enquiries, send it to RAF Innsworth and the letter would be passed on to the last known next of kin address for the crew member. This I did and put the letters in plain white envelopes and sent them to Innsworth, making sure that I wrote a return address on the outside of the envelope.

As expected all letters were returned by Royal Mail a few weeks later marked 'not known' or, in some cases 'address no longer exists'. However, on the front of the envelope was the address that the RAF held for the next of kin so immediately I knew where in the country the crew member came from. John Brownlie, my father's wireless op, came from Aberdeen and so I wrote to the *Aberdeen Independent* explaining what I was trying to do and they carried a feature in the paper asking if anyone knew the family from the war years or knew any relatives of John. Two days after the article came out I received a call from Bill Brownlie, John's son, then living in Auchterarder near Gleneagles and he was able to supply much needed info on his father (and also I reciprocated about what I knew of the crew). This same approach also helped me locate Ken Jones, the brother of rear gunner Tommy Jones, and John Andrews a cousin of Bernard Happold, the pilot. Unfortunately, the approach drew a blank for relatives of John Baxter, the bomb aimer, who was from Glasgow and it was to be another sixteen years before I finally located a relative of his.

Joining online associations and forums linked to the RAF, Bomber Command and ex-Prisoners of War helped me to locate a relative of Gordon Bowles the flight engineer and the Commonwealth War Graves Commission helped with information on the home town of Duncan McGregor, the mid upper gunner. Via another newspaper appeal I was able to contact Duncan's sister Helen and she gave details about her brother that helped me create a rounded pen portrait of him. Finally, in 2020, the last piece of this particular puzzle fell into place when I was able to make contact with Alastair Hunter, a distant relative of John Baxter, who was living on the other side of the world but was able to furnish me with a picture of John and details of his life.

As I mentioned before, the internet is teeming with groups and forums on a wide range of subjects and I would heartily recommend joining as many as you can. Also it is worth keeping any old email addresses active and check back on old forum posts. I once had a reply some six years after my original post on a forum by someone who had stumbled across the site and my post and by contacting them I was able to trace a member of my father's crew.

Good luck and happy hunting.

Notes

Chapter 1

1. Wolverhampton City Council.
2. Cannock Chase District Council.
3. The author has the watch in his possession and wore it on his Wedding Day in 2016. Sadly, the stand does not survive after falling into the hands (or should that be jaws) of my Boxer dog Kayleigh in 1991 who made short work of it.
4. Infant Mortality and the health of survivors: Britain 1910 – 1950 p.34. *Economic History Review*, 2011.
5. Mines Inspectors Report. HM Inspector of Mines – published in the *Colliery Guardian*, 18 January 1918, p.134, 22 February, p.383, 23 August. p.393. Coal Mining History Resource Centre.
6. *Colliery Guardian*, 5 January 1911, p.38.
7. www.vconline.org.uk/thomas-stokes-em-1911/4595271408.html. The Edward Medal was established in July 1907 to recognise acts of bravery by miners and quarrymen. It was divided into Silver and Bronze class and the Silver was awarded only 77 times, making it one of the rarest of the medals awarded for gallantry. The Edward Medal was replaced in 1971 by the George Medal.
8. *Miner's Lung: a history of dust disease in British coal mining*, Aldershot, Ashgate, 2007 pp. xviii, 355.
9. 'Snap' was the colloquial name miners gave to their lunch, probably derived from the waterproof snap-shut tins that they wore on their belt containing their lunch. *miningheritage.co.uk*

Chapter 2

1. www.cannock-chase.co.uk/about-the-aonb/facts-and-figures/
2. Cannock Chase District Council.
3. Uffz Alfred Mueller, Gefr Gerhard Neumann and Uffz Rudolf Langhans perished when their Heinkel He-111 P2 5/KG crashed at Busbridge Lakes in Godalming after being attacked by a Defiant from 264 Squadron, crewed by Sergeants E.R. Thorn and F.J. Barker, on 9 April 1941. Gerf Heinrich Berg was the only survivor from the Heinkel. On 9 April 1997 a statue was erected at the crash site depicting a German crewman gazing at spot where the Heinkel came down. The three who died were originally buried in the author's local village, Milford, before they were exhumed in 1962 and reburied at the German Military Cemetery in Cannock Chase.
4. http://cinematreasures.org/theaters/38632
5. The author in discussion with his father.
6. https://www.nationalarchives.gov.uk/cabinetpapers/alevelstudies/strike-buildup.htm
7. https://1sthednesfordscouts.co.uk
8. Written correspondence between the author and Percy Carruthers in 1997.
9. Written correspondence between the author and Dennis Emes in 1998.
10. The German Workers Party (*Deutsche Arbeiterpartei*) was founded in January 1919 and on 24 February 1920 changed its name to The National Socialist German Worker's Party (*Nationalsozialistische Deutsche Arbeiterpartei*), commonly referred to as the Nazi Party.
11. The Reichstag building, home to the German Parliament, was the subject of an arson attack on 27 February 1933. Many considered that the Nazis themselves had laid the fire or were complicit in the act but the most likely explanation remains that

Dutch communist sympathiser Marinus van der Lubbe, who was arrested at the scene, acted alone.

12. The Decree for the Protection of People and the Reich, otherwise known as the Reichstag Fire Decree, was issued by Hindenburg the day after the catastrophic fire that destroyed the parliament building. As a consequence, Germany became a police state.

13. Almansor, Heine: *Christian Johann Heinrich, 1821.*

14. The Treaty of Versailles, signed on 19 June 1919.

15. Speech in the House of Commons, 3 September 1939.

Chapter 3

1. Details of Henry Tanday's military achievements can be found at the website of the Duke of Wellington's regiment (West Riding) Regimental Association http://www.dwr.org.uk/history/victoria-cross-recipients/

2. *Sunday Graphic*, Coventry, December 1940.

3. Comments made by my mother in discussion with the author. A veteran of the battlefields of France in the First World War, my grandfather was too old to fight in the Second World War but he served as a Fire Watcher.

4. Comments made by my mother in discussion with the author.

5. Ellis, Major L.F. (2004) [1st. pub. HMSO 1953]. Butler, J.R.M. (ed.). *The War in France and Flanders 1939–1940. History of the Second World War* United Kingdom Military Series. Naval & Military Press.

6. The gains made and the sheer speed of the German advance were startling, and the reasons for these successes have been debated by military historians for decades. Compared to their French, Belgian and Dutch counterparts German troops were well trained, well equipped and versed in the tenets of Blitzkrieg ('Lightning War') following recent successful

operations in Poland. Also they were extremely well-led and Guderian and Rommel were arguably two of the greatest field commanders of their era and each knew how to mobilise large groups of men and armour effectively in order to punch a hole through weak defensive lines. More recently the German writer Norman Ohler in his book *Blitzed: Drugs in Nazi Germany* put forward an additional preposition that psychoactive drugs, especially metamphetamine, were routinely issued to German troops under the brand name Pervatin which allowed them to remain stimulated and focused sometimes staying awake for days without the need for food or rest. Between April and July 1940 more than 35 million doses of Pervatin, and it's modified sister product Isophan, were distributed among the German Wehrmacht and Luftwaffe. Source: Ohler, Norman: *Blitzed: Drugs in Nazi Germany*, (Penguin Books, 2017).

7. Source: National Army Museum.
8. The usual methods employed were to remove the oil sump plugs from vehicles and leave the engines running so that eventually they seized as the oil ran out. Grenades were pushed down the barrels of tanks and artillery pieces to burst the gun barrels ('spiking').
9. Comments made by my father in discussion with the author.
10. The original leave pass with handwritten directions and contact details for the ACSB is in the author's possession.

Chapter 4

1. The original copy of my father's visa paperwork is in the author's possession.
2. The original hand-typed menu from this journey is in the author's possession.
3. Speech made by Charles Lindbergh on 23 April 1941 reported in *The New York Times*, 24 April 1941.

4. Source: Bauer, Daniel *Fifty Missions: The Combat Career of Col. Charles A. Lindbergh*, Air Classics, 1989.

5. My father's logbook is in the author's possession and, as one would expect, provides a complete and fascinating record of every flight undertaken including the date, take-off and flying time, serial number of the a/c, name of the pilot and details of the specific tasks undertaken by my father as either 1st or 2nd Navigator on the flight.

6. Raids by the Luftwaffe on the town were commonplace. On 23 May 1942 one such raid on Bournemouth, at low level, destroyed 22 buildings, damaging a further 3,000. A number of hotels were destroyed including the Metropole in Lansdowne Square, and in total almost 200 people – including 22 British, Canadian and Australian airmen – lost their lives. It was to be the town's heaviest and bloodiest raid of the war (Source: IWM/ Wartime Heritage Association 2021).

7. The author recalls sitting down with his father to watch the recovery of this aircraft on television and particularly his amusement when, after 45 years at the bottom of a Scottish Loch, the aircraft's electrics were connected up to a battery and the navigation lights promptly lit up. R-Robert now resides back at Brooklands Museum in Surrey where she was built, undergoing restoration. By a strange quirk of fate she was on charge with 20 OTU flying from Lossiemouth at the time she went down.

8. During the early part of research for this book the author was fortunate in tracing Bernard Happold's cousin, John R. Andrews, an historian and researcher at Exeter University. Through many hours of discussion, both face to face, over the telephone and by letter John was able to provide much information and allow me to form a very in-depth and informed picture of the type of man Bernard was, and for that I am very much indebted to him.

9. Wellington R1060 was something of a warhorse. Built to contract B.992424/39 by Vickers Armstrong Limited at Hawarden, it was taken on charge by 20 OTU at Lossiemouth on 7 April 1941 and suffered two sets of minor damage on 4 Feb and 16 Feb 1943 after which it passed to 18 MU (Maintenance Unit) and 105 (Transport) OUT. Further damage on 24 February 1944 (clearly not a good month for this aircraft!) meant that it was eventually struck off charge as Cat.E on 9 August 1944.

10. Wellington W5690 was initially the aircraft of Wing Commander David Halford DSO, DFC during his time at 103 Squadron. At 22 he was one of the youngest airman ever to hold that rank. Sadly he was killed while Officer Commanding 100 Squadron on 16 December 1943 when his Lancaster flew into the ground in poor visibility returning from a raid on Berlin. W5690 went to 301 Polish Bomber Squadron at RAF Hemswell before finding it's way to 20 OTU and then to 15 OTU. On 16 November it crashed while on a night training exercise at RAF Hamstead Norris in Berkshire with the loss of the crew (Source: *Bomber Command Losses of the Second World War*, W.R. Chorley, Midland Counties, 1996).

11. Wellington R1707 was lost on the night of 2 June 1943 approaching RAF Morpeth. The aircraft was observed to be on fire by a witness and is believed to have been hit by lightning before it crashed in flames at Benbridge Farm with the loss of the crew.

12. Wellington N2758 was later lost with all crew when it flew into a cliff near Macduff in Aberdeenshire whilst on a night navigation exercise.

Chapter 5

1. https://www.yorkshire-aircraft.co.uk/aircraft/planes/dales/jb926.html

2. Sergeant William Ambrose Griffiths (service number 1316333) son of Martha Griffiths and stepson of John Peel of Hakin, Milford Haven was subsequently posted to 102 Squadron flying a number of Ops in Halifax DT747 DY-P 'Popsie'. Sadly, the aircraft was brought down by flak on Stettin raid of 20 April 1943 with the loss of Sergeant Griffiths and the entire crew.

3. Comments made by the crew of HR663 DY-T in debriefing. Air 27/809/10 Operations Record Book (ORB) for 102 Squadron February 1943. Interestingly this aircraft would be lost on 17 April over France returning from a raid on Pilsen. It was shot down by night fighter pilot Hauptmann Wilhelm Herget of the Stab.1/ NJG 4. Six of the seven crew managed to survive with four crewman successfully evading including Squadron Leader Wally Lashbrook, the former Officer Commanding 1652 HCU and who signed off my father's logbook. The other two were captured and became PoWs, one in Stalag Luft IV where my father and the Wireless Operator John Brownlie would eventually end up.

4. For readers interested in more about Wally Lashbrook's successful evasion from capture I would recommend Chris Goss's excellent history of 102 Squadron where he describes the events in detail (Source: *It's Suicide But It's Fun – The Story of 102 (Ceylon) Squadron 1917 – 1956*, Chris Goss, Crecy Books, 1995. Pages 85-88).

Chapter 6

1. Source: Harvey, Maurice: *The Allied Bomber War 1939-1945*, p.84 (Spellmount Books 1992).

2. Source : Bombing the European Axis Powers: *A historical Digest of the Combined Bomber Offensive 1930-1945*, Air University Press, Maxwell AFB 2009. Source: Longmate, Norman: *The Bombers: The RAF Offensive against Germany 1939-1945* (Hutchinson 1983).

3. Hansard 25 February 1942 vol 378 c317.
4. Middlebrook, Martin & Everitt, Chris. *The Bomber Command War Diaries – An Operational Reference Book 1939-1945* (Penguin, 1990).
5. Hamilton, Hamish *The Goebbels Diaries*, p146 (1948).
6. Squadron Leader (later Air Commodore) Gilchrist DFC and his crew, flying in Halifax L9489 F-Freddie were unfortunately shot down by a British night fighter whilst returning from the raid and the aircraft crashed at what is now part of Merrist Wood Golf Course, Worplesdon near Guildford with the loss of four crew. The author met local historian Dennis Hoppe in 1997 who wrote a book about the action and was at the site when one of the Merlin 20 engines from the Halifax was excavated by Croydon Aviation Archaeological Society in the late 1990s.
7. Bingham, Victor: *Halifax – Second to None*, p.16 (Airlife 1986).
8. Iveson, Tony: *Lancaster: The Biography*, (Deutsch 2010).

Chapter 7

1. Cooper, Alan: *Air Battle of the Ruhr*, (Airlife Books, 1992).
2. Middlebrook, Martin & Everitt, Chris: *The Bomber Command War Diaries – An Operational Reference Book 1939-1945* (Penguin, 1990).
3. HE159 QB-P 'Popsie' came down at Hexden Marshes. A monument to the crew was unveiled in 2003 at Lambsland Farm, Rolvenden Layne in Kent and paid for by public subscription with Sergeant Lees attended its unveiling. After his death in 2004 his name was also added to the memorial.
4. Once the engine has been shut down, 'feathering' a propeller is the means by which the blades are angled to the direction of flight thereby reducing drag on the aircraft (and the resultant strain put on the remaining operational engines).

5. Taken from Air 27/809/10 Operations Record Book (ORB) for 102 Squadron April 1943.
6. A regular haunt of Battle of Britain pilots during wartime, The Jackdaw (then known as The Red Lion) near Denton is there to this day and features a variety of BoB and Spitfire memorabilia. The pub also features in the 1969 film *Battle of Britain* during one of the scenes between Christopher Plummer and Susan Hampshire. A few years ago my wife and I attended the funeral of one of my aunts (one of my father's sisters, Doris) at Barham. After the funeral we were invited to attend the wake – it was held at The Jackdaw.
7. On 11 December 1943, W7912 underwent an inspection at 1658 Heavy Conversion Unit. The inspection found wrinkling of the main plane surface. It was considered likely that the problem was due to the age of the aircraft and that general wear and tear on the aircraft with continual use for circuits and landings on training flights that were perhaps rougher than would normally be expected (Yorkshire-aircraft.co.uk/aircraft accidents in Yorkshire).
8. *Military Aircraft Crash Sites*, English Heritage, 2002.
9. The so-called 'Tollerton' or 'Z' nose was produced by Tollerton Aircraft Services for Halifaxes of 4 Group. This was primarily to reduce drag caused by the rather clumsy looking original front turret which led to a saving in weight as well as a claimed increase in speed of around 16mph (but only when the mid-upper turret was also removed). There are several variations of Halifax nose treatments that can be seen at this time in archive photos – some had the Tollerton nose but retained the newer, less bulbous mid-upper gun turret design that can be seen on later aircraft. There are no known pictures of JB869 in existence but comparisons with other aircraft from the same build batch suggest that this was the case with this aircraft. Eventually

the design was standardised with the introduction of a single Perspex front 'nose' which incorporated a single .303 Browning machine gun. Source: Bingham, Victor: *Halifax – Second to None* (Airlife Books 1986).

Chapter 8

1. Sadly, Flying Officer John Dartry Ezinger RCAF (J/7023) would later perish along with the crew of JB799 DY-E when he was shot down by Leutnant Heinz Struning 2. /NjG 1 after raiding Duisberg (Source: Boiten Theo: *Nachtjagd Combat Archive 1943 Part 1 – Theo Boiten*, (Red Kite Press 2018). F/O Erzinger has no known grave and is commemorated on the Runnymede Memorial (Panel 173).

2. Taken from Air 27/809/10 Operations Record Book (ORB) for 102 Squadron April 1943.

3. From 1941 to 1952 the Air Ministry categorised aircraft into 10 different grades ranging from Cat.U (Undamaged) through to Cat.Em (Missing from an operational sortie) and these grades were recorded on the Form 78 Aircraft Movement Card belonging to each aircraft. As a result of the collision with the unlit signals van JB869 DY-H was categorised as Cat.A (Aircraft can be repaired on site) so presumably the damage was light. On 5 May 1943 the aircraft was classed as Cat.Em and then finally Struck Off Charge (SOC) on 8 May after confirmation of destruction.

4. For the Allied Strategic Bomber Offensive all major German cities were given codenames by Bomber Command, Dortmund's was 'Sprat'.

5. Based on course coordinates taken from the official loss card for JB869 DY-H (ref 15 of 15.9 299F).

6. Please see note 3.

7. Interview with Helen McGregor by the author in 1997.

8. Hastings, Max: *Bomber Command – The Strategic Bombing offensive:1939-45* (Pan Books, 1979).

9. Taylor, James & Davidson, Martin: *Bomber Crew*, p.347 (Hodder & Stoughton, 2004).

10. For a more in depth understanding of LMF I would recommend the whole of Chapter 9 'Schräge Musik' which details various cases and the different outcomes for the unfortunate airmen involved.

11. Bomb load taken from the official loss card for JB869 DY-H (ref 15 of 15.9 299F).

12. http://www.bombercommandmuseum.ca/s%2Cwhennaturecalls.html

13. Cooper, Alan: *Air Battle of the Ruhr* (Airlife Books 1992). In fact this raid was to be the largest loss of civilian lives reported until the Dams Raids of 16/17 May where the number of dead were calculated at 1,294* (the majority of them in the vicinity of the Moehne Dam). * Cooper, Alan: *The Men Who Breached The Dams* (Kimber 1982).

14. Taken from Air 27/809/10 Operations Record Book (ORB) for 102 Squadron May 1943.

15. Comments made by crew of JB864 in debriefing. Air 27/809/10 Operations Record Book (ORB) for 102 Squadron May 1943.

16. Theo Boiten, *Nachtjagd Combat Archive 1943 Part 1*, Red Kite Press 2018.

17. Cooper, Alan: *Air Battle of the Ruhr*, p.60 (Airlife 1992).

18. A detailed account of the ditching of this aircraft can be found on page 88 of Chris Goss' excellent book about 102 Squadron. Goss, Chris: *It's suicide but it's fun – The Story of 102 (Ceylon) squadron 1917 – 1956* (Crecy Books, 1995). Air Chief Marshal Arthur Harris visited 102 at Pocklington on 5 May, 1943 for a photo opportunity with the crew. Most notable is the fact that this was the first use of the Uffa Fox Life Raft and the crew became members of the coveted Goldfish Club.

254 The Greatest Escape

19. Details related to the author in conversation with his father.

20. During correspondence with John Baxter's nephew when researching for this book it emerged that after the war one of the survivors had spoken with F/O Baxter's relatives and confirmed that they had seen him leave the aircraft but he had been caught in the blast and killed when it exploded and broke up in the air.

21. Site identified by researcher Steve Heppenstall in 2020. Crash site is in the field directly north of grid ref N51 35 37 E6 13 01.

22. As well as the damage to his legs and back my father also carried scars from bayonet wounds inflicted by German Kriegsmarine during the infamous 'Heydekrug Run' atrocity that took place in 1944 at Stalagluft 6. The incident is described in detail in a later chapter of this book, but I would also recommend the reader to dip into Carruthers, Percy Wilson: *Of Ploughs, Planes and Palliases* (Woodfield Press, 1992). Percy knew my father in the camp along with the Wireless Op John Brownlie and we conversed for several years before his death.

23. Information provided by researcher Steve Heppenstall, 2020

24. See note 10. Theo Boiten, the author of the Nachtjagd Combat Archive series of books, has been extremely helpful to me in my research for this book and has made extensive enquiries about JB869 but sadly no further information has come to light about who (or what) brought the aircraft down. We most likely will never know for sure but the most likely scenario is that they were hit by anti-aircraft fire.

25. Sergeants Happold, Bowles, McGregor and F/O Baxter were originally buried at the Stadtfriedhof Cemetery in Monchengladbach in Section F 08 Row 3 graves 168 to 171 (Source: *Graves Concentration Report Form 20.09.48 BAGR/ GR/CON/2813*).

26. On 2 August 1946 the four crewmen were exhumed and reburied at Rheinberg War Cemetery in Germany where they rest today. Plot 2 Row F graves 8-11.
27. Kevelaer Archiv, Kevelaer, Germany.
28. This aircraft was HE 530 and was shot down by Oberleutnant Lothar Linke12.NJG1, the aircraft came down in the vicinity of De Wijk.

Chapter 9

1. Cooper, Alan: *Air Battle of the Ruhr* (Airlife Books,1992).
2. O Orange was brought down by Leutnant Robert Denzel 12/ NJG 1 at Weestergest about 7km south of Dokkum in Holland. A claim was also made by the Flak at 3./M.Flak Abt 246 battery based at Vlieland-West (their 43rd 'kill') – both were duly confirmed. Five of the crew, including the pilot Squadron Leader Flowerdew have no known grave and are commemorated on the Runnymede Memorial, the two gunners (Sgt Buck and F/Sgt Rose) lie in Westergeest Protestant Cemetery. Sources: Boiten, Theo: *Nachtjagd Combat Archive 1943 Part 1* (Red Kite Press 2018) and also see note 1.
3. The original handwritten pencil telegram is in the author's possession, as is the follow up telegram advising that my father was being held as a Prisoner of War. Similarly, I have the original of every letter that he wrote to my grandmother from a Prisoner of War camp. The fact that this precious archive survives at all is down to my grandmother, Elizabeth Barratt, who kept everything relating to my father's wartime service including letters to the RAF, the Irvin Parachute Company, the Air Ministry and the British Red Cross.
4. Flight Sergeant Bowman's crew was the first to use the new motorised life raft developed by English boat designer and

sailing enthusiast Uffa Fox. As well as the photos with Bomber Command C-in-C Arthur Harris the crew were also featured in a range of newspapers including *The Tottenham Gazette*. On 29 January 1963 the crew appeared alongside Eamon Andrews in 'This is Your Life' with Uffa Fox.

5. ED910 AJ- C piloted by P/O Bill Ottley DFC was hit by flak near Hamm on the way to the target. Sergeant Frederick 'Freddie' Tees was the only survivor, suffering extensive burns to his hands and body. Born in Chichester in 1922 Fred Tees can be seen in a Pathé clip of the 617 Squadron Dambusters reunion at Scampton in 1967. Fred's mother was killed after an American Liberator bomber crashed at her works returning from a raid on 11 May 1944, he did not find out until he returned home. After the war he ran a barber's shop in Letchworth. Freddie Tees took his own life on 15 March 1982. He was cremated and in line with his wishes his ashes were scattered over the graves of his crew at Rheinberg Cemetery, Germany. The author is in touch with Mick Tees, Fred's nephew.

6. Clutton-Brock, Oliver: *Footprints On The Sands of Time - RAF Bomber Command Prisoners of War in Germany 1939-1945* (Grub Street 2003).

7. Source: Hall, K.T. *Luftgangster over Germany: The Lynching of American Airmen in the Shadow of the Air War.* (Historical Social Research, 2018) Creative Commons Licence 4.0 https:// creativecommons.org/licenses/by/4.0/

8. John Brownlie's son, Bill, very kindly sent the author photocopies of two letters written by his father from Dulag Luft and then later from Stalag Luft 1, Barth. In addition, Bill very kindly gave me the original of my grandmother's letter to his grandmother where they spoke about the news of their son's capture.

9. Some of the letters in the author's possession have large purple censor ink (blocks) through a few sentences making it impossible to decipher what was written underneath.

10. RAF Loss Card for Halifax JB869 DY-H and also Chorley, W R: *Bomber Command Losses of the Second World War: Volume 4 Aircraft & Crew Losses 1943* (Midland Counties 1998).

Chapter 10

1. The Mauser Kar 98k had been around from 1935 and was the standard issue bolt-action rifle for the Wehrmacht, chambering a 7.62 round. Reliable and robustly made the rifle had an effective range of around 500 – 600 yards using iron sights and up to 1,000 yards when fitted with a telescopic sight. Many remain in service around the world today. Bishop, Chris: *The Encyclopaedia of Weapons of World War II* (Metrobooks New York, 1998).
2. WWII PoW German Stalag Luft Camps for Airmen (b24.net)
3. An exceptional leader of men, Deans was to receive an MBE when he returned home from the war and worked as an Executive Officer at the London School of Economics. Sadly he was diagnosed with MS (Multiple Sclerosis) which he bore with characteristic stoicism and he continued to play an active part in the ex-PoW associations.
4. Carruthers, Percy W: *Of Ploughs, Planes and Palliases* (Woodfield Press, 1992).
5. Conversation with my father.

Chapter 11

1. Brickhill, Paul: *The Great Escape*, (Norton, 1955).
2. In a remarkable feat of endeavour and ingenuity the men had built a simple radio receiver from parts stolen and purloined from with the camp. It was hidden behind a removable wall panel, screwed to an upright – despite many exhaustive searches the Germans never found it.

3. The SS *Insterburg* was finally sunk on 3 May 1945 in the Bay of Kiel following an attack by Typhoons of the 83rd and 84th Bomb Group. (Haworth, Roger: Miramar Ship Index.)
4. Taken from the original in my father's Wartime Log in the author's possession.
5. Kiefhelde station was approximately three miles away from the camp.
6. There are many accounts of what became known as 'The Heydekrug Run' or the 'Run up the Road'. For a detailed description I would recommend Percy Carruther's book (see appendices). Percy was a participant and knew my father 'quite well'.
7. After liberation Vic Clarke and other veterans gave detailed reports about what had happened on the 'Run' to Gross Tychow and the injuries that had been received.

Chapter 12

1. Carruthers, Percy W: *Of Ploughs, Planes and Palliases* (Woodfield Press, 1992).
2. All of these men, plus David Joseph, are listed at the back of my father's Wartime Log with their home addresses at the time. The author wrote to all of these last known addresses and corresponded with Dennis Emes and David's son who was clearing out his father's house following the former's death.
3. Having been raised on jam as a child and then again as a Prisoner of War my father professed to detesting it and on his return to England vowed never to eat it again for the rest of his life.
4. Discussion with my father and others.
5. There is evidence in existence, uncovered after the end of the war, that the Germans had indeed been digging mass graves as, at one point, Hitler had intended that all airmen held as PoWs would be executed and buried at the various camps.

6. Nicol, John & Rennell, Tony: *The Last Escape – Untold story of Allied Prisoners of war in Germany 1944-1945* (Viking Penguin 2002).

7. In one of the very few breakdowns in military discipline by American forces in the Second World War men of the 45th Division were shaken by the discoveries they were making at Dachau with scores of decomposing, unburied corpses found rotting on trains. Some men broke down and sobbed, others hunted down any guards they could find and meted out their own punishment. Though a formal investigation was ordered General George S. Patton dismissed all charges and no further action was taken against the allied soldiers involved. Some SS guards were beaten to death by inmates at the camp using whatever came to hand.

Chapter 13

1. Between 3 April and 31 May 1945 the RAF carried home almost 354,000 allied ex-prisoner who had been stranded in various camps after liberation. Collection airfields were Lübeck in Germany, Brussels in Belgium and Juvincourt in France. Reception Centres were located at RAF Dunsfold in Surrey, RAF Wing and RAF Westcott in Buckinghamshire. At the heart of Operation Exodus it is estimated that sixteen aircraft an hour were arriving back home via a fleet made up of 443 Lancasters, 103 Dakotas, 51 Halifaxes, 31 Liberators, 3 Stirlings, 3 Hudsons and 2 B17 Flying Fortresses. Source: International Bomber Command Centre.

2. The author in discussion with his mother.

3. Clutton-Brock, Oliver: *Footprints On The Sands of Time - RAF Bomber Command Prisoners of War in Germany 1939-1945* (Grub Street 2003).

4. Related to the author in discussion with John Brownlie's son Bill and Tommy Jones' brother Ken in 1996 and 2007 respectively.
5. Wendell Phillips (1811–1884). American abolitionist, advocate for native American rights, orator and attorney.

Bibliography

The author has read and thoroughly recommends all of the following:

Air 27/809/10 Operations Record Book (ORB) for 102 Squadron May 1943, PRO.

Graves Concentration Report Form 20.09.48 BAGR/GR/CON/2813).

Bingham, Victor: *Halifax – Second to None* (Airlife Books 1986).

Blanchett, Chris: *From Hell, Hull and Halifax – Illustrated history of No 4 Group 1937 – 1948* (Midland Counties Publications 1992).

Boiten, Theo: *Nachtjagd Combat Archive 1943 Part 1* (Red Kite Press 2018).

Bowman, Martin: *The Men Who Flew The Halifax*, (Pen & Sword Aviation 2020).

Bowman, Martin: *Bomber Command Reflections of War Volume 2: Live to Die Another Day: June 1942 – Summer 1943* (Pen & Sword, 2012).

Brickhill, Paul: *The Great Escape* (Norton, 1955).

Bushby, John: *Gunner's Moon: Memoir of the RAF Night Assault on Germany* (Ian Allan 1972).

Carruthers, Percy W: *Of Ploughs, Planes and Palliases* (Woodfield Press, 1992).

Chorley, W. R: *Bomber Command Losses – 1943* (Midland Counties Publications, 1996).

Clutton-Brock, Oliver: *Footprints On The Sands of Time - RAF Bomber Command Prisoners of War in Germany 1939-1945* (Grub Street 2003).

Cooper, Alan: *Air Battle of the Ruhr* (Pen & Sword Books, 2013).

Ellis, Ken: *Bomber Command* (RAF Media, MoD Crown Copyright, 2012).

Fowler, Elliott, Nesbit & Goulter: *RAF Records in the PRO: Reader's Guide No 8* (Public Records Office, 1994).

Gibson, Guy: *Enemy Coast Ahead (Uncensored)* (Crecy 2003).

Golley, John: *So Many – Bomber Command*, (W.H. Smith, 1995).

Goss, Chris: *It's Suicide But it's Fun – The Story of 102 (Ceylon) Squadron* (Crecy Books, 1995).

Halifax – *Aeroplane Monthly*, Kelsey Publishing, 2005.

Harvey, Maurice: *The Allied Bomber War 1939-1945*, p.84 (Spellmount Books 1992).

Hastings, Max: *Bomber Command*, (Michael Joseph, 1987).

Hope, Barry: *'And in the Morning', 102 Squadron (Ceylon)* (BHP 2022).

Hoppe, Dennis: *A Rather Sad Beginning - The Story Of Halifax L9489* (VaaVee Books, 1998).

Jefford, CG: *RAF Squadrons* (Airlife Books, 1988).

Jefford, CG: *Observers & Navigators* (Grub Street 2001).

Johnson, George *'Johnny' The Last Dambuster* (Edbury Press, 2014).

Kaplan, Philip & Currie, Jack: *Round The Clock* (Cassell, 1993).

Lake, John: *Halifax Squadrons of World War 2* (Osprey Publishing, 1999).

Lomas, Harry: *One Wing High – Halifax Bomber – the Navigators Story* (Airlife Books, 1995).

Middlebrook, Martin & Everitt, Chris. *The Bomber Command War Diaries – An operational reference book 1939-1945* (Penguin, 1990).

Nichol, John: *Lancaster* (Simon & Schuster, 2020).
Nicol, John & Rennell, Tony: *The Last Escape – Untold story of Allied Prisoners of war in Germany 1944-1945* (Viking Penguin 2002).

Overy, Richard: *Bomber Command 1939-1945 – Reaping the Whirlwind* (Collins, 1997).

Probert, Henry: *Bomber Harris – His Life & Times* (Greenhill Books, 2001).

Taylor, James & Davidson, Martin: *Bomber Crew* (Hodder & Stoughton, 2004).

Ward, Chris: *4 Group Bomber Command – An Operational Record* (Pen & Sword , 2012).

Younger, Calton: *No Flight from the Cage* (Fighting High 2013).

Index